# Algorithmic Information Theory for Physicists and Natural Scientists

# Algorithmic Information Theory for Physicists and Natural Scientists

**Sean D Devine**

*Victoria University of Wellington, Wellington, New Zealand*

**IOP** Publishing, Bristol, UK

ISBN    978-0-7503-2640-7 (ebook)
ISBN    978-0-7503-2638-4 (print)
ISBN    978-0-7503-2641-4 (myPrint)
ISBN    978-0-7503-2639-1 (mobi)

DOI    10.1088/978-0-7503-2640-7

Version: 20200601

IOP ebooks

British Library Cataloguing-in-Publication Data: A catalogue record for this book is available from the British Library.

Published by IOP Publishing, wholly owned by The Institute of Physics, London

IOP Publishing, Temple Circus, Temple Way, Bristol, BS1 6HG, UK

US Office: IOP Publishing, Inc., 190 North Independence Mall West, Suite 601, Philadelphia, PA 19106, USA

# Contents

# Preface

I was originally a research physicist in a government laboratory, with a modest publication record. On the way to becoming a manager in the New Zealand science system, I became an economist inquiring into wealth creation through technological change. In doing this, I saw serious difficulties with the neoclassical equilibrium view of economics as the view failed to recognise that an economy is far from thermodynamic equilibrium. From an economic equilibrium point of view, the development path is irrelevant yet, as the Soviet Union and China moved towards market economics at the end of the 20th century, it became obvious that the development path is critical. Again, following the 2007–2008 shock to the US and the world economy, the neoclassical equilibrium point of view was unable to adequately account for the complexity of the actual economic drivers and it became obvious that things, if left to themselves, were not just going to return to normal equilibrium.

In looking for a way to approach non-equilibrium issues, I stumbled across Chaitin's work on algorithmic information theory (AIT) outlined in John Casti's book *Complexification*. This introduced me to the works of Gregory Chaitin and ultimately Li and Vitányi's [1] comprehensive book. While the latter book is a treasure trove, I, as an outsider, found it difficult to master. The context of much of the development and the notation was daunting to a non-mathematician. Nevertheless, that book pointed to Kolmogorov's work on algorithmic complexity, probability theory and randomness in a way that had potential to be applied to the organised systems studied in the natural world. I found that the earlier work of Zurek and Bennett on algorithmic entropy provided rich understandings of non-equilibrium systems; those that were outside the most probable set of states—yet these contributions seem to have become lost in the mists of time.

While it seemed that AIT was able to provide a useful tool for scientists to look at natural systems, if not economics, the advances already made needed to be put in an accessible form. In addition, some critical conceptual issues needed to be explored to ensure the approach was consistent. The most important of these is the thermodynamics of replication processes, as these processes are critical to creating and maintaining ordered systems distant from equilibrium. Once these issues were resolved, it became clear that even an economic system, like an ecology was an example of a far-from-equilibrium system that could also be explored by the same techniques.

This book has been written in the hope that readers will be able to absorb the key ideas behind AIT so that they are in a better position to access the mathematical developments and to apply the ideas to their own areas of interest.

Sean Devine

## Reference

[1] Li M and Vitányi P M B 2008 *An Introduction to Kolmogorov Complexity and Its Applications* 3rd edn (New York: Springer)

# Author biography

**Sean D Devine**

 After obtaining a PhD in physics at the University of Canterbury, Christchurch, New Zealand, and a stint overseas, Sean spent 20 years as a government research scientist working mainly on materials science. After becoming a science manager, with the funding cuts to New Zealand science during the science reforms of the mid-1980s, Sean studied economics, arguing that if you cannot beat them join them. But the real aim was to answer the question of why should government provide more funding for science than say ballet?

In 1990 with the economics background, Sean became manager of the newly formed Public Good Research Fund at the Foundation for Research Science and technology, responsible for allocating most of New Zealand's non-university government research funding. From 1995 until 2001, Sean became the Executive Director of The Association of Crown Research Institutes, the association of Crown-owned research companies.

In the late 1980s, Sean was a Director of Superlink (a subsidiary of Electricorp New Zealand) involved with the development of the new high-temperature super-conductors. This has now become HTS-110 a subsidiary company of Scott Technology that produces high-temperature superconductor wire.

In the mid-1990s, Sean became the founding Chairperson of Robinson Seismic Limited, established by a colleague, Dr Bill Robinson. This private company was involved in developing and commercialising seismic protection devices, exploiting the intellectual property, such as the lead rubber bearing, developed by Bill Robinson (https://http://www.wgtn.ac.nz/robinson/about/bill-robinson).

Since 2002 until the present, Sean has been a research fellow at the Victoria Management School, Victoria University of Wellington, with research interests on the economics of technological change and innovation, complex systems and algorithmic information theory applied to the natural world.

# Symbols

| | |
|---|---|
| $\lvert\ldots\rvert$ | The number of bits in the string between the vertical lines |
| $A$ | A formal logical system |
| $\mathcal{B}$ | The collection of subsets of a metric space |
| $C(s)$ | The algorithmic complexity of string $s$ using codes with end-markers |
| $d(x\lvert n)$ | The randomness deficiency in bits of a string of length $n$ |
| $\delta_0(x\lvert P)$ | A universal Martin-Löf test of randomness |
| $D$ | Data used in hypothesis testing |
| $D_{\mathrm{ord}}$ | The degree of order, or the distance from equilibrium, in bits |
| $\eta$ | A microstate outside a viable set of states |
| $e_i$ | A microstate that embodies stored energy |
| $\Gamma$ | $6N$-dimensional phase space |
| $\Gamma_x$ | The cylinder set. The set of all reals on the number line that start with the sequence $x$ |
| $\zeta$, or $g$ | A string that encapsulates reversibility requirements in a closed system |
| $h$ | Entropy rate |
| $H(s)$, | The algorithmic complexity using self-delimiting coding, or equivalently, the |
| $H_{\mathrm{algo}}(s)$ | algorithmic entropy of string $s$ in bits |
| $H_{sh}$ | The Shannon entropy in bits |
| $H_{\mathrm{prov}}(s)$ | The provisional entropy in bits |
| $l\hat{o}gn$ | The lexicographic specification of the natural number $n$ |
| $\mathcal{H}_i$ | Hypothesis $i$ |
| $k_B$ | Boltzmann's constant in J K$^{-1}$ |
| $\kappa_0(x\lvert P)$ | A Martin-Löf sum P-test for randomness |
| $p_i, p_{xi}$ | The string specifying the momentum coordinate of species $i$, $x$ component of momentum coordinate of species $i$ |
| $\mathrm{p}_i, \mathrm{q}_i$ | A binary programme that generates string $i$ |
| $\mathrm{p}_i^*$ | The shortest programme that generates string $i$ |
| $\mu$ | A general measure on a set |
| $m(x_i)$ | The universal semi-measure for outcome $x_i$ |
| $M_U$ | The universal semi-measure for the continuous case evaluated on UTM $U$ |
| $N, R$ | Integers representing numbers of particles or characters |
| $\mathcal{N}$ | The number of magnetic spins |
| $P$ | A discrete, computable probability distribution |
| $P_i$ and $P(x_i)$ | The probability of outcome $i$ or outcome $x_i$ |
| $\mathcal{P}_k(i)$ | The probability of selecting string $k$, $i$ from the set of all strings in a macrostate |
| $q_i, q(x_i)$ | The string representing the position coordinate of species $i$, $x$ component of position coordinate of species $i$ |
| $Q$ | The halting probability |
| $\mathcal{P}$ | The probability of a particular configuration in an isolated system |
| $s_i$ or $x_i$ | The binary string representing the $i$th configuration or microstate |
| $s_i^*$ | The shortest algorithm that generates $s_i$, equivalent to $p_i^*$ |
| $\lvert s_i^*\rvert$ | The number of bits in the shortest algorithm that generates $s_i$ |
| $\sigma$ | An input string specifying computational resources |
| $T_i$ | The $i$th Turing machine |

| | |
|---|---|
| $U$, or $W$ | A universal Turing machine |
| $\Omega$ | The number of available states in a system |
| Chaitin's $\Omega$ | The halting probability for all outcomes |
| $\mathfrak{R}$ | The set of reals |
| $S$ | The thermodynamic entropy in J $K^{-1}$ |

IOP Publishing

# Algorithmic Information Theory for Physicists and Natural Scientists

Sean D Devine

# Chapter 1

# Introduction

This chapter introduces algorithmic information theory (AIT) as a tool to complement the insights of traditional thermodynamics. Key is the insight that natural laws can be understood as computations on a real-world universal computer or universal Turing machine (UTM). The algorithmic entropy, or the information content, of a configuration in the natural world is given by the number of bits in the shortest binary programme that generates the configuration using an instruction set that needs no end-markers. The number of bits aligns with the thermodynamic entropy. Where computational end-markers are needed for the instructions, the terms algorithmic complexity or Kolmogorov complexity are used instead of algorithmic entropy. As only entropy differences matter in nature, and as one UTM can simulate another to within a constant, the number of bits required to change one state to another in the natural world is the same as the number that exactly simulates the process in a laboratory UTM.

The history of AIT or Kolmogorov complexity is outlined with the contributions of key researchers while the ambiguity over terms such as information and complexity is clarified. As real-world computations are reversible, a simulation of a real-world process must also be structured to maintain reversibility. Once bits are tracked in a reversible computation, bits are conserved. Bits specifying the momentum degrees of freedom, allowing for units, align with the thermodynamic entropy, whereas bits carried in stored energy states or in computational instructions correspond to potential thermodynamic entropy. Only when these bits, under the second law of thermodynamics, are transferred to thermal degrees of freedom will the thermodynamic entropy increase.

The historic application of AIT to mathematical issues such as randomness, Gödel's theorem, is discussed. Here, the mathematical tools of AIT are presented in a coherent form and the conceptual framework is extended to enable the science community to apply the technique to problems in the natural world. As AIT

doi:10.1088/978-0-7503-2640-7ch1

provides a bridge between the detailed bottom-up and the top-down approaches to complex systems, linking the thermodynamic entropy to the detailed microstates of the system, the focus is on linking the detailed physics of a system from a bottom-up perspective to understand emergent properties. In so doing, interesting philosophical issues that emerge are explored.

## 1.1 Brief outline of the book

There are three traditional approaches to entropy. The first is the entropy of classical thermodynamics, the second the entropy of statistical mechanics and the third the entropy of Shannon's information theory. The book shows how the concept of algorithmic entropy provides a fourth understanding that is consistent with the traditional entropies. The concept of algorithmic entropy arises from AIT, or Kolmogorov complexity as it is known to mathematicians. The tools of AIT have been developed over some 60 years, but have mainly been applied to mathematics, computational information issues and data analysis. The approach has not been widely used for natural systems (with a few exceptions related to data compression and modelling), as the underlying mathematics is not readily accessible to non-specialists. Here, AIT is used to provide a simple conceptual framework that allows entropy to be visualised in terms of computational bits, i.e. as distinct entities being carried by energy, avoiding much of the mystery surrounding the idea of entropy. The number of such bits needed to specify a natural system defines its algorithmic entropy. These bits can be tracked and their interactions can model the behaviour of a thermodynamic system to provide rich insights into modelling, far-from-equilibrium living systems and the resource dependence of economic systems.

The following are key understandings of the algorithmic approach:

- The actions of natural laws can be understood as computations involving bits as real entities, consistent with Lloyd's approach that sees the Universe as a computational system [1].
- The algorithmic entropy is the number of bits needed to exactly specify the microstate of a system. However, like energy, the thermodynamic entropy is seen as the property of a macrostate or a set of states, even though it is actually embodied in a microstate at a particular instant.
- The approach shows that, allowing for units, the number of computational bits specifying a microstate in the most probable set of states aligns with the thermodynamic entropy. Where bits characterise stored energy states or instructions implementing physical laws, they do not contribute to the thermodynamic entropy. Only when the energy is released to become bits specifying the momentum degrees of freedom can the system settle in a microstate belonging to the most probable set of states. In which case, the bits measuring the algorithmic entropy become the realised entropy corresponding to the thermodynamic entropy.
- Rather than 'equilibrium', the terms the 'most probable set of states' or the 'equilibrium set' are preferred to specify the decayed state of a natural system when energy sources are no longer available to sustain it. The phrase 'distant-

from-equilibrium' or more accurately 'distant from the most probable set of states', identifies a state of a natural system that, without the throughput of energy, will decay under the processes implementing the second law of thermodynamics.

- Significantly, once entropy is understood in terms of information or bit flows, and the energy needed to carry a bit, a coherent framework emerges that provides a new tool to understand thermodynamic systems.

- In a reversible natural system, bits are conserved provided all bits are tracked. Tracking bits that flow in and out of a thermodynamic system becomes a tool to identify the entropy flows needed to maintain the system distant from its most probable set of states.

- Landauer's principle outlined in chapter 8 is used to show that for a reversible system one computational bit carries $k_B \ln 2T$ Joules.

- Replication processes generate highly ordered structures distant from the most probable set of states and can be specified with far fewer bits than the decayed structures that eventuate under the second law of thermodynamics. Replicating systems are maintained distant from the equilibrium set by utilising the bits in the stored energy as computational nutrients, but at the same time, rejecting waste as decayed products and heat.

- It is shown that seeing an ecology as a far-from-equilibrium coupled system of a myriad of diverse replicators provides insights into evolutionary processes and the thermodynamic requirements of the ecology. Similarly, an economy can be seen as a system of replicating families. A sophisticated economy emerges from a simple hunter–gatherer economy, once trade allows computational resources to be shared, while tools amplify human effort, off-setting death and decay. The difference between a sophisticated highly connected economy and a hunter–gatherer economy is that the former is further from the decayed equilibrium set of states and can only be maintained by accessing resources that, from an algorithmic perspective, carry computational bits.

The theoretical underpinning of AIT is outlined in the earlier chapters, while later chapters focus on the applications drawing attention to the thermodynamic commonality between ordered physical systems, such as the alignment of magnetic spins, the maintenance of a laser distant from equilibrium, and ordered living systems, such as a bacterial system, an ecology and an economy.

## 1.2 What are complex systems?

In recent years, there has been increased interest in complexity and organised complex systems whether these be physical, biological or societal systems (see, e.g. [2]). However, there is not always a consistent understanding of the meaning of the word complexity. Those approaching complexity from a mathematical viewpoint identify complexity with randomness—i.e. the most complex structures are those embodying the least redundancy of information. These show no structure or pattern and so have the greatest entropy. However, others from a physical, biological, or social sciences perspective use the phrase, 'complex system' to identify systems that show order or structure, but cannot be simply described. From this perspective, these systems do not have a relatively high entropy and, because they are far from equilibrium, outside the most probable set of states, they are anything but random. As this book is written from the perspective of the natural sciences, the phrases 'organised system', or 'organised complex system' and, in the case of economics,'sophisticated system' will generally be used to apply to ordered systems that are non-random and are far from the most probable set of states, i.e. those that natural scientists might call complex.

Nevertheless, as at times these organised systems will also be described as 'complex', exhibiting 'complexity' or 'complex behaviour', a distinction is needed between the use of the term 'complex' in these cases and 'complex' in the mathematical sense of more random. Hopefully, the context will make the meaning clear so that no ambiguity arises.

A critical question is whether one should enquire into a complex organised system from the 'bottom up' so to speak, by striving to understand the system at the most fundamental level. But, while a bottom-up understanding may provide insights into how organised systems can be constructed from simpler systems, at some level of complexity the bottom-up process of sense making becomes too involved—there is just too much detail. If deeper understandings are to emerge, high-level approaches are needed to enquire into the system from the 'top down'. The bottom-up approach uses the simplest pattern-making structures, such as a cellular automaton (see [3]) or a Turing machine (see section 2.1), to determine whether understandings at the fundamental level throw insights into high-level structured or ordered systems. Moving up to a higher level of detail, a few steps from the bottom, these pattern-making structures may be interpreted as adaptive agents responding to an external environment (e.g. [4]). In practice, the observed complex behaviour at the higher level may be said to be emergent, because it cannot be understood in simple terms. For example, one can discuss the adaptive responses of a life form in a biosystem in these higher level terms. Understandings at these higher levels are primarily phenomenological, often seeing the whole as more than 'the sum of the parts' because this is the best that can be done with the way humans make sense with limited information.

However, the argument here is that algorithmic information theory can suggest ways to 'sum the parts' in order to provide insights into the principles behind the phenomenological approach. The approach of AIT (see, for example, [5, 6]) provides a thread that can link fundamental descriptions of simple systems to understandings of the behaviour of emerging systems and, furthermore, is helpful in providing insights into underlying processes implicit in the more phenomenological descriptions. Where the high-level description makes reference to underlying structures, e.g. where nesting occurs, as it does for Stafford Beer's viable systems model [7, 8], AIT can provide a bridge between a top-down phenomenological approach to structure and a bottom-up, atomistic or microsystem's, approach.

## 1.3 Some approaches to complex or organised systems

Crutchfield and his colleagues have developed computational mechanics [4, 9] using the concepts of 'causal states' and statistical complexity to characterise pattern, structure and organisation in discrete-valued, discrete-time stationary stochastic processes. The computational mechanics approach recognises that, where a noisy pattern in a string of characters is observed as a time or spatial sequence, there is the possibility that future members of the sequence can be predicted. The approach [10, 11] shows that one does not need to know the whole past to optimally predict the future of an observed stochastic sequence, but only what causal state the sequence comes from. All members of the set of pasts that generate the same stochastic future belong to the same causal state. Measures associated with the causal state approach include the statistical complexity, which is the Shannon entropy of the set of causal states, the excess entropy $E$ and the entropy rate $h$—the entropy per symbol. The approach has been extended to spatial sequences using the example of one-dimensional spin chains [12].

Wolfram [3] has shown that a simple cellular automaton can generate rich patterns. He suggests that the Universe itself should be able to be explained in terms of simple computational systems. Bennett [13] has suggested that 'logical depth'; a measure of how many steps are required for a computational system to produce the desired pattern or structure, is an alternative measure of a system's organisation.

Each of these bottom-up approaches offers insights into organised systems. However, the purpose of this book is to focus on how algorithmic information theory (AIT), the measure of the complexity of a structure or object by its shortest description, can provide a comprehensive understanding of organised systems. The development of an AIT approach that allows for noise or variation in pattern [14, 15] is not inconsistent with the causal state approach of Crutchfield and his colleagues. Wolfram's approach [3] (last chapter) can also be interpreted in an AIT framework, while Bennett's logical depth is a measure of the time or number of steps required to complete a computational process. The following section outlines the key points of AIT.

## 1.4 Algorithmic information theory (AIT)

AIT has emerged to offer insights into several different mathematical and physical problems. Solomonoff [16] was interested in inductive reasoning and artificial intelligence. Solomonoff argued that to send the result of a series of random events (such as the outcome of a series of football games) would require each outcome to be transmitted as a string of numbers. On the other hand, the first 100 digits of $\pi$ could be transmitted more efficiently by transmitting the algorithm that generates 100 digits of $\pi$. The Soviet mathematician Kolmogorov [17] developed the theory as part of his approach to probability, randomness and mutual information. Gregory Chaitin [18] independently developed the theory to describe pattern in strings and then moved on to enquire into incompleteness in formal systems and randomness in mathematics. Significant developments took place within the Kolmogorov school but these did not become readily available to those in the West until researchers from the school moved to Europe and the US.

While the next chapter will describe the theory in more depth, the core of AIT is that where a structure can be represented by a string of symbols, the shortest algorithm that is able to generate the string is a measure of what mathematicians call the 'complexity' of the string and therefore its structure. (Here, to avoid ambiguity, the phrase 'algorithmic complexity' will be used to denote this concept.) As the length of any algorithm will depend on the computational system used, such a measure would appear to be of little use. Fortunately, the length of the set of instructions that generates the string is not particularly computer dependent (see section 3.2). As a consequence, a structure represented by a string showing pattern or order can be generated by an algorithm much shorter than the actual string representing the structure. On the other hand, a string that is a random sequence of symbols represents a system that has no discernible organisation. Such a string can only be generated by an algorithm that is at least as long as the random string.

For example, a string made up of a thousand repeats of '01', has 2000 characters and is of the form $s = 010101...0101$ can be described by the algorithm:

$$OUTPUT\ 01,\ 1000\ times.$$

The algorithm is relatively short. Its size will be dominated by the code for '1000', which is close to $\log_2 1000$ for a binary algorithm. On the other hand, a random binary string, of the same length $s = 10011...0111$ can only be produced by specifying each symbol, i.e. $OUTPUT\ 10011...0111$. The instruction set will be at least 2000 characters long, plus some extra instructions to specify the output statement.

In order for each computational instruction to be uniquely decoded, either an end-marker is required, or the codes are constructed in a way that no code is a prefix of any other code. The latter codes, which in effect can be read instantaneously, come from a prefix-free set. Because they contain information about their length, they are called 'self-delimiting' coding (or for some strange reason 'prefix' coding). Throughout this work, code words from a 'prefix-free set', or code words that are 'self-delimiting' will be used to describe these codes. As is discussed later, algorithms that do not need end-markers have properties that align with the Shannon entropy measure as they obey the Kraft inequality (see section 3.3). Similarly, if an algorithm without end-markers is to halt in a unique state, no subroutine can be a prefix of another; otherwise, it would halt too early. In this case, subroutines and algorithms must also come from a prefix-free set and be self-delimiting.

As is shown later (section 3.3), the extension of the Kraft inequality to an infinite set of programmes can be used to ensure programmes themselves are self-delimiting. This then:

- allows algorithms and subroutines to be concatenated (joined), with little increase in overall length;
- provides a connection between the length of an algorithm describing a string and the probability of that algorithm in the set of all algorithms—thus tying AIT more closely to information theory; and

- allows a universal distribution to be defined and by so doing provides insights into betting payoffs and inductive reasoning.

### 1.4.1 Algorithmic information theory and entropy

The algorithmic entropy of a string is taken to be identical to the algorithmic complexity measure using self-delimiting coding. That is, the algorithmic entropy of the string equals the length of the shortest programme, using self-delimiting coding, that generates the string. Once provision is made for the computational overheads (see sections 4.2 and 7.2), a calculation of the algorithmic entropy for a string representing an equilibrium state of a thermodynamic system, i.e. one from the most probable set, is virtually identical to the Shannon entropy of the system [19]. Furthermore, allowing for different units, the algorithmic entropy virtually equals the entropy of statistical mechanics. However conceptually, the algorithmic entropy is different from the traditional entropies. The algorithmic entropy is a measure of the **exact microstate** of a system and therefore has meaning outside of the so-called equilibrium set and would appear to be more fundamental.

The normal way of defining the binary string representing the instantaneous position and momentum or phase space coordinates of each particle in a Boltzmann gas involves specifying six position and momentum coordinates in the binary notation for each atom in turn. The specification is taken to the required degree of precision and, just as in statistical mechanics, this process imposes a cellular or grid structure on the phase space.

Zurek [20] has shown how the grain or cellular structure of the phase space can first be defined using an appropriate algorithm. Zurek also uses an alternative approach to specifying the instantaneous configuration of the gas particles. These are described by a sequence of 0's and 1's depending on whether a cell in phase space is empty or occupied. This notation can be converted to the normal notation using a short algorithm.

Zurek has defined the concept of 'physical entropy' to quantify a system where some information can be described algorithmically and the remaining uncertainty encapsulated in a Shannon entropy term. Gell-Mann and Lloyd [21], recognising that the mathematical use of complexity is counter-intuitive, define total information, in their equation (7). This total information is identical to Zurek's physical entropy as it combines Shannon uncertainty with the effective complexity. The latter is a term that captures the regularity expressed in algorithmic terms. However, it is now clear, as is discussed in section 7.2.3, that a new type of entropy, such as physical entropy, is unnecessary, as an algorithm that is able to generate a given string with structure, but also with uncertainty due to the variations of the structure, can be found. The length of this algorithm returns the same value as Zurek's physical entropy (see also chapter 4). The limiting value of the physical entropy of Zurek, where all the patterned information is captured, can be identified as the true algorithmic entropy of a noisy or variable patterned string.

## 1.4.2 Problems with AIT

There are, as Crutchfield and his colleagues Feldman and Shalizi [11, 22] point out, a number of apparent difficulties with AIT. Some of these are to do with custom or notation. For example, the use of the word 'complexity' by mathematicians to measure degree of randomness does not fit in with the intuitive approach of the natural scientist where the most complex systems are neither simple nor random, but rather are those systems that show emergent or non-simple behaviour. Provided everyone is consistent (which they are not), there should be little problem. As is mentioned earlier, the approach here is to use the phrase 'organised systems' to refer to what a natural scientist might call a 'complex system', and to use 'algorithmic complexity' or 'algorithmic entropy' to mean the measure of randomness used by mathematicians. The remaining two key problems that these authors identify with the AIT approach are:

- the algorithmic entropy is not computable because of the Turing halting problem; and
- the algorithmic description of a string must be exact; there is no apparent room for noise, as the description of the noise is likely to swamp an algorithmic description of a noisy patterned string.

However, the so-called halting problem is a fact rather than a problem. Any measure of complexity that avoids the halting problem inevitably sacrifices exactness. Nevertheless, when pattern is discovered in a string by whatever means, it shows a shorter algorithm exists. The second bullet point above is more critical. It seemed to the author that AIT could not be applied to even the simplest natural system because of the assumed inability to deal with noise or variation. However, it has since become clear there is no problem. AIT is able describe noisy strings effectively [14, 15]. In essence, the algorithmic entropy of a string exhibiting a noisy pattern or variation of a basic structure or pattern, is defined by a two-part algorithm. The first specifies the structure, as a model, a hypothesis or a pattern, characterising the set of all similar strings. The second algorithm identifies the particular string, given the specification of the set. The second stage algorithm turns out to have a value virtually identical to the Shannon entropy of the patterned set, i.e. the uncertainty inherent in identifying a particular string in a set of similar strings. As the algorithmic description of the pattern using this approach may not be the shortest possible, the algorithmic complexity or the algorithmic entropy is not defined in an absolute sense. Rather, it is a measure of the upper limit to the algorithmic entropy. Here, this upper limit will be called the 'provisional' algorithmic entropy, with the understanding the true algorithmic entropy may be less (see chapter 4). Previously, Devine [14] used the word 'revealed' entropy. However, 'provisional' may be better as it ties in with Zurek's 'physical entropy' and the algorithmic minimal sufficient statistic measure of a particular string section outlined in 4.3.1. These different measures, and that of Gács [23, 24], which extends the idea to infinite strings are all essentially the same. They provide an entropy measure for each string that is a different variant of the set of strings with a common observed pattern or structure.

As mentioned, where an individual string is a typical string in the set, the algorithmic description or provisional entropy returns a value the same as the Shannon entropy for the set of all such strings. However, a few non-typical or non-representative strings may exhibit further pattern or structure. In which case, the algorithmic entropy for these strings will be less, as they are only typical in a restricted set of strings.

An approach based on the minimum description length (MDL) (see section 5.3) also provides a description of a string fitting noisy data that aligns with the algorithmic description. The ideal MDL approach models a system by finding the minimum description length, i.e. the shortest model that fits the data. This description requires an algorithm that specifies the hypothesis or model (equivalent to the description of the set) together with an algorithmic code that identifies a particular data point given the model. Given the model, the particular string $x_i$ is identified by a code based on the probability $p_i$ of the occurrence of the string. If two vertical lines are used to denote the length of the string between the lines, the length of this code is $|code(x_i)| = -\log_2 P_i$. The expectation value of $|code(x_i)|$ is the Shannon entropy of the set of noisy deviations from the model. However, while the MDL approach compresses the data, it does not actually fulfil the requirement of AIT that the algorithm must generate the string. The MDL approach only explains it. The full algorithmic description must take the MDL description and combine this with an $O(1)$ decoding routine to actually generate a specific string.

## 1.5 Algorithmic information theory and mathematics

Most of the developments of AIT have taken place within the discipline of mathematics to address problems related to randomness, formal systems and issues that would appear to have little connection with the natural sciences. Furthermore, because these theorems are cast in mathematical terms, they are not readily available to the typical scientist.

A key application of AIT is to formal axiomatic systems. The assumptions and rules of inference of a formal system can be described by a finite string. Chaitin [25] has shown that the strings representing the theorems of the formal system can be recursively enumerated through a programme that implements the axioms and rules of inference. Consider an algorithm of length $n$ that specifies a potential theorem, or its converse. To be a theorem the algorithm must be able to be derived from this programme that manipulates the axioms and rules of inference to generate the potential theorem. Where this is possible, the derivation is a compressed version of the theorem. But not all potential theorems, or their converse, can be compressed as they cannot be enunciated in terms of a simpler set of axioms and rules and instructions. The associated potential theorems are undecidable. While these can be made decidable by including new axioms in a more complex formal system (in the sense of having a longer description), the number of random strings corresponding to unprovable statements, grows faster than the provable ones. This is of course Gödel's theorem, but with the twist that unprovable theorems are everywhere. As Chaitin [26] put it: 'if one has ten pounds of axioms and a twenty-pound theorem, then that theorem cannot be derived from those axioms'. This leads Chaitin to speculate that mathematics should accept this uncertainty and become experimental [27–29]. Randomness, Gödel's theorem and Chaitin's view of mathematics are discussed later in section 3.8.

## 1.6 Real-world systems

There are two ways of specifying the instantaneous state of a natural system. The first is to specify the system from an external perspective, the second is to see the system as emerging from an ongoing computation based on physical laws. Wolfram [3] gives examples of cellular automata that, operating under simple rules, produced highly patterned structures. The rules that generate the structure after a fixed number of steps are more likely to provide a shorter description than an algorithm that just describes the result.

Another example is a flock of geese flying in V formation (see *New Scientist* [30]). This formation can also be described by an algorithm developed by an external observer. However, the pattern arises because each goose optimises its position with respect to other geese to minimise energy use, to maintain an adequate separation from other geese and to allow for sufficient vision to see ahead. The formation that emerges is a consequence of the computational process of each goose. The algorithmic description, as an entropy measure, will be the shortest of these two different computational descriptions. This will either be the computations under-taken by each goose as computing machines, or that observed externally. However, which of these is the minimal description will depend on what degrees of freedom the observer is interested in. It is likely that, where the entropy measure must include all degrees of freedom, the ongoing computation, based on physical laws that gives rise to the system is likely to be more compressed than one just derived from observation. Indeed, the Universe itself is often assumed to be a computational machine undertaking an ongoing computation that steps through all the valid states of the Universe. However, if we are only interested in a small part of the Universe, the algorithmic description can be compressed more succinctly than one describing the whole Universe.

The AIT approach contributes to making sense of real-world systems in a number of ways. While the main focus of this book is on emergence, and linking bottom-up with top-down approaches to understanding systems, reference will be made to these other contributions. AIT has provided a set of tools to address some deep philosophical questions. These might be to do with the conservation of information in reversible systems and issues to do with why the Universe is as it is. For example, Paul Davies in *The Fifth Miracle* [31] taps into algorithmic information theory. Some of the questions raised and approaches taken will be outlined below. Later, in chapter 12, section 12.3, it is argued that the reason scientific reductionism is such a successful way of making sense is because much of the observable universe can be described algorithmically in terms of subroutines nested within subroutines. That is, the Universe appears to be algorithmically simple. Reductionism is possible when the physical realm mapped by a subroutine can be studied at the subroutine level.

For example, a stone falling under gravity can be described by a simple algorithm because interaction with the rest of the Universe, including the observer, can usually be ignored. The subroutine that describes this behaviour has low algorithmic entropy and, as a consequence, it can be analysed by our own very limited cognitive capability. If the Universe were not algorithmically simple, the reductionist process would bear little fruit as the computing capability of the human brain, which itself is part of the Universe, would be inadequate to make any sense of a physical system (see also [32]). In general, it would be expected that our brains would be insufficiently algorithmically complex to decide on the truth or falsity of propositions belonging to a more algorithmically complex universe. Even allowing for the ability to extend our brain's capability by the linking of human brains, or utilising computational machines, we are no more likely to understand the Universe than an ant is able to understand us. Much of the Universe appears simple and for that reason is amenable to a reductionist approach.

The length of the string that describes the total universe is mind bogglingly long. Clearly, as Calude and Meyerstein [33] point out, sections of the string might appear to show algorithmic order on a large scale—e.g. the scale of our existence, yet the string could be completely random over the full time and space scale of the Universe that embeds this ordered section. In other words, the ordering of our universe may be a fluctuation in a region of the much larger random string that specifies a larger universe. While this may be so, it is argued in this work that, where large-scale order exists, no matter how it arises, AIT can be used to show how the laws of the Universe can generate new ordered structures from existing order. This is discussed in detail in chapter 10.

### 1.6.1 AIT concepts need to explore the natural world

The first, perhaps obvious, point is that real-world computational instructions do not have end-markers. For a laboratory computer to adequately simulate real-world computations, self-delimiting codes, i.e. those without end-markers, must be used.

As the real-world system is reversible under natural laws, any algorithm that tracks natural processes must account for reversibility. As is argued in section 8.5.2, because non-reversible algorithms eliminate information about the prior state, the information required for reversibility must be kept, or the computational device must involve reversible gates. The requirement for reversibility has a number of conceptual implications as is discussed below.

*Bits are conserved*
As Lloyd argues [1] bits, the binary equivalent of real-world computational instructions, are physical entities and are carried by energy. In an isolated natural system, because energy is conserved, bits are conserved. As the loss of bits due to irreversible processes involves energy transfer, the loss of bits implies an entropy transfer. Furthermore, when bits as computational instructions flow into or out of the system of interest, bits can be tracked if the system of interest is seen as a subsystem in a wider system. This understanding resolves a puzzling issue.

The algorithmic description of a string requires the algorithm to halt. For example, the following algorithm, which generates the integers one at a time, is very short because it does not halt.

$$N = 0$$
$$1.\ N = N + 1$$
$$OUTPUT\ N \tag{1.1}$$
$$GO\ TO\ 1.$$

However, as the algorithm that specifies a particular integer must halt when that integer is reached, it is much longer. Consider the following algorithm that generates $N_1$ which, for example, could be the $1\,000\,000$th integer.

$$N = 0$$
$$1.\ N = N + 1$$
$$IF\ N < N_1\ GO\ TO\ 1 \tag{1.2}$$
$$output\ N$$
$$HALT$$

About $\log_2 N_1$ bits are required to specify $N_1$. For example, if $N_1 = 1\,000\,000$ the algorithm is about 20 bits longer than the programme given by (1.1) that generates integers in turn without stopping.

A similar issue arises with the algorithm that describes the Universe. The Universe would appear to be more like a non-terminating Turing machine (at least so far) so one might expect equation (1.1) to be the most appropriate. But, the definition of algorithmic entropy requires that the algorithm that defines a particular state halts. The specification of the number of steps, that either implicitly or explicitly forces the algorithm to halt at an instant of time, is extremely large compared with the algorithm that just cycles through all the Universe's states without stopping.

But an algorithm of the form (1.1) cannot specify a real-world state, when $N + 1$ overwrites $N$, as information in equation (1.1) is lost. As it is not reversible, the computation cannot describe a real-world process. Only the second of the above equations represents the true algorithmic measure for a real-world state, but only if all information is kept for reversibility. As is discussed in chapter 9, the programme bits that determine the integer specifying the halt state are in effect a counter that determines how many bits external to the system flow into it in order to generate the halt state. When an isolated system is distant from the most probable equilibrium set of states, most of the bits characterise stored energy states. As bits are conserved, the computation implementing the second law of thermodynamics shifts the system to the most probable set of states. In which case, the bits in stored energy states are released, becoming bits specifying the degrees of freedom in the momentum states increasing the thermodynamic entropy. Section 8.5.1 argues that bits in the momentum states measure what can be called the **realised thermodynamic entropy**, whereas bits in the stored energy and programme states represent what can be called the **potential thermodynamic entropy**.

# References

[1] Lloyd S 2000 Ultimate physical limits to computation *Nature* **406** 1047–55

[2] Casti J L 1995 *Complexification: Explaining a Paradoxical World Through the Science of Surprise* (New York: Harper Collins)

[3] Wolfram S 2002 *A New Kind of Science* (Champaign, IL: Wolfram Media)

[4] Crutchfield D 1994 The calculi of emergence: Computational, dynamics, and induction *Physica* D **75** 11–54

[5] Li M and Vitányi P M B 2008 *An Introduction to Kolmogorov Complexity and Its Applications* III edn (New York: Springer)

[6] Chaitin G J 1987 *Information, Randomness & Incompleteness: Papers on Algorithmic Information Theory* (Hackensack, NJ: World Scientific)

[7] Beer S 1979 *The Heart of Enterprise* (Chichester: Wiley)

[8] Beer S 1981 *Brain of the Firm* II edn (Chichester: Wiley)

[9] Crutchfield J P and Young K 1989 Inferring statistical complexity *Phys. Rev. Lett.* **63** 105–8

[10] Crutchfield J P and Shalizi C R 1999 Thermodynamic depth of causal states: When paddling around in Occam's pool shallowness is a virtue *Working Paper* 98-06-047

[11] Shalizi C R and Crutchfield P 2001 Computational mechanics pattern and prediction, structure and simplicity *J. Stat. Phys.* **104** 819–81

[12] Feldman D P and Crutchfield J P 1998 Discovering noncritical organization: Statistical mechanical, information theoretic, and computational views of patterns in one-dimensional spin systems. *Technical Report SFI Working Paper* 98-04-026, Department of Physics, University of California and the Santa Fe Institute

[13] Bennett C H 1988 Logical depth and physical complexity *The universal Turing Machine—A Half-Century Survey* ed R Herken (Oxford: Oxford University Press) pp 227–57

[14] Devine S D 2006 The application of algorithmic information theory to noisy patterned strings *Complexity* **12** 52–8

[15] Vereshchagin N K and Vitányi P M B 2004 Kolmogorov's structure functions and model selection *IEEE Trans. Inf. Theory* **50** 3265–90

[16] Solomonoff R J 1964 A formal theory of inductive inference: Part 1 and Part 2 *Inf. Control* **7** 224–54

[17] Kolmogorov K 1965 Three approaches to the quantitative definition of information *Prob. Info. Trans.* **1** 1–7

[18] Chaitin G 1966 On the length of programs for computing finite binary sequences *J. ACM* **13** 547–69

[19] Shannon C E 1948 A mathematical theory of communication *Bell System Tech. J.* **27** 379–423

[20] Zurek W H 1989 Algorithmic randomness and physical entropy *Phys. Rev. A* **40** 4731–51

[21] Gell-Mann M and Lloyd S 1996 Information measures, effective complexity and total information *Complexity* **2** 44–52

[22] Feldman D 1988 Computational mechanics of classical spin systems *PhD Thesis* University of California, Davis

[23] Gács P 1994 The Boltzmann entropy and randomness tests—Extended abstract *Proc. Workshop on Physics and Computation* (Morristown, NJ: IEEE Computer Society Press) pp 209–16

[24] Gács P 2004 The Boltzmann entropy and random tests *Technical Report* Boston University Computer Science Department (http://www.cs.bu.edu/ gacs/papers/ent-paper.pdf)

[25] Chaitin G J 1974 Information—Theoretic limitations of formal systems *J. ACM* **21** 403–24

[26] Chaitin G J 1982 Gödel's theorem and information *Int. J. Theor. Phys.* **22** 941–54

[27] Chaitin G J 1982 Algorithmic information theory *Encyclopedia of Statistical Sciences* (New York: Wiley) vol 1 pp 38–41

[28] Chaitin G J 1994 Randomness and complexity in pure mathematics *Int. J. Bifurcat. Chaos* **4** 3–15

[29] Chaitin G J 2005 *Meta Math! The Quest for Omega* (New York: Pantheon)

[30] 2007 Flying in V-formation gives best view for least effort *New Scientist* 21 April 2007 https://www.newscientist.com/article/dn11679-flying-in-v-formation-gives-best-view-for-least-effort/

[31] Davies P C W 2003 *The Fifth Miracle: The Search for the Origin of Life* (Harmondsworth: Penguin)

[32] Chaitin G J 2003 *The Limits of Mathematics* (London: Springer)

[33] Calude C S and Meyerstein F W 1999 Is the Universe lawful? *Chaos Solitons Fractals* **106** 1075–84

**IOP** Publishing

# Algorithmic Information Theory for Physicists and Natural Scientists

Sean D Devine

---

# Chapter 2

# Computation and algorithmic information theory

This chapter provides the basic framework of algorithmic information theory (AIT) before applying the approach to natural and complex living systems. As natural world computations that shift one state to another are self-delimiting, i.e. no end-markers are needed to specify when an instruction finishes, laboratory computations that track real-world processes must also be self-delimiting. Somewhat surprisingly, this requirement ensures that length of the computational instructions in bits can align with the thermodynamic entropy. However, to understand AIT, the concept of the Turing machine (TM) needs to be explored. A TM is not so much a device, but a set of procedures that can evaluate any function that is computable. The universal Turing machine (UTM), which is a universal computer like the typical laboratory computer, can simulate any other computational device or process. As real-world processes that enact natural laws to shift one state to another can be seen as computations on a UTM, the laboratory UTM that exactly simulates these processes requires the same number of computational bits as the real-world counterpart.

The properties of the TM and the UTM are outlined leading to the concept of non-computable functions and cylinder sets (i.e. the set of real numbers where all members have the same prefix). Also, measure theory, the overarching mathematical framework is discussed to provide a consistent understanding of probability, of the number of members of a set, of the distance measure, etc. As the algorithmic entropy is a semi-measure, measure theory provides the basis for establishing some of its critical properties.

doi:10.1088/978-0-7503-2640-7ch2

## 2.1 The computational requirements for workable algorithms

AIT defines the complexity of a structure or an object by the length of the shortest algorithm that generates the binary string defining the structure. This length is known as the Kolmogorov complexity, the algorithmic complexity or the programme sized complexity of the string. However, there are two variations of the complexity measure. The first is where end-markers are required for the coded instructions or subroutines, to ensure the computer implementing the instructions knows when one instruction is completed before implementing the next. In this case, the hypothetical computational device known as TM (see section 2.2) that implements an instruction from an input tape will need to distinguish successive instructions by separating them with blanks, or some other marker. As is discussed further later, the computational instructions where end-markers are used gives rise to what is known as the plain algorithmic complexity.

Alternatively, when no code or algorithm is allowed to be a prefix of another, the codes, routines and algorithms are self-delimiting. That is, there can be no blanks on the input tape to the TM in order to indicate when an instruction finishes. Rather, by restricting instructions to a prefix-free set, the machine knows when an instruction is completed, as these can be read instantaneously [1, 2]. Chaitin [3] points out that an operational programme, such as a binary algorithm implemented on a UTM, also needs to be self-delimiting as it runs from start to finish and then halts. Self-delimiting subprogrammes can operate within a main programme, behaving rather like parenthesis in a mathematical expression. The length of the algorithmic description, using self-delimiting coding will be termed the 'algorithmic entropy' as it turns out to be an entropy measure for physical situations and is therefore preferred over the plain algorithmic complexity.

However, irrespective of the coding used, the type of computer determines the details of the algorithm and its length. Fortunately, the computer dependence is usually of no great significance as a measure of the algorithmic complexity. Firstly, an algorithm written for a universal Turing machine (i.e. one that is sophisticated enough to simulate any another computer) can be related to any other computing machine, once the simulation instructions are known. The length of the simulation algorithm just adds a string of fixed length to the algorithm run on the given universal machine. Secondly in science, only the entropy difference is the relevant physical measure as entropy is a function of state. Where algorithmic entropy differences are measured on different UTMs, any simulation constant cancels. Algorithmic entropy differences are therefore machine independent. A further consequence is that common algorithmic instructions, such as those referring to physical laws, or describing common physical situations (e.g. the resolution of the phase space) also cancel. In which case, the algorithmic entropy closely aligns with the Shannon entropy.

The following sections deal with the theory of the computing devices known as a TM. For those who want to skip the detail, the take home messages are:

- A TM is a standard procedure for generating any computable function (see section 2.2). Where a set of instructions allows one to unambiguously compute a particular function from a given input, such instructions can be written for a TM or for any computing device that is equivalent to a TM. Each TM is equivalent to a function. For example, given an integer $n$, there exists a set of instructions that can turn $n$, as an input, into the function $n^2$ as an output. That is, the TM that implements this set of instructions corresponds to the function $n^2$.

- There are many different computational processes and devices that are equivalent to a TM.
- A TM may only halt on some inputs. If the machine does not halt, no output is generated. If a procedure implemented on a TM is designed to prove whether a mathematical theorem is true or not, because there is no certainty that the TM will halt, there is no certainty that the theorem is provable. This throws some insights into Gödel's theorem.
- It follows from the above bullet point that not all functions can be computed by a Turing machine. Those that cannot be are said to be non-computable.
- A UTM is one that can simulate any TM or any UTM. The typical programmable computer, familiar to scientists, is a UTM (see section 2.2.2). Often it is desirable to use a simpler UTM and longer programme where the programme instructions are transparent. The alternative is to use a sophisticated UTM where much of the computation is embodied in the hardware or the computer's instruction set. The classical universe, driven by deterministic physical laws is a reversible UTM where much of the computation is embodied in the hardware, i.e. the interactions between atoms and molecules, etc. This is why we can use computers and rational laws to map the behaviour of the Universe.

First time readers may wish to skip the details of Turing machines and cylinder sets and jump to chapter 3 and come back to the following section later.

## 2.2 The Turing machine

A TM is a simple computational device or, more accurately, a computational procedure that is able to compute any function that is intuitively computable. This is captured in the Church–Turing thesis that any effective computational procedure can be represented by a TM. Generally, a TM is considered to be deterministic as there is a well-defined output for each step; otherwise, the machine halts. The TM may be described as follows (see [4] for a worked example):

- It has an arbitrary long tape (extending in one direction) divided into cells. Each cell contains a symbol from a finite alphabet. One of these symbols corresponds to a blank. The finite number of non-blank cells on the tape represents the input data.
- The TM has a read/write head that can read a symbol, move one cell left or right and write a symbol. At the beginning of each computational step, the read/write head is poised to read the current cell.

- The machine is in one of a finite set of states which determine the action of the machine at each step.
- Given the symbol read, and the state of the machine, a transition table shows what is to be written in the cell, what the new state of the machine is, and whether the head moves right or left. That is, the transition from the old configuration to the new configuration can be written as a quin-tuple of symbols.

(current state, current symbol read) $\rightarrow$ (new symbol written, move left/right, new state).

(Readers should be aware that some definitions express these moves as a quad-tuple where the specification in the transition table is an instruction to either write a new symbol, or move right or move left.) The transition table is in effect the programme that determines what calculation the machine undertakes. A physical machine is unnecessary, as one can undertake a Turing computation on an Excel spreadsheet, or by following instructions using a piece of paper. It is the instructions, not the structure that embodies the machine. As each Turing machine implements one computation, there are an infinite number of TMs, a different one for each transition table.

The so-called machine starts in an initial configuration and during the computation process steps through the different configurations, reading and writing on the tape at each step, as determined by the transition table. If there is no effective instruction for the current configuration to implement, the machine halts and the symbols remaining on the tape become the computational output. A TM uses two or more symbols. Where a binary alphabet is used, symbols need to be coded in binary form. A simple, but inefficient, form of coding for the natural numbers is to represent the number $n$ by a zero and $n + 1$ ones followed by another zero, i.e. $01^{n+1}0$. For example, the number 5 can be represented by 01111110. The use of $n + 1$ rather than $n$ allows the number zero to be represented by 010.

Each separate TM corresponds to a single programme that generates a function given the input on the tape. In modern terms, the tape serves as the memory of the machine. There are equivalent variations of the simple TM. The two tape machine outlined by Chaitin [2] is a more straightforward representation of the computational processes underpinning the measurement of algorithmic complexity. This machine has both a work tape and a programme tape. The work tape initially contains the input string $y$. The computation can be represented by $T(p, y) = x$ which implies, given input $y$, and programme $p$, the machine $T$ halts to give output $x$. The two tape machine is more efficient in a time sense and, because most of the instructions are on the programme tape, the machine is more like a conventional computer as the programme controlling the output can be manipulated externally to the computational system.

### 2.2.1 Alternative Turing machines

There are a number of alternative computing procedures or processes that are equivalent to a TM or are extensions of Turing machines. These are briefly outlined below for completeness.

1. Register machines. The register machine is Turing equivalent and gets its name from its one or more 'registers' which replaces a TM's tapes and head. Each register holds a single positive integer. The registers are manipulated by simple instructions like increment and decrement. An instruction that, on a simple condition, jumps to another instruction provides programming flexibility

2. Tag system. A tag system may also be viewed as an abstract machine that is equivalent to a TM. It is sometimes called a Post tag machine as it was proposed by Emil Leon Post in 1943. It is a finite state machine with one tape of unbounded length. The tape symbols form a first in first out queue, such that at each step the machine reads the symbol at the head of the queue, deletes a fixed number of symbols and adds symbols. One can construct a tag machine to simulate any TM.

3. Lambda calculus, developed by Church and Kleene in the 1930s, is the smallest universal programming language. It is a formal system specifically designed to investigate function definition, function application and recursion. While it is equivalent to a TM, its focus is on the transformation rules rather than computational steps.

4. A reversible TM. A TM can be made reversible where information about past states is either stored, or its instructions themselves are reversible. As the laws of physics are reversible, they can only be simulated adequately by a reversible UTM. The physical implications of this are discussed in chapter 8.

5. Probabilistic TM. Generally, a TM is deterministic as there is a well-defined output for each step; otherwise, the machine halts. But, a probabilistic TM, can be envisaged where, at some points in the computation, the machine can randomly access a 0 or a 1. The output of such a machine can then be stochastic. However, as there is no valid random number generator, only pseudo-probabilistic machines would seem to exist. Nevertheless, Casti and Calude [5] have proposed that a quantum number generator be used to provide a true random input. Their article in *New Scientist* suggests some intriguing applications of a truly probabilistic TM. However, at least at the present time, AIT restricts itself to deterministic computation.

It should also be noted that if quantum computers become possible (e.g. *New Scientist* [6]), the Strong Church–Turing Thesis would not apply and efficient quantum algorithms could perform tasks quickly in polynomial time.

### 2.2.2 The universal Turing machine

Each possible TM can be viewed either as a machine that implements a specific algorithm, or as an algorithmic process to enumerate a function. As has been mentioned, a TM is defined by its set of quin-tuples (or quad-tuples). These map the before and after states of the transition table. It becomes possible to identify the string of a quin-tuple by a number that codes for the specified transition. The numbers defining each quin-tuple can be joined to give a single number representing the transition table. This number is unique for each TM and is known as the Turing number or sometimes the Gödel number. This is possible as the set of all TMs is countable, but infinite.

A UTM is one that can simulate any other TM by including the instructions defining a particular TM as part of a UTM programme. Once the Turing number $i$ for the TM, denoted by $T_i$, is established, its transition table can be generated from the integer $i$. That is, the UTM denoted by $U$ can simulate the computation $T_i(p) = x$ by prefixing a simulation programme to $p$. Noting that instructions in the following computation are implemented from the left, the computation that generates $x$ on the UTM $U$ is $U(e1^i0p) = T_i(p) = x$. The routine $e$ is relatively short. It counts the 1's until the 0 is reached. This gives $i$, which is the number that specifies the transition table for the $i$th TM, allowing it to be simulated. The number of bits needed to specify $x$ on the UTM now becomes $|e| + i + 1 + |p|$. Hence, $|e| + i + 1$, which is the simulation constant $sim(T_i)$, is the number of extra bits needed to specify $x$ on the universal machine. While this constant is $O(1)$, as $i$ represents a natural number, it can be very large for TMs specified by a large $i$.

While there are an infinite number of possible universal TMs, Marvin Minsky has described a 7-state 4-symbol UTM [7] and Stephen Wolfram has described a 2-state 3-colour TM that has recently been shown to be universal by Alex Smith [8].

### 2.2.3 Non-computable functions

A computable number is one for which there exists a defined procedure that can output the number to an agreed level of precision. That is, there exists a TM that can implement the procedure. For example, as $\pi$ can be evaluated to, for example, 100 decimal places by a defined procedure, it is a real number that is said to be Turing-computable. One envisages a TM as a function that maps natural numbers as inputs on to a natural number as an output. For example, if the inputs are two numbers, the output can be the sum of these. But there is only a countably infinite number of TMs. Countably infinite means one can order each TM by its Turing or Gödel number. But, as the number of TMs is only countably infinite, and as functions of the natural numbers, are infinite and uncountable, there are insufficient TMs to compute every function. The set of all real numbers are also uncountable and therefore most reals are not computable. As a consequence, a TM cannot halt for all inputs. If a TM halts after a designated finite number of steps, the function specified by the TM is computable. However, if it does not halt in the designated number of steps, it is uncertain whether it will halt if allowed to continue running.

Turing showed [9] that, where a possibly true proposition in a formal system can be articulated as a decision algorithm, the inability to know whether a computation will halt implies that there are some propositions that are undecidable. These cannot be shown to be true or false. The proof of the halting problem as it is known relies on a self-referential-algorithm analogous to the Epimenides' paradox 'this statement is false'. As a consequence, the halting problem is equivalent to Gödel's incompleteness theorem and leads to Rice's theorem, which shows that any nontrivial question about the behaviour or output of a TM is undecidable.

A partially recursive function or a partially recursive computation is one that is computable for some inputs. That is, the TM expressing the function halts on some inputs but not all. A Turing computer can therefore be envisaged as a partially recursive function; a procedure that maps some members of an input set of natural numbers on to an output set of natural numbers. On the other hand, a recursive function (or more strictly total recursive function) is defined for all arguments (inputs) and the TM that embodies the procedure halts on all inputs.

A recursively enumerable or computably enumerable set is one for which an algorithmic or decision procedure exists that, when given a natural number or group of numbers, will halt if the number or group is a member of the set. Equivalently if a procedure exists to list every member of the set, it can be established that a particular string is a member of the set. The set is in effect the domain of a partially recursive function. However, as there is no certainty that the computation will halt, a partially recursive function is semi-decidable; the result of any computation is yes/possibly yes. All finite sets are decidable and recursively enumerable, as are many countable infinite sets, such as the natural numbers. From the point of view of this book, the provisional entropy measure requires the set of all strings that satisfies a particular requirement to be recursively enumerable. That is, a procedure exists to determine whether a string is a member of the set or not.

From a scientific perspective, a primitive recursive function needs to be distinguished from a recursive function. Primitive recursive functions form a subset of the recursive functions and correspond to functions that can be generated by a recursive process applied to a few simple functions. Most functions used in science are in fact primitive recursive as they can be implemented by a computation involving a 'Do' or a 'FOR' loop that terminates after a specified number of cycles.

## 2.3 Measure theory

Useful measures, such as probability, the counting measure (the number of elements in subsets), and the Lebesgue measure, i.e. the distance measure, or volume measure in a multidimensional space, all have similar properties. Measure theory has been developed to provide a framework to establish the properties of these measures on sets, such as the set of real numbers, or reals, $\Re$ that may be infinite.

The critical feature of measure theory is that it provides the tools to determine how a measure on separate subsets is related to the measure for a larger set containing the subsets. For example, in the case of the counting measure, one expects the total number of elements in separate subsets that have no elements in common to be the sum of the elements in each subset. A general measure of a property of a set, and its members, will be denoted by $\mu$. A measure must have appropriate additive properties like the counting measure just mentioned. The measure for all possible events, and arrangements of events, must also be able to be defined. Key to providing a framework for measure theory is the understanding of the Borel sigma algebra or Borel field. This framework is just a series of definitions that provide the rules for manipulating members of a set (e.g. the set of reals, i.e. real numbers), to allow the properties, such as probability, to be defined consistently. The Borel algebra is what is called a sigma algebra that is restricted to a set $\Omega$ which is a metric space; i.e. a space, such as the collection of open sets on the reals, where there is a distance function. Keeping this in mind, the collection $\mathcal{B}$ of subsets of a metric space has the following properties:

- the empty set is in $\mathcal{B}$;
- if subset $B$ is in $\mathcal{B}$ then its complement is in $\mathcal{B}$;
- for any collection of a countable number of sets in $\mathcal{B}$ their union must also be in $\mathcal{B}$. That is, if $B_1$ and $B_2$ are in $\mathcal{B}$, then $B_1 \cup B_2$ are in $\mathcal{B}$, or for countably infinite members, $\bigcup_{i}^{\infty} B_i$.

The axioms also imply that the collection of sets is closed under countable intersection and the collection also includes the full set $\Omega$. For infinite reals, the Borel sigma algebra defines the smallest sigma algebra family that contains all the intervals; but it does not include all the subsets $\Omega$. (The set of all subsets is known as the power set.) In case you want to know, this restriction avoids the Banach–Tarski paradox. With these definitions of the properties of the subsets of the metric space, the definition of a general measure $\mu$, such as probability or number of members, on the Borel algebra is as follows:

- $\mu(\mathcal{B}) \geqslant 0$ and for the empty set $\mu(\varnothing) = 0$;
- the measure is additive;
- for any collection $B_1$, $B_2$, $B_3$ with union $\mathcal{B}$ of countable disjoint sets (i.e. $B_1 \cap B_2 = 0$), $\mu(\mathcal{B}) = \sum_i (B_i)$; noting that $\mathcal{B}$ can be a countable infinite union of sets.

This last bullet point states that if there are no elements in common between the (sub)sets, the measure is just the sum of the measure for each subset.

In the particular case where the measure $\mu$ is over the whole sample space and $\mu(\Omega) = 1$, the measure is termed a probability and is usually denoted by $P$. The measure definition of $P$ corresponds to the Kolmogorov definition of probability used in AIT. However, for infinitely many events, the Kolmogorov probability requires the following extra axiom (see [10] (p 18)) namely:

- for a decreasing sequence of events $B_1 \supset B_2 \supset B_n$ such that the set of intersection of all such events is empty; $\bigcap_n B_n = 0$, then the probability in the limits is given by $lim_{n \to \infty} P(B_n) = 0$.

The Kolmogorov approach to probability provides a fundamental definition of probability that is more useful than the traditional probability based on the frequency of occurrence of events. However, it has some counter-intuitive features. When the approach is applied to the number line of reals [0,1], the probability of the set of irrationals is 1 and the probability of one particular irrational is zero, as there are an infinite number of irrationals. It follows that the probability of the set of all rationals is zero. In other words, the Kolmogorov probability of drawing a rational at random from the set of all numbers on the number line is not just virtually zero, it is zero.

### 2.3.1 Cylinder sets

Not all numbers are rational. Often in science a measurement, for example one that specifies the position and momentum coordinate of an atom, can be treated as a rational number when it is specified to a certain level of precision. However, it is sometimes necessary to develop the mathematical tools to handle the irrational numbers. These are numbers whose decimal or binary expansion is infinite, as they cannot be expressed as a simple fraction in the form of $a/b$ where $a$ and $b$ are integers and $b$ is non-zero. The reals, or real numbers, include both the rational and irrational numbers. Normally, one considers the set of reals to be represented by the set of infinite numbers lying on the number line between 0 and 1, as the properties of any real greater than 1 depends on its properties between 0 and 1. Similarly, using binary notation, there are an infinite set of reals starting with the sequence $x$, i.e. the number on the number line represented by $0.x\dots$ The concept of a cylinder set provides a convenient notation for dealing with such sequences. The cylinder set allows sets of reals belonging to the same region of the number line to be specified by their common prefix, which is $x$ in the above example. The cylinder set is denoted by $\Gamma_x$ and is the set associated with prefix $x$ just after the decimal point. For example, the binary string $0.1011\dots$, where the dots indicate the sequence continues, is the one way set of infinite sequences starting with 1011 and is represented by $\Gamma_{1011}$. The cylinder set $x$ represents the reals from $0.x0^\infty$ to $0.x1^\infty$. (i.e. $0.x$ to $0.x111\dots$ where the $\infty$ sign refers to a repeated 0 or 1). Just as in decimal notation $0.00009^\infty = 0.0001$, so in binary notation $0.00001^\infty$ is equal to $0.0001$. A useful fact is that the infinite set of 1s in the sequence $0.00001^\infty$ can be replaced by $2^{-|0000|}$ $(= 2^{-4})$. In general, $0.x1^\infty$ can be replaced by $0.x + 2^{-|x|}$. (Note here that the vertical lines denote the number of digits enclosed.) This allows one to see that $\Gamma_x$ represents the half open set $[0.x$ to $0.x + 2^{-|x|})$. For those not familiar with the notation, the square bracket '[' indicates the start point is a member of the set while ')' indicates that the endpoint is not.

For a measure $\mu$ based on the set of reals, such as the probability measure, $\mu(\Gamma_x) = \sum_b \mu_b(\Gamma_{xb})$, or in simplified notation $\mu(x) = \sum \mu_b(xb)$. This means that a measure, such as the probability on a cylinder set starting with the prefix $x$, is the sum of the measure of all the strings starting with this prefix. For example, the probability measure denoted by $P$ for all strings starting with 10 is given by $P(\Gamma_{10}) = P(\Gamma_{1010}) + P(\Gamma_{1011})$. This is just the sum of the probabilities of strings starting with 1010 and 1011.

Useful measures include the following.
- *The Lebesgue measure $\lambda$ is a measure of distance between reals and is an invariant under translation. For the real line interval [a,b], this corresponds to*

our intuitive concept of distance and $\lambda = (b - a)$. The Lebesgue measure for a three-dimensional space (i.e. $\mathfrak{R}^3$) is formed from the Cartesian product of the one-dimensional space and is a volume measure. The $6N$-dimensional equivalent is the measure used to quantify volumes in phase space in statistical entropy calculations. The Lebesgue measure $\lambda(\Gamma_x)$ is a measure on the cylinder represented by $[0. \; x$ to $0. \; x + 2^{-|x|})$. An important point that is used later is that the measure corresponds to $2^{-|x|}$, which is the distance between the ends of the cylinder. For example, the cylinder starting with the empty set $\emptyset$ denoted by $\Gamma_\emptyset$ has the Lebesgue measure $\lambda(\emptyset) = 1$ as this cylinder embraces the whole number line from $.\emptyset 0000000...$ to $.\emptyset 1111...$, i.e. $.00000...$ to 1.

- The *Kolmogorov probability measure* on the reals $[0,1]$, with cylinder sets as the subsets, has been mentioned earlier. It is a consistent measure.
- The *counting measure* is straightforward; it is the number of members in a set or subset $\mathcal{E}$ and is denoted by $|\mathcal{E}|$.

*The semi-measure.* A semi-measure does not have the simple additive properties of a true measure. It is a sort of defective probability measure as the definition is loosened. The semi-measure $\mu$ for the set of strings $\Omega$ has

$$\mu(\Omega) \leqslant 1.$$

In the discrete case, this corresponds to $\Sigma_i \mu(s_i) \leqslant 1$. For a continuous semi-measure, specified on the real number line between 0 and 1, the measure has different additive properties than a true measure. That is,

$$\mu(\Gamma_x) \geqslant \Sigma_b \mu(\Gamma_{xb}).$$

The semi-measure is particularly important in AIT as $2^{-H(x)}$, where $H(x)$ is the algorithmic entropy, is a semi-measure. Later section 3.3 shows, $\sum 2^{-H(x)} \leqslant 1$ because of the Kraft–Chaitin inequality.

This connection means that the semi-measure is useful in dealing with the halting probability and in developing the idea of a universal semi-measure to deal with inference as is outlined in section 3.9. The semi-measure is computable from below, i.e. one can approximate it from below.

This is probably all a bit heavy going for the non-mathematician. However, the take home message is that set theory, with the idea of cylinder sets to represent all strings with the same initial sequence, allows a number of different measures, such as volume, probability and number of elements in a set, to be defined in a way that can cope with infinite sets.

# References

[1] Levin L A 1974 Laws of information (nongrowth) and aspects of the foundation of probability theory *Probl. Inf. Trans.* **10** 206–10
[2] Chaitin G 1975 A theory of program size formally identical to information theory *J. ACM* **22** 329–40

[3] Chaitin G J 1988 Randomness in arithmetic *Sci. Am.* **259** 80–5

[4] Casti J L 1995 *Complexification: Explaining a Paradoxical World Through the Science of Surprise* (New York: Harpercollins)

[5] Casti J L and Calude C 2004 Randomness: The Jumble Cruncher *New Scientist* **183** 36–7

[6] Das S 2007 Quantum threat to our secret data *New Scientist* 12 September 2007 https://www.newscientist.com/article/mg19526216-700-quantum-threat-to-our-secret-data/

[7] Minsky M 1962 Size and structure of a universal turing machine using tag systems *Recursive Function Theory: Proceedings, Symposium in Pure Mathematics* (Providence, RI: American Mathematical Society) vol 5 pp 229–38

[8] Smith A 2020 Universality of Wolfram's 2, 3 Turing machine *Complex Syst.* **29** 1–44

[9] Turing A 1936 On computable numbers, with an application to the entscheidungsproblem *Proc. London Math. Soc., Ser. 2* **42** 230–65

[10] Li M and Vitányi P M B 2008 *An Introduction to Kolmogorov Complexity and Its Applications* 3rd edn (New York: Springer)

**IOP** Publishing

# Algorithmic Information Theory for Physicists and Natural Scientists

**Sean D Devine**

# Chapter 3

# AIT and algorithmic complexity

This chapter outlines the history of algorithmic information theory or Kolmogorov complexity as it is known. The principle is that the more structured or ordered an object, the simpler it is to exactly describe by an algorithm. Ice is more ordered and structured than steam, and the algorithm needed to define the position and momentum coordinates of water as ice is much shorter than one that defines water as steam.

This chapter illustrates how a configuration represented by a string of characters that shows order can be described by a shorter algorithm than a string that shows none. Critical to this application is the invariance theorem that shows the number of bits in a program that specifies how a natural system can move from one state to another is independent of the universal Turing machine (UTM) used to undertake the computation.

It is shown that, from the natural world perspective, computational instructions that are uniquely coded eliminate the need for end-markers. In which case, the number of programme bits specifying a real-world structure aligns the algorithmic entropy with the thermodynamic entropy. Related is Shannon's noiseless coding theorem (section 3.4), which shows that optimal coding is achieved when shorter codes are used for outcomes with higher probability.

The algorithmic concept of conditional entropy is analogous to the Shannon conditional entropy. In the algorithmic case, this allows common information such as the bits specifying natural laws to be taken as given or to define a zero of algorithmic entropy. The relevant bits in the algorithmic entropy are the extra bits needed to change one state in the natural world to another.

The idea of the provisional entropy is introduced to specify the algorithmic entropy of the members of a set of natural configurations that exhibit a common pattern but with variation that appears as noise. The relevant example is the set of all microstates in a thermodynamic macrostate. The provisional entropy is identical to

doi:10.1088/978-0-7503-2640-7ch3

Kolmogorov's algorithmic minimal sufficient statistic. Both require a two-part code—one to specify the set, and the other to specify the particular variation to identify the string of interest.

The halting probability is the probability that an algorithm chosen at random and fed into a computer will halt. While not strictly a probability but rather a semi-measure, the algorithmic entropy can be identified with the negative logarithm of the universal semi-measure. The universal semi-measure can be used as the prior in the Bayesian approach to induction, as it is a measure of maximum ignorance.

The concept of the halting probability gives rise to Chaitin's measure Omega (section 3.6). Because this is the sum of the halting probability of all strings, it embodies all algorithms that enact natural laws.

Chaitin [1] has also used algorithmic information to express a formal axiomatic system as a process of stepping through all possible theorems. He provides an alternative proof of Gödel's theorem, showing that valid statements exist that cannot be proven from the axioms (section 3.8).

## 3.1 Shorter algorithms imply order

As was pointed out in section 1.4, algorithmic information theory (AIT) was originally conceived by Ray Solomonoff [2]. The approach was formalised by Andrey Kolmogorov [3] and independently by Gregory Chaitin [4]. These two authors showed how the machine dependence of the algorithmic complexity measure could be mostly eliminated. Later, the approach was extended to self-delimiting coding of computer instructions by Leonard Levin [5, 6], Peter Gács [7] and also Gregory Chaitin [8].

AIT is based on the idea that, what might be considered a highly ordered structure with recognisable pattern, can be more simply described than one that has no recognisable features. For example, the sequence representing $\pi$ can be generated by a relatively short computer programme. This allows the AIT approach to provide a formal tool to identify the pattern or order of the structure represented by a string. In this approach, the algorithmic complexity of a string '$s$' is defined as length of the shortest binary algorithm $p^*$ of length $|p^*|$ that is able to generate that string. Here, * indicates that it is the shortest programme and $|...|$ denotes the length in bits of the programme between the vertical lines.

The length of the shortest algorithm or programme that generates a string is also known as the Kolmogorov complexity or the programme sized complexity. Furthermore, it is also a measure of the information contained in the string. If the programme that generates $s$ is much shorter than the programme that separately specifies each character of $s$, the string is said to be algorithmically ordered. This contrasts with a programme that is as long as the string itself and clearly shows no order.

The importance of AIT for the natural sciences is that a physical or biological system can always be converted to a binary string that represents an instantaneous configuration of the system in an appropriate state space. As an example, consider how one might represent the instantaneous configuration of $N$ players on a sports field. If jumping is to be allowed, three position and three velocity (or more strictly momentum) dimensions are required to specify the coordinates for each player at an instant. The specification of the instantaneous configuration of $N$ players requires a binary string in the $6N$-dimensional state space of the system. The state space is known as the phase space for the particular case of position–momentum coordinates.

If the configuration is ordered, as would be the case if all the players were running in line, the description would be simpler than the situation where all players were placed at random, jumping or running at different speeds and directions. An actual configuration in the state space of a collection of particles will specify the position of the particle, its momentum or the equivalent and the electronic and other states. If the string that describes a particular structure shows order, features or pattern, a short algorithmic description can be found to generate the string.

In practice, strings and algorithms are usually represented in binary form. A simple example might be that of a magnetic material such as the naturally occurring loadstone. The magnetic state of each iron atom can be specified by the direction of its magnetic moment or spin. When the spin is vertically aligned, the direction can be specified by a 1, and by a 0 when the spin is aligned in the opposite direction. This allows the instantaneous configuration of the magnetic system to be specified by a string of 0's and 1's representing the alignment of each spin. Above, what is called the Curie transition temperature, all the spins will be randomly aligned and there will be no net magnetism. In which case, the configuration at instant of time can be specified by a random sequence of 0's and 1's. However, where the spins become aligned, either through unlikely random processes or because the system is below the Curie temperature, the resultant configuration is highly ordered from an algorithmic perspective. It can be represented by a relatively short algorithm generating the sequence of 1's and 0's, as shown below.

Consider the following two sequences, which might represent the configuration of physical system. The first is an ordered string of $N$ repeated 1's, and the second is string of length $N$ with a random sequence of 0's and 1's. If these sequences emerged by tossing a coin $N$ times where a head is denoted by a 1 and tail by a 0, the first sequence is unlikely to occur unless the coin was tampered with. However, in the second case, the outcome would most likely be the results of a toss of a fair coin. Alternatively, these two outcomes could be considered to represent the orientation of spins in a magnetic system as mentioned in the previous paragraph. The algorithms corresponding to two different cases are discussed in the following bullet points.

1. The first case is where the outcome is ordered and is represented by a string of $N$ 1's in a row, i.e. $s = $ '11111 ...'. This string can be described by a simple algorithm $p'$ of the form

$$FOR\ I = 1\ to\ N$$
$$OUTPUT\ '1' \quad\quad (3.1)$$
$$NEXT\ I.$$

In this situation, the algorithm only needs to code the number $N$, the character outputted and the loop instruction that repeats the OUTPUT command. Readers need to keep in mind that in the natural world, the output command sets a bit and this requires energy. However, in the laboratory computer, a bit or bits are set in the code that sends an instruction to the printer to print the character '1'.

In what follows, the notation $|......|$ is used to denote the length of the binary string representing the characters or computational instructions between the vertical lines. In which case, the length of the algorithm $p'$ is

$$|p'| = |N| + |1| + |OUTPUT| + |loop\ instruction|. \qquad (3.2)$$

The integer $N$ is usually specified by the length of its lexicographic representation, i.e. its representation in dictionary order. This is discussed in more detail in section 3.4.1. In the lexicographic representation, $|N| = \lfloor \log_2(N + 1) \rfloor$. Here, the floor function around the log term represents the greatest integer $\leqslant \log_2(N + 1)$. In what follows, $l\hat{o}gN$, without the subscript, will be used to denote this integer—i.e. the length of the lexicographic representation. If $N$ is large, the algorithm will be dominated by the length of $N$ which is close to $\log_2 N$ bits. If $p'$ is a binary algorithm that generates $s$ on a computer $C$, then $|p^*|$, the size of the shortest algorithmic description $p^*$ that generates $s$ must be $\leqslant |p'|$.

2. In the second case, the string is a random sequence of 0's and 1's. This string can be represented by $N$ characters of the form '110010...1100'. Because the sequence is random, it can only be generated by a binary algorithm that specifies each character individually. That is, the algorithm is of the form

$$p' = OUTPUT\ s'.$$

If $p^*$ is the shortest algorithm to do this, then its length is

$$|p^*| \approx |p'| = |s'| + |OUTPUT|.$$

As the length of this algorithm must include both the length of the sequence and the length of the $OUTPUT$ instruction, it must be somewhat greater than the sequence length.

In the AIT framework, the most complex strings are those that show no pattern and cannot be described by a shorter algorithm. However, as is outlined below, to be consistent, standard procedures are required to code the algorithms that specify the structure and to minimize the computer dependence of the algorithm. There are two types of codes that can be used for the computational instructions. The first is where an end-marker, such as a blank, is required at the end of each coded instruction or routine to tell the computer when one instruction or set of instructions finishes and the next starts. This coding gives rise to the plain algorithmic complexity denoted by $C(s)$.

Alternatively, when no code or routine is a prefix of another, the codes or routines can be read instantaneously requiring no end makers. This requires the codes to be restricted to a set of instructions that are self-delimiting. That is, they come from a prefix-free set [6, 8]. The algorithmic complexity using this form of coding will be denoted by $H(s)$. Because $H(s)$ has the properties of entropy and is a measure of string $s$ that represents a configuration in the natural world, it will be termed the 'algorithmic entropy'. To sum up, any natural configuration that can be represented by a string $s_i$ that shows order can be described by a shorter algorithm than one where the string $s_i$ shows no order and which can only be described by specifying each character.

## 3.2 Machine dependence and the invariance theorem

Nothing has been said about the computational device that implements the programme $p^*$. Fortunately, as is shown below, this machine dependence can be managed. Let $p$ be a programme that generates $s$ on a UTM denoted by $U$, i.e. $U(p) = s$. The algorithmic complexity measure on machine $U$ is given by the shortest programme $p^*$ that does this. However, as mentioned above, there are two forms of the algorithmic complexity. The first is called the 'plain algorithmic complexity' where each instruction or code has an end-marker to show that it is completed. This plain algorithmic complexity is denoted by $C_U(s)$. However, the second version of the algorithmic complexity uses self-delimiting coding and no end-markers are required. This is possible where no instruction or algorithm is a prefix of any other. In which case, there is no ambiguity about when one instruction finishes and another starts (section 3.3). The algorithmic complexity for self-delimiting coding, denoted here by $H_U(s)$, is called the algorithmic entropy rather than complexity, as it aligns with the Shannon entropy of information theory.

The following are the equations for plain algorithmic complexity and the algorithmic entropy, the only difference being that the entropy version requires self-delimiting coding. The definitions of $c_U$ and $H_U$ are

$$C_U(s) = min_{U(p)=s} |p| \tag{3.3}$$

and

$$H_U(s) = min_{U(p)=s} |p|. \tag{3.4}$$

That is, the number of bits in the shortest value of $p$, where $U(p) = s$.

When the UTM generates $s$ with input string $y$, i.e. $U(p,y) = s$ the measure becomes

$$C_U(s|y) = min_{U(p,y)=s} |p|, \tag{3.5}$$

and

$$H_U(s|y) = min_{U(p,y)=s} |p|. \tag{3.6}$$

As any UTM can simulate the computations made on any other, when another UTM $W$ implements a similar programme to generate $s$, the invariance theorem shows these two computations are related by

$$C_U(s) \leqslant C_W(s) + c, \qquad (3.7)$$

and

$$H_U(s) \leqslant H_W(s) + c. \qquad (3.8)$$

Here, the constant $c$ allows for the length of an extra term needed to instruct machine $W$ to simulate machine $U$. Although the constant $c$ can be large, it is independent of the string generated and is of the order of 1. It can be denoted by $O(1)$. In practice, algorithmic complexity can be evaluated on a standard reference UTM.

This allows a machine independent measure of algorithmic complexity or entropy as the shortest programme to generate string $s$ defined by

$$C(s) \leqslant C_U(s) + O(1), \qquad (3.9)$$

and

$$H(s) \leqslant H_U(s) + O(1). \qquad (3.10)$$

When string $y$ is given as an input to compute $s$, i.e. $U(p,y) = s$

$$C(s|y) \leqslant C_U(s|y) + O(1), \qquad (3.11)$$

and

$$H(s|y) \leqslant H_U(s|y) + O(1). \qquad (3.12)$$

The UTM invariance theorem is intuitively reasonable as a UTM can be designed with a few simple instructions and an interpreter or compiler can simulate another. The proof of the theorem can be made robust as outlined in section 2.2.2. However, a critical point is that, in the natural world, only entropy differences matter and the $O(1)$ term can often be ignored.

However, it makes sense to use a simple UTM with a minimal instruction to be a reference machine as, in the physical situation, only entropy differences matter. This approach encapsulates most of the instructions in the programme, as the relatively long programme can be compiled from the minimal set of instructions. For this reason, Chaitin uses LISP as the programme language. He has shown that for LISP programming the simulation or $O(1)$ term is of the order of 300 bits. Li and Vitányi [10] (p 210) using combinatory logic based on lambda calculus get

$$C(x) \leqslant |x| + 8 \; and \; C(\varnothing) = 2.$$

There is an alternative but equivalent definition of $C(s)$ and $H(s)$. This involves a two-part definition which involves minimizing the combined description the Turing machine and the programme as given in Li and Vitányi [10] (p 107) as

$$C(s) = min_{i,p}\{|T_i| + |p|: T_i(p) = s\} + O(1), \qquad (3.13)$$

and

$$H(s) = min_{i,p}\{|T_i| + |p|: T_i(p) = s\} + O(1). \tag{3.14}$$

As has been mentioned, $T_i$ is a function, which might, for example, specify a straight line, or a parabola intended to exactly specify a noisy string trending upwards. In this context, $p$ is the argument of $T_i$ and for each random variation of the function a different $p$ is needed to exactly specify the output. The simplest TM might need a long $p$ to generate $s$, while a complex one might need a shorter $p$. This definition minimises the description of the Turing computer that implements the programme combined with the specification of the programme. This formulation is useful if the string has structure, as the approach shows how to capture structure and variation. Just as there is an optimum curve to fit a set of noisy data, i.e. one could have a highly complex curve attempting to pass through each data point, or a simple curve with deviations from the simple curve specified (see sections 4.2 and 4.3.1). The optimum is where the deviations are random. In the same way, using the approach of equations (3.13) or 3.14, one can put most of the description in the TM, in which case the programme will be short, or put most of the description in the programme having a simple TM. Articulating the computation in this way implies that the optimum occurs when all the pattern is included in the machine description which represents a function, and all the random structure is in the programme $p$.

The alternative definition of equation (3.13) indicates how one could use the algorithmic approach to specify noisy data in chapter 4 and also how to find a suitable model to fit data, as is discussed in chapter 5.

Section 7.2 and the following sections focus on the relationship between the algorithmic entropy $H(s)$ and the traditional entropies.

### 3.2.1 Issues with AIT

Crutchfield and his co-workers [11, 12] have noted the following difficulties with the AIT approach to measuring the complexity of strings:

- there is no way to know in advance whether the string $s$ has a shorter description. Even if a shorter description, $s'$, is found, there is no certainty that it is the shortest description. This is equivalent to the Turing halting problem;
- the AIT approach must specify a single string exactly. It appeared that irrelevant information from an observer point of view, including noise, must be exactly specified making the description excessively long and possibly useless for most observed patterns. As chapter 4 shows, noisy strings or strings with variation can be succinctly specified;
- the computational resources (time and storage) to run an AIT algorithm can grow in an unbounded manner;
- the complexity is greatest for random sequences;
- the use of a UTM may restrict the ability to distinguish between systems that can be described by less powerful computational models and the UTM lacks uniqueness and minimality;
- the AIT approach does not capture algebraic symmetries.

The first two bullet points were discussed in section 1.4.2 of the Introduction. The halting problem is a fundamental problem and using some other measure of complexity only hides the problem. The ability of AIT to include noise and variation in strings is no longer a problem. As is discussed further in chapter 4, the concept of provisional entropy, or algorithmic minimal sufficient statistic, or equation (3.13) circumnavigates this perceived problem. The following bullet points discuss the remaining issues:

- the third bullet depends on what measure of complexity is appropriate for a particular application. Certainly, for many physical situations, simple AIT provides insights. For example, Bennett [13] has developed the additional concept of logical depth to capture issues related to resource use, while several other authors have discussed the trade-off between size and resources [10, 14, 15];
- the fourth bullet point is a matter of definition as the critics recognise;
- the fifth bullet point arises because Crutchfield [16] is able to show that stochastic processes can be explained by a hierarchy of machines. Simple processes can be described by computing devices that are less powerful than a UTM. This is not a problem that can be seen if one uses the definition of algorithmic complexity that optimises the sum of the computer device description and the programme as in equation (3.13). Whenever a simple TM captures the pattern, the description of the simpler device is short. One always needs to be aware of the issues related to uniqueness and minimality. But for many physical situations, such as the measurement of the algorithmic entropy of a system, differences rather than absolute values are the critical measure and these concerns are of no significance. Related to this is Rissanen's development of stochastic complexity outlined in section 5.3.3;
- the author is not sure what to make of the last bullet point. Unless the point has been misunderstood. Where algebraic symmetries and scaling symmetries are recognised, any algorithmic description recognising the symmetry will be shorter than one that does not.

Crutchfield and his colleagues [16, 17] developed the causal state approach to provide a systematic process to highlight structure in a stationary stochastic series. However, the purpose of AIT, in contrast to the causal state approach, is to describe the pattern, not to discover it. Hence, any pattern recognition process, that is able to highlight hitherto unobserved structure, can be used to shorten the algorithmic description. These include the causal state approach, the practical minimum description length perspective (see section 5.3), and other systematic processes, whether based on symmetry or physical understanding. Once pattern is identified by whatever means, further compression of the string of interest is possible as a shorter algorithm can be used to capture the pattern.

## 3.3 Self-delimiting coding and the Kraft inequality

A computer implementing an algorithm must recognise where one instruction ends and another begins.

This can simply done by using an end-marker to delimit the code or the instruction. In this case, the complexity measure is the plain algorithmic complexity. However, as Levin [6], Gács [7] and Chaitin [8] have shown, there are many advantages if the coding of each instruction or number is taken from a prefix-free set. In this case, the number of bits needed to specify a structure is the algorithmic entropy. In such a set, no code can be the prefix of any other code. As no end-markers are necessary, these codes can be called instantaneous codes, because they can be decoded as they are read, or alternatively self-delimiting codes, as the code indicates its own length. They are sometimes termed prefix codes which would seem confusing as, strictly, they come from a prefix-free set. As computations in the natural world implementing physical laws are self-delimiting, the algorithmic entropy complexity measure better aligns with the real-world situation.

As has been mentioned, the Kraft inequality holds for self-delimiting codes. Let the codeword length of the $i$th code from the $n$ codes in the prefix-free set be $|x_i|$; then for binary coding the Kraft inequality states:

$$\sum_i 2^{-|x_i|} \leqslant 1. \tag{3.15}$$

This can be generalised to other non-binary alphabets. Figure 3.1 shows the restriction on allowable codes if no code is to be a prefix of any other. The Kraft inequality can be understood by noting that whenever a codeword is assigned, such as the codes in bold type in the figure, the assigned code cannot have a direct connection with a prior code or a subsequent code in the code tree as no code can be a prefix of another. Thus any branch in the binary tree that starts with an already assigned code is blocked from further use as indicated by the dashed lines in the tree in figure 3.1.

For example, if a code is assigned as 100, then 101 can only be assigned if no more codes are needed for this branch. If more codes are needed the potential codes starting with 101 must be extended to 1011 and/or 1010. In general, more codes can only be assigned if an unused code is extended further before being assigned. At each branch, an allowable code of length $|x|$ contributes $2^{-|x|}$ to the Kraft sum.

Whenever a code is assigned, e.g. 0111 and/or 0110 as in figure 3.1, at most the contribution to the Kraft sum is $2^{-|0111|} + 2^{-|0110|}$. This is at most $2^{-3}$, which is the same as the contribution of the parent code '011'. As the contributions are halved at each split, inspection shows that the overall sum can never be greater than 1. Calude's theorem 2.8 [9] provides a neat proof for the Kraft inequality where the codes are not restricted to a binary alphabet.

The converse, the 'Kraft–McMillan' inequality also holds. This inequality states that whenever the codeword sizes satisfy the above inequality, each member in the set of codewords can be replaced by a self-delimiting code of the same length that will also satisfy the inequality.

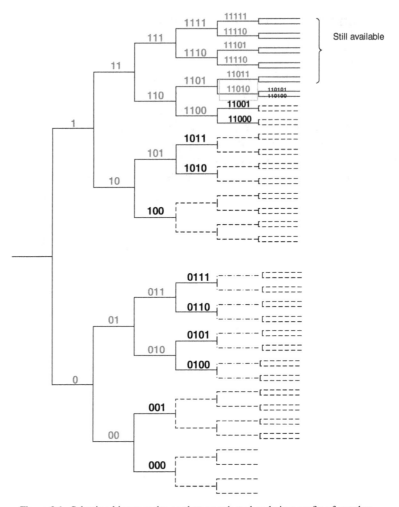

**Figure 3.1.** Selecting binary codes so that no selected code is a prefix of another.

The approach can be extended to complete programmes, not just instructions. If algorithms do not have end-markers, no halting algorithm (e.g. the string $x$ representing an algorithm) can be a prefix of any other algorithm (e.g. string $xy$ is not allowed) as, reading from the left, the machine would halt before undertaking the computation $y$. Thus, if there are no end-markers, the algorithms must also come from the prefix-free set. As the number of possible algorithms is infinite, the Kraft inequality needs to be extended to an infinite set of prefix-free algorithms. Chaitin [8] has proved the extension, known as the Kraft–Chaitin inequality to infinite recursively enumerable sets.

Chaitin argues that, as no valid algorithm can be the prefix of any other for self-delimiting coding, where an algorithm $p$ of length $|p|$ is valid, any other algorithm starting with $p$ and of the form $pxxxx\ldots\ldots$ is invalid. The restriction on prefixes for valid algorithms requires the region on the number line between $0.p0$ and $0.p1$ to be blocked out and unavailable for further algorithms. As for each valid $p$, the region blocked out on the number line is $2^{-|p|}$, the sum of all the non-overlapping regions blocked out for all valid $p$ can at most equal 1, i.e. the length on the number line between 0 and 1.

More formally, consider computer $T(p) = x$ where programme $p$ is a natural number in binary form. If $p$ is a self-delimiting programme, no other programme can start with $p$. If one considers all the real numbers between $[0,1]$, the infinite set of strings starting with $0.p$ must be blocked out and cannot be used for another programme. Section 2.3.1 introduces the idea of cylinder sets, where the cylinder $\Gamma_p$, representing the reals between $0.p0^\infty$ to $0.p1^\infty$, covers all these non-allowed programmes. As section 2.3.1 shows, the Lebesgue or distance measure $\lambda(\Gamma_p)$ on this cylinder is $2^{-|p|}$. If all $p$ come from a prefix-free set, none of the cylinder sets can overlap (i.e. they are disjoint). The measure property means that the sum over all possibly infinite $p$ satisfies $\sum_p \lambda(\Gamma_p) = \sum_p 2^{-|p|}$. This sum can be no greater than 1, the value of the Lebesgue measure on all the reals $[0,1]$. That is, the Kraft inequality holds and $\sum_p 2^{-|p|} \leqslant 1$. Equality occurs when the union of all the cylinder sets completely covers the reals.

However, two standalone programmes cannot be concatenated (joined) as the first implemented will halt before implementing the second. Nevertheless, Bennett [13] shows these halting programmes can be joined (see 3.5) by the insertion of an appropriate linking instruction. At the most, the joining code adds $O(1)$ to the length of the combined routine.

The Kraft inequality holds for all codes or algorithms that come from a prefix-free set. That is, the algorithmic entropy $H(x)$ satisfies $\sum_{all\ x} 2^{-H(x)} \leqslant 1$. As a consequence, in contrast to the plain algorithmic complexity, the algorithmic entropy is more useful for physical situations. Also, in the physical situation, the algorithmic entropy is the preferred concept as it avoids the ambiguity over the meaning of the word complexity, and secondly, as is shown later (see section 7.2), the algorithmic entropy is virtually the same as the Shannon entropy and leads to the algorithmic equivalents of mutual information. Because of the similarity with the Shannon entropy, here $H(x)$ is used to denote the measure with self-delimiting coding, rather than the alternative $K(x)$ as used by Li and Vitanyi [10]. The algorithmic entropy $H(x)$ differs from the $C(x)$, the plain algorithmic complexity, because self-delimiting coding leads to a slightly longer algorithm.

## 3.4 Optimum coding and Shannon's noiseless coding theorem

If one wishes to code a message efficiently, it makes sense to use the shortest codes for the message symbols that occur most frequently. In a sense, an algorithm is a message made up of instruction strings and strings representing structures. These correspond to the set of message symbols. If one instruction or structure occurs more often than another, the shortest algorithm will code the most common message symbols with shorter codes. Shannon's noiseless coding theorem shows how to do this optimally. Consider a set of message symbols $s_1, s_2, s_3, s_4, s_5, \ldots s_k$ that occur in the expected message with probabilities $P_1, P_2, P_3, P_4, P_5, \ldots P_k$. Let the self-delimiting or prefix-free binary codewords for these be $code(s_1)$, $code(s_2)$, $code(s_3)$, $code(s_4)$, $code(s_5)$, ...$code(s_k)$. If $code(s_k)$ is chosen so that the length of the code is given by $-\log_2 P_k$ rounded up, the Kraft inequality is satisfied, as $\sum_k 2^{-\log_2 P_k} = \sum_i P_k$, cannot be greater than 1. In which case, the length of each codeword is within one bit of the probability of its occurrence. That is:

$$-\log_2 P_k \leqslant |code(s_k)| \leqslant 1 - \log_2 P_k. \tag{3.16}$$

The Shannon–Fano method of coding satisfies this requirement. The Shannon–Fano coding can be implemented for a set of symbols that are used to create a message by ordering the set of symbols in a list from the most probable to the least probable. Divide the list into two subsets so that the total probabilities in each half are as near equal as possible. Assign a 0 as the first bit of the code for the members of one subset and a 1 to the first bit for the codes in the other subset. The process is repeated for each subset. That is, each of the two subsets is again divided into halves so that the total probabilities of the two halves are as equal as possible. The second bit in the code is found by assigning a 0 to one of the sub-subsets and a 1 to the other. The process is repeated till each symbol has a unique code. By splitting in this way, the process ensures that no code for a symbol is a prefix of any other, and the code lengths are no more than $-\log_2 P_k + 1$. An alternative, Huffman coding combines probabilities to form even more efficient coding. An arithmetic code [18] is a slightly more efficient entropy-based code.

Equation (3.16) leads to Shannon's noiseless or source coding theorem. As the Shannon entropy, $H_{sh}$, of the set of source symbols is given by $H_{sh} = -\sum_k P_k \log_2 P_k$, given the probabilities $P_k$ of the symbols in the message, the average length of each can be made very close to the Shannon entropy, that is, the entropy based on the expected occurrence of symbols. The expected code length per symbol $\sum P_k |code(s_k)|)$ in a such a coded message is found by multiplying equation (3.16) by the probability $P_k$ and summing over all $k$. This gives

$$H_{sh} \leqslant \sum P_k |code(s_k)| \leqslant H_{sh} + 1. \tag{3.17}$$

In other words, by choosing codes based on their probability, the expected length of a message consisting of $N$ symbols can be made close $NH_{sh}$. As this is optimal for the given probability distribution and cannot be bettered, it provides the basis for choosing codes for a set of computational instructions. While equation (3.17) is known as Shannon's noiseless coding theorem and was originally conceived for codes used in communication, it applies to any system requiring codes such as coding algorithms. An algorithm is a coded message sent to a computer.

The following subsection shows how to optimally code the natural numbers when the probability distribution of the natural numbers in the set of message symbols is not known. Later, in section 3.9, the algorithmic equivalent of Shannon's coding theorem will be discussed.

### 3.4.1 Delimiting coding of a natural number

The algorithmic entropy is given by the number of bits needed to specify a string where the computations are self-delimiting. But two problems emerge.

The first is that the conventional binary representation of a natural number is ambiguous as it is unclear whether the string '010' is the same as the string '10'. This ambiguity can be avoided by coding the number using lexicographic (dictionary) ordering. For example, the integers from 0 to 6 are coded lexicographically as $\varnothing$, 0, 1, 00, 01, 10, 11, etc, where $\varnothing$ is the empty string. It can be seen that the lexicographic equivalent of a natural number $n$ is the binary equivalent of $n + 1$ with the leading 1 removed. This is equivalent to $|n| = \lfloor \log_2(n + 1) \rfloor$ where the floor function in the equation is the integer below the term in the L shaped brackets. Here, this will be denoted by $l\hat{o}gn$, i.e. $|n| = l\hat{o}gn$, noting that this is, at worst, one bit less than $\log_2 n$.

But the second problem is that the algorithmic entropy does not allow end-markers on the codes for symbols representing instructions or structures to indicate where a particular code starts or ends. The codes must be self-delimiting where each code carries information about its length.

While it is straightforward to assign self-delimiting codes to a finite set of instructions or numbers with a known probability distribution using Shannon's noiseless coding theorem (see section 3.4), it is not obvious how to efficiently code a natural number, which may be of an arbitrary length. For example, such numbers often are needed to determine how many times a routine cycles through a computational loop. The lexicographic code for natural numbers codes can be made self-delimiting by appending a prefix that specifies the length of the code to be read.

An inefficient form of doing so is to prefix a string of 1s to indicate the size of $n$ followed by a zero. This prefix takes the form $1^{|n|}0$, where $|n|$ represents the number of bits specifying $n$. This is added to the front of $n$, giving the code $1^{|n|}0n$ to represent $n$. The machine counts the number of 1's before the 0, and this determines the number of bits needed to read $n$. The length of the code is then $2l\hat{o}gn + 1$. For example, if the number 5 is coded by '10' lexicographically, the universal self-delimiting form is 11010 (i.e. two 1's to specify the length of '10' for 5, followed by a zero and finally 10, the code for 5 itself). The machine reading the code counts the number of '1s' until the '0' is reached.

While this code is universal and is effective for any unknown probability distributions, it is lengthy and is not asymptotically optimal [10] (pp 78–79).

Another way of compressing the representation is to shorten the code specifying the number of ones that need to be read rather than using the longer code of the sequence of $|n|$ 1's. This can be achieved by coding the number of bits in $|n|$ by $1^{||n||}0|n|$. This establishes the number of bits specifying the size of $n$, i.e. $|n|$. This step requires $1 + 2l\hat{o}g\hat{o}gn$ bits which then instructs the algorithm to read the next $l\hat{o}g_2n$ bits to determine $n$. The total number of bits including those in $n$ is $1 + l\hat{o}gn + 2l\hat{o}gnl\hat{o}gn$ bits. This is shorter than the previous code which required $1 + 2l\hat{o}gn$ bits. In principle, this compression process can be repeated to code for—the size of, (the size of (the size of (n))) etc. The result is a code for $n$ of length $H(n)$ given by the infinite series;

$$H(n) = 1 + l\hat{o}gn + l\hat{o}gnl\hat{o}gn + l\hat{o}gl\hat{o}gl\hat{o}gn....$$

In practice, the size of the representation of $n$ can be taken to be $\leqslant 1 + l\hat{o}gn + l\hat{o}gl\hat{o}gn + 2l\hat{o}gl\hat{o}gl\hat{o}g$ or a higher expansion.

The additional information required over $l\hat{o}gn$ needed for simple coding is the cost of using self-delimiting coding.

However, it is cumbersome to keep track of the $l\hat{o}gn$ expansion. In what follows, $\log_2$ will be used to replace $l\hat{o}g$ and the full series will be expressed succinctly by $H(n)$. In other words, the self- delimiting code for a string $s_i$, where $s_i^*$ is an $n$ bit string is given by

$$H(s_i) = n + H(n) = n + |n| + H(|n|), \quad (3.18)$$

Noting that $H(n)$ can be expressed as $|n| + H(|n|)$, where $|n|$ can be represented by $\log_2 n$. In which case, the higher loglog terms are captured in $H(|n|)$. Later, this nomenclature is used to identify the increase in bits due to a randomising process. A highly ordered string of $n$ repeated 1's can be coded with $H(n) = |n| + H(|n|)$ bits, whereas a random string requires $n + H(n)$ bits. Randomising an $n$ bit ordered string adds an extra $n$ bits to the self-delimiting representation of the string.

An important question is how significant is the length information embodied in the code representing a natural number? Are these loglog terms significant? The answer is that for a so-called equilibrium (or a typical) state in a thermodynamic system, the extra length information is insignificant. For example, there are about $N = 10^{23} \approx 2^{77}$ particles in a mole of a Boltzmann gas. The algorithmic entropy of a typical state requires the position and momentum of each of the $2^{77}$ particles to be specified to a required degree of precision. Assume that both the position and momentum coordinates of each particle are defined to 1 part in $2^8$. This requires 16 bits per particle. If there are $2^{77}$ particles, $16 \times 2^{77}$ bits are required. The algorithmic entropy of a typical configuration is therefore approximately $2^{81}$ bits. The loglog term, which is the first in the sequence capturing the length information, is $\log_2 2^{81} = 81$ bits. This is an insignificant contribution to the algorithmic entropy. The next term in the series is $\log_2(81)$ which is smaller still. However, in comparing a partially ordered system with a disordered one, as illustrated in figure 4.1, the length or self-delimiting contribution needs to be identified for consistency.

The discussion here is relevant to the evaluation of the provisional entropy of a string in a set of states discussed in section 4.2. The provisional entropy consists of a two-part code, one part defines the set of strings exhibiting a particular structure or pattern, the other identifies the string within the set representing a variation of the structure. In this case, it may be possible to embody the length information in the description of the set.

### 3.4.2 The relationship with entropy, conditional entropy, etc

An important question is, when is it more efficient to compute two strings $x$ and $y$ together, using a single algorithm, rather than separately? In other words, when is

$$H(x, y) < H(x) + H(y)? .$$

If $x$ and $y$ are independent, there is clearly no gain in calculating them in a combined algorithm. However, if $y$ has information about $x$ it would suggest that computing $y$ first will lead to a shorter description of $x$ given $y$.

A similar question arises from the Shannon information theory perspective. In this case, given random variables $X$ and $Y$, when is the Shannon entropy

$$H_{sh}(X, Y) < H_{sh}(Y) + H_{sh}(X)? \tag{3.19}$$

The following discussion shows that the algorithmic relationships between strings closely resembles the Shannon relationships between random variables. However, care is needed as seen in the discussion below.

In the Shannon case in general,

$$H_{sh}(X, Y) = H_{sh}(Y) + H_{sh}(X|Y). \tag{3.20}$$

In the special case where the random variable $X$ depends on $Y$, $H_{sh}(X|Y) < H_{sh}(X)$ and $H_{sh}(X, Y) < H_{sh}(Y) + H_{sh}(X)$. If the random variable $X$ does not depend on $Y$, knowing $Y$ does not decrease the uncertainty in $X$ and the equal sign is appropriate in equation (3.19)[1].

Similarly, for the algorithmic entropy, if the strings $x$ and $y$ are to be described together, information about $y$ may simplify the computation of $x$. However, in contrast to the Shannon case, Chaitin [19] has shown that, unless the compressed description $y^*$ of $y$ is used, logarithmic corrections are required. This means that, while $U(y^*) = y$, rather than using $y$ as an input to compute $x$ given $y$, $y^*$ should be used instead to eliminate the logarithmic corrections. Hence, if the programme $p^*$ generates $x$ by the computation $U(p^*, y^*) = x$, then as $|p^*| = H(x|y^*)$,

$$H(x, y) = H(y) + H(x|y^*) + O(1).$$

In contrast to the Shannon equation, 3.20, $y^*$ is needed as it contains information about both $y$ and the length of the shortest description of $y$. The alternative is to use $y$ and $H(y)$, in which case the above equation becomes

$$H(x, y) = H(y) + H(x|y, H(y)) + O(1).$$

The above equation recognises that, in many cases, string $x$ can be computed more efficiently once the minimal description of string $y$ is known. Where this is the case $H(x|y^*) \leqslant H(x)$, i.e.

$$H(x, y) \leqslant H(x) + H(y) + O(1).$$

---

[1] Note for the Shannon entropy, upper case labels are used to indicate the sets of random variables.

As computing $x$ independently may be achieved by a shorter programme than one that computes both $x$ and $y$, $H(x) \leqslant H(x, y)$. In general,

$$H(x) \leqslant H(y) + H(x|y^*) + O(1). \qquad (3.21)$$

When the full description of $y^*$ is essential to compute $x$, the equal sign is necessary as $y^*$ must be computed as part of the shortest computational path that computes $x$. An important example of this is where $y^*$ represents the compressed version of the subroutines that express the physical laws that are essential to specify $x$ in a physical situation. In general, equation (3.21) shows that programmes can be joined or concatenated in a subadditive manner to within $O(1)$. Here, the $O(1)$ term is the few extra bits required to join two separate algorithms as was outlined in section 3.3 and is further discussed in section 3.5. As the discussion is about physical situations, an appropriate algorithmic entropy zero can be chosen to avoid the computer dependence of the entropy measure.

Shannon has defined the mutual information between two sets $X$ and $Y$ as

$$I(X: Y) = H(X) + H(Y) - H(X, Y).$$

The mutual information is a measure of how many bits of uncertainty are removed if one of the variables is known. In the algorithmic case, the mutual information between the two strings is denoted by $I(x: y)$ (or $H(x: y)$). Given the minimal programme for $x$, the mutual information $I(x: y)$ can be defined as

$$I(x: y) = H(x: y) \equiv H(x) - H(x|y^*)$$

or

$$I(x: y) \equiv H(x) + H(y) - H(x, y) + O(1).$$

Readers should be aware that the definition of mutual information can differ slightly between authors. For example, authors in [19, 20] have defined a symmetric version of the mutual information by using the second equation but without the $O(1)$ term. In which case, an $O(1)$ term is transposed to the first equation. However, in the more fundamental paper [8], Chaitin uses the definitions above. Nevertheless, the difference in the definition is insignificant for measures on large strings.

The remarkable similarity of the similarity of algorithmic entropy relationships and those of the Shannon entropy should not be overlooked. Allowing for the use of $y^*$ instead of $y$ and the $O(1)$ term, they look identical. But the two approaches are not the same. The Shannon relationships show how the uncertainty in observing a random variable can be reduced by knowing about a dependent random variable. The algorithmic relationships show how computing one string simplifies the computation of a related string where there is common information. The algorithmic expression is about actual information shared between two strings.

From the above algorithmic results other important results also follow.

$$H(x, y) = H(y, x) + O(1).$$

Because self-delimiting coding is used, the algorithmic entropy may be slightly greater than $|x|$. The general equation is

$$H(x) \leqslant |x| + H(|x|) + O(1).$$

The equation immediately above shows that for a typical, or close-to-random string, which is the case for most strings, the algorithmic entropy is the length of the string plus the cost of requiring self-delimiting coding embodied in $H(|x|)$. This was discussed earlier in equation (3.18). If the string can be compressed, the entropy will be less than the right-hand side. Also,

$$H(x) = H(x||x|) + H(|x|) + O(1),$$

which for the case of a random string of length $n$ gives

$$H(x) = n + H(n) + O(1),$$

as in equation (3.18). In algorithmic information theory, the information embodied in a string that specifies a state of a system or structure is the minimum number of bits needed to specify the string and hence the system. The measure of information $I(x)$ and the algorithmic entropy are identical and

$$I(x) = H(x).$$

One further point of interest is that section 3.6 defines a halting probability $Q$. While $Q$ is not a true probability, the algorithmic mutual information between two specific strings $x$ and $y$ can be defined in terms of the halting probability, $Q$, i.e.

$$I(x: y) = \log_2(Q(x, y)/(Q(x)Q(y)) + O(1).$$

The expectation value of the mutual information takes the same form as the Shannon definition of mutual information using probabilities, but with $Q(x, y)$ instead $P(X, Y)$, etc.

## 3.5 Entropy relative to the common framework

If $y$ is essential as an input to generate $x$, and $q^*$ is the routine that given $y$, halts on generating $x$, then $U(q^*, y) = x$. However, if $y$ can be generated by programme $p^*$ with the computation $U(p^*, w) = y$, can $q^*p^*w$ be a programme to generate $x$ directly without $y$ as an input? That is, can we generate $y$, and from $y$ generate $x$. The answer is that this is not straightforward, as the string $q^*p^*$ is not a valid algorithm. The halting requirement forces the computation to stop when $y$ is generated, as $p^*$ is self-delimiting. That is, $U(q^*(p^*, w))$ halts once $y$ is produced and does not continue to generate $x$. But as has been shown [8, 13], the situation can be remedied as a prefix $r$ can be introduced to stack an instruction to restart the computation when the computation would otherwise end. Hence $U(q^*r((p^*, w))) = x$. Here, brackets are used within brackets to indicate the priority order of the computations. The algorithmic entropy is then the combined entropy given by $|p^*| + |q^*| + |r^*|$. While the contribution of $r$ is trivially small, if necessary it can be specified in an $O(1)$ term. It follows for this particular case where $y$ is necessary to generate $x$, $H(x) = H(x, y)$.

The algorithmic entropy of string $x$ can then be expressed as $H(x) = H(y) + H(x|y, H(y)) + O(1)$ as $y$ must be generated in the computational path that generates $x$. Nevertheless, this simple additive expression only covers the case of optimally compressed essential routines. In the case where string $y$ is not an essential input to $x$, $H(x) \leqslant H(x, y)$ and $\leqslant H(y) + H(x|y, H(y)) + O(1)$.

However, as is discussed further in section 8.4, the above argument is not needed for real-world, reversible non-halting computations. Although self-delimiting algorithms know when to halt, a real-world computation is reversible and continues indefinitely. It is when an on-going computation puts a string representing a real-world configuration such as $y$, in a region of computational space accessible to an algorithm $q^*$, that $x$ can be produced. The bit flows (section 8.5) show that the algorithmic entropy of $x$ is identical to the length of the concatenated programmes $q^*$ and $p^*$.

As the entropy difference rather than the absolute entropy has physical significance, in any physical situation, common information strings, in effect the common instructions, can be taken as given. Effectively, this information plays the role of the critical routine $p^*$ in the previous paragraph. Common information can include the binary specification of common instructions equivalent to 'OUTPUT' and 'FOR/NEXT' and the $O(1)$ uncertainty implied by the reference UTM. In a physical situation, the common information can include the physical laws and for thermodynamic systems, the algorithmic description of the phase space grain size [21]. In what follows the common information routines will be represented by '$CI$' and, given the common information, the physically significant entropy will be denoted by the conditional entropy $H_{algo}(x|CI)$. As the entropy difference between two configurations $x$ and $x'$ is $H_{algo}(x|CI) - H_{algo}(x'|CI)$, $H(CI)$ can be taken as the algorithmic entropy zero and the common contribution ignored.

An algorithmically ordered sequence is recognized because there is an implicit reference to a patterned set that will be recursively enumerable. Any sequence $x$ of this set can be at least partially compressed (see chapter 4) and the primary entropy contribution will depend on parameters such as the length of the string and the number of possible states in the system. The conditional algorithmic entropy of a typical member of this patterned set will be termed the 'provisional' entropy. As section 4.2 shows, it is the upper measure of the conditional algorithm for a member given the set. However, a very few non-typical members of the set may be further compressed. Whenever a member of a set can be compressed further, a more refined model is needed to capture the pattern in those particular strings. This is discussed further in section 4.3.1 on algorithmic minimal sufficient statistic.

## 3.6 Entropy and probability

Let the algorithmic halting probability $Q_U(x)$ be the probability that a randomly generated programme string will halt on the reference UTM, denoted by $U$ with $x$ as its output [8]. The randomly generated programme that has a halting probability $Q_U(x)$ can be considered as a sequence of 0's and 1's generated by the toss of a coin.

The probability of any particular random programme of length $|p|$ occurring will be $2^{-|p|}$. In which case, $Q_U(x)$ is defined by

$$Q_U(x) = \sum_{U(p)=x} 2^{-|p|}. \tag{3.22}$$

The sum of all such probabilities, $\Omega_U = \sum_x Q_U(x)$. As each algorithm that generates $x$ comes from a prefix-free set $\Omega_U \leqslant 1$ because of the Kraft–Chaitin inequality. But, whenever $\Omega_U \neq 1$, $Q_U(x)$ cannot be a true probability. It is instead termed a semi-measure as discussed in section 2.3.1. Furthermore, in this case there is no gain in normalising $Q_U(x)$ by dividing by $\Omega_U$, as $\Omega_U$ is not computable. Even so, this concept allows a very important connection to be made between the algorithmic entropy of a string and the halting probability. The argument is as follows.

- $Q_U(x) \geqslant 2^{-H_U(x)}$ as $H_U(x)$ is the minimum $|p|$ to generate $x$, while the sum defining $Q_U(x)$ includes not just one, but all programmes that generate $x$. Basically, the shortest programme generating $x$ in the sum for $Q_U(x)$ is $H(x)$ and is a dominate contribution. This leads to the inequality,

$$H_U(x) \geqslant -\log_2 Q_U(x). \tag{3.23}$$

- But, $H(x)$ cannot be much greater than $-\log_2 Q_U(x)$ as only a few short programmes are able to generate $x$ on the UTM, $U$. All the longer descriptions contribute little to the sum as is shown immediately below. Furthermore, if it can also be shown that

$$H_U(x) \leqslant \lceil -\log_2 Q(x) \rceil + c, \tag{3.24}$$

then because of equation (3.23), it must follow that

$$H_U(x) = -\log_2 Q(x) + c, \tag{3.25}$$

where $c$ is a small constant.

The upper limit on $H_U(x)$ (equation 3.24) can be seen by noting (Downey, private communication) that, as $H_U(x)$ is an integer, $H_U(x) \geqslant \lceil -\log_2 Q_U(x) \rceil$. But $\lceil -\log_2 Q_U(x) \rceil$ can also be used in an algorithm to generate string $x$. More specifically, a routine $p$ that takes $\lceil -\log_2 Q_U(x) \rceil$ and decodes it to give the string $x$, would be a measure of algorithmic complexity of $x$. Basically, the routine $p$ can be found by taking the integral value of $-\log_2 Q(x)$ and, starting with the lowest programme of this length step through all allowable routines in lexicographic order to see which, if any, generate the string $x$. If no routine generates $x$, the programme increments the length by one, and again steps through all allowable routines of this length. (This is a thought experiment as some routines may not halt. However, we are only interested in finding those that do.) Eventually one, close to $-\log_2 Q(x)$ will generate $x$. The length of this routine cannot be less than $H_U(x)$ by definition. That is, the programme $p$ with length $|p| = \lceil -\log_2 Q(x) \rceil + |stepping\ routine|$ is an upper measure of the algorithmic entropy or complexity. From the second bullet point above, it follows that $H_U(x) \leqslant |p|$ and because of equation (3.23)

$$H_U(x) \leqslant \lceil -\log_2 Q(x) \rceil + c \tag{3.26}$$

where $c$ represents the length of the stepping routine. This upper limit can be combined with equation (3.23) leading to the relationship;

$$-\log_2 Q(x) \leqslant H_U(x) \leqslant -\log_2 Q(x) + c.$$

Equation (3.25) follows by including the fraction that rounds up $-\log_2 Q(x)$ in the constant $c$. This is similar in form to equation (3.16) that leads to Shannon's noiseless coding theorem. Here, however, the upper limit is determined by the constant $c$ rather than 1, noting that the $O(1)$ constant, $c$, is not dependent on $x$. This indicates that the algorithmic code for a string, i.e. its algorithmic entropy, is just a constant away from the halting probability of that string. Also, as the result will only vary slightly for different UTMs, one can drop the suffix $U$ representing the specific UTM. It can be seen that the constant $c$ indicates that there are $2^c$ programmes close to $H(x)$. If there are $2^c$ programmes of a size close to $H(x)$, and one ignores the significantly longer programmes, it follows that $Q(x)$ would be $\leqslant 2^c 2^{-H(x)}$. As was stated above, this implies that $H_U(x) \leqslant -\log_2 Q_U(x) + c$. In effect, the constant $2^c$ becomes a measure of the small number of short programmes that make a significant contribution to $Q(x)$.

$Q(x)$ is an un-normalised measure of the probability that a string generated at random will produce $x$ on the UTM. However, it can be envisaged as an actual probability by assigning the unused probability space to a dummy outcome. This allows $Q(x)$ to be treated as a probability measure for a particular algorithm $x$ in the set of all algorithms that generate $x$. Relative to this probability, the expectation value of $H(x)$, $\langle H(x) \rangle$ over the set of strings is close to $\langle H(x) \rangle = -\sum_x Q(x) \log_2 Q(x)$. That is the algorithmic equivalent of Shannon's coding theorem 3.17, as $\langle H(x) \rangle$ is within a constant $c$ of a term that represents the Shannon-type entropy derived from the halting probability. This again reinforces what has been shown earlier that, while the algorithmic entropy and the Shannon entropy are conceptually different, the expectation value of the algorithmic entropy for a set of states is closely aligned to the Shannon entropy. A more general approach to prove the same relationship that relies on the properties of a universal semi-measure will be outlined in section 3.9.

## 3.7 The fountain of all knowledge: Chaitin's Omega

Chaitin [8] asked the question; 'What is the probability that a randomly selected programme from a prefix-free programme set, when run on a specific UTM will halt with a given output $x$?' section 3.6 defined $Q_U$ as this probability. Strictly, it is a defective probability and should be termed a semi-measure (see section 3.6). The halting probability $\Omega_U$ for all $x$ is obtained by summing $Q_U$ over all halting outcomes $x$ generated by a random input.

$$\Omega_U = \sum_{U(p)halts} 2^{-|p|} = \sum_x Q_U(x).$$

$\Omega_U$ is between 0 and 1. As $\Omega$ contains all possible halting algorithms, if the Universe operates under computable laws, $\Omega$ contains everything that can be known about the Universe; it embodies all possible knowledge as it embodies all halting programmes. While the value of $\Omega$ is computer dependent, it can be converted between UTMs. Unfortunately, all the contributions to $\Omega_U$ can only be established by running all possible programmes to see if they halt. Every $k$ bit programme $p$ that halts (i.e. where $|p| = k$) contributes $2^{-k}$ bits to $\Omega_U$. $\Omega$ is random in the Chaitin or Martin–Löf sense (section 6.2). If $\Omega$ could be generated by a simpler programme, it would then be possible to predict whether a particular programme contributing to $\Omega$ will halt. This cannot be possible, as doing so would violate the Turing halting theorem. Chaitin (who named this number $\Omega$) showed that, just as there is no computable function that can determine in advance whether a computer will halt, there is also no computable function able to determine the digits of $\Omega$. $\Omega$ is uncomputable and can only be approximated by checking each possible programme from the smallest upwards to see which might halt in a given time. Interestingly, Calude, Dinneen and Shu [22] have calculated $\Omega$ to 64 places and get the binary value $\Omega = 0.000\,000\,100\,000\,010\,000\,011\,000\,100\,001\,101\,000\,111\,111\,001\,011\,101\,110\,100$ $001\,000\,0....$

## 3.8 Gödel's theorem and formal axiomatic systems

Chaitin [1] has developed the algorithmic equivalent of Gödel's theorem. He has shown that in a formal axiomatic system, valid propositions exist that are true, but which cannot be shown to be true. That is, they cannot be proven from a simpler set of axioms and rules. For example, most strings are random, as there are, at most only $2^n - 1$ strings shorter than a string of length $n$. This indicates that there are insufficient strings to provide a shorter description of most strings. Once $n$ becomes reasonably large, most strings of length $n$ are random and cannot be algorithmically compressed into an appreciably shorter string. One would therefore expect to be able to identify a random string and prove it is random, by a theorem in the formal system. Chaitin has shown that this is not possible.

Given the axiomatic system and the rules of inference, any valid theorem, represented by a string, can be generated by a computational procedure that systematically steps through all possible derivations until the theorem is proven. However, as is shown below, no theorem can be found that identifies a particular string as random for large $n$. While random strings clearly exist, a proposition that a particular string is random is undecidable in the system. This is of course Gödel's theorem showing that certain truths are unprovable.

In order to explore Chaitin's approach using AIT, consider a formal logical axiomatic system that is as rich as arithmetic with multiplication, and which is required to be both consistent and sound. No statement in such a system can be both true and false, and only true statements can be proven to be true. Let '$A$' be a string of symbols that represents the axioms of the system and the rules of inference. The length of the shortest algorithmic description of the string $A$ is denoted by $|A|$. The set of all provable theorems is recursively enumerable. This means that one can generate all theorems by a process that steps through all possible theorem proofs in ascending order of length and uses a proof checking algorithm to determine whether a particular statement or proposition generated is a valid theorem. Those strings that might represent theorems, but which do not belong to the recursively enumerable set of true theorems, cannot be proven. As they do not appear in the list of theorems, they are undecidable. This is of course Gödel's theorem but with an upsetting twist that unprovable theorems are everywhere; the provable theorems are only a small selection of the space of all possible theorems. Worse, as the length of the derivation of possible theorem strings increases, the number of strings associated with unprovable statements grows faster than the provable ones.

An alternative way of looking at this is to tie the argument into the halting problem. The undecidability of the halting problem underpins the undecidability of a rich formal system.

The above argument can be made more robust. Denote $n$ as the length of string $x$, where '$H(x) \geq n$' is a statement to be proved in the formal system. This statement asserts that a random string $x$ can be found that satisfies the inequality; i.e. one where the algorithmic complexity of the string is at least as great as its length $n$. It has already been argued that many such strings must exist, but can one always find such a string?

The proof relies on developing a procedure to step through all the valid proofs that can be derived from the axioms and the laws of inference until an algorithmic proof $p$ finds the first $x$ such that $H(x) \geq n$. As has been mentioned, this is akin to stepping through all the integers until one is found with a particular property. The proof $p$ will contain the axioms, embody the algorithm stepping through and checking the proofs, as well as the specification of $n$ to indicate when the string of interest has been found. As the size of $n$ can be represented by a little more than $\log_2 n$ bits in the algorithm, the length of this algorithm is

$$|p| = |A| + \log_2 n + |stepping\ algorithm\ and\ proof\ checker| + O(1). \quad (3.27)$$

This implies a computational procedure, $p$ where $U(p) = x$ can be found. But $|p|$ cannot be less than the shortest possible description defined by $H(x)$; otherwise, $p$ could be used to provide a more compressed definition of $x$. If the finite constant $c$ is taken to be the length of the description of the system, $|A|$, and the stepping algorithm, and because $|p|$ cannot be less than the shortest description of $x$, it follows that

$$H(x) \leq |p| = \log_2 n + c.$$

This implies that a proof has been found that outputs the first $x$, where $H(x) \geq n$. As $\log_2 n + c > H(x)$, it follows that $\log_2 n + c \geq n$. But this is only possible when $\log_2 n \geq n - c$. As for finite $c$, $n - c$ grows faster than $\log_2 n$, eventually, for large values of $n$ the inequality cannot be satisfied. In which case, any search for an algorithm $p$ can never halt.

While there are mathematical propositions in any formal system that are not decidable, it is impossible to determine which these are, even though the number of such undecidable propositions grows faster than the decidable ones as the description length of the propositions increases. While some undecidable statements could be made decidable by judiciously incorporating them as new axioms in a more complex formal system (in the sense of the system having a longer description), there is no certainty that the system would remain consistent.

This leads Chaitin to speculate that mathematics should accept this uncertainty and become experimental [19, 23, 24]. Chaitin suggests that apparently undecidable statements that would seem to be true based on compelling evidence to date, could be incorporated as additional axioms in the formal system to extend its capability. Presumably after several decades or even centuries of exploration of the consequences of the new axioms, when no inconsistency is found, there could be confidence in their truth. For example, the Riemann hypothesis may be undecideable (although, for an update see the article by Kvaalen [25] in *New Scientist* that suggests it might be provable), yet experimentally it seems likely to be true. This hypothesis could then be taken as an extra axiom with the possibility that more new and interesting theorems could then be proved. This can tell us something about Chaitin's somewhat mystical number $\Omega$. $\Omega$ can be constructed from the provable theorems in a logical system—there is no contribution from undecidable theorems as the generating computation will not halt for these. If $\Omega$ represents the logical system that encapsulates all the physical laws, knowing $\Omega$ is equivalent to knowing everything. If $\Omega$ were computable, all the physical laws could be expressed simply. As mentioned, Calude, Dinneen and Shu [22] have calculated $\Omega$ to 64 places and get the binary value given in section 3.7.

There is a further implication that many have wrestled with. Does the human mind operate as a finite TM when undertaking logical thought? If so, it will be constrained by Gödel's theorem. Barrow [26] (chapter 8) scopes the views of some of the key players in the debate, while more recently Feferman [27] discusses the historical development. The particular issues surrounding strong determinism and computability have been explored by Calude *et al* [28]. It seems to the present author that, while the human brain or mind need not act as a finite TM to hit upon new truths about the Universe, formal logical processes would appear to be needed to prove that these are truths. In which case, the proof process, rather than the discovery, will be constrained by Gödel's theorem. While the human mind can add new theorems and use external devices to extend its computational capability, once the axioms and laws of inference become too great, the mind may not have sufficient capability in terms of its complexity to be assured of the consistency of the formal processes. Thus, there may well be laws that are beyond human comprehension in that these laws will not be able to be deduced from simpler principles or be understood in simpler terms. Clearly not all agree.

## 3.9 The algorithmic entropy, the universal semi-measure and inference

It was shown in section 3.4 that, for an enumerable probability distribution $P$, where the source alphabet of symbols has probabilities as $P_1$, $P_2$, ... , $P_k$..., a set of optimal codes denoted by $code(s_j)$ can be found for each symbol $s_j$. The expected code length of a message made up of these symbols is related to the Shannon entropy, $H_{sh}$, by

$$H_{sh} \leqslant \sum P_k|code(s_k)| \leqslant H_{sh} + 1.$$

This, known as Shannon's noiseless coding theorem, shows that the expected length of a coded message originally of length $N$, is close to $NH_{sh}$. As section 3.6 showed, algorithmic information theory has a coding theorem, called the algorithmic coding theorem, which is analogous to Shannon's noiseless coding theorem. This section looks at an alternative approach to the algorithmic coding theorem based on establishing a universal semi-measure that is optimal.

Just as one can have a universal TM that, within fixed boundaries, can simulate any other TM, one can have a universal code that is asymptotically optimal in coding a message independently of the distribution of the source words. As is outlined below, and implied in section 3.6, this code for $x$ is given by the semi-measures $H(x)$ or $\log_2 Q(x)$. The two are equivalent to within an $O(1)$ constant.

The derivation is based on the fact that there is a universal enumerable semi-measure that is an optimal code for a discrete sample space. It is optimal in the sense that it must multiplicatively dominate all other constructive semi-measures. That is, up to a multiplicative constant it assigns a higher probability to an outcome than any other computable distribution. In other words, if $m(x)$ is the universal enumerable semi-measure, then $m(x) \geqslant c\mu(x)$ where $\mu(x)$ is any other semi-measure in the discrete sample space. The significance of this will become apparent, but firstly it should be noted that the universal property only holds for enumerable semi-measures, not for the class of all semi-measures or the more restricted class of recursive semi-measures (see Li and Vitányi (p 246) [10] and Hutter [29]). Gács [30] has shown that $m(x)$ is also constructive (i.e. computable from below).

While there are a countably infinite number of universal semi-measures, the universal halting probability $Q(x)$ can be taken to be a reference universal semi-measure. All semi-measures can in principle be enumerated by establishing the halting probability $Q_T(x) = \sum_{T_i(p)=x} 2^{-|p|}$ for every Turing machine, $T_i$. Let the universal halting probability $Q(x)$ be defined for a universal machine that can simulate any TM. The set of all random inputs giving rise to $Q(x)$ will include the simulation of every TM and every programme $p$ that runs on each $T_i$. As $Q(x)$ includes every semi-measure, it multiplicatively dominates them all. The universal probability is therefore a universal semi-measure. However, $2^{-H(x)}$ is also a constructive semi-measure, and because $H(x)$ is equal to $-\log_2 Q(x)$ to within an additive constant, $2^{-H(x)}$ is equal $Q(x)$ to within a multiplicative constant. $H(x)$ must also be a universal semi-measure. In other words, the semi-measures, $m(x)$, $Q(x)$ and $2^{-H(x)}$, are all universal and are all equal to within a multiplicative constant, as they all multiplicatively dominate each other and their logarithms additively dominate each other.

Taking logarithms, the following equality, which is the algorithmic equivalent of Shannon's coding theorem [6], holds to within an additive constant $c_p$ or an $O(1)$ term:

$$H(x) = -\log_2 m(x) = -\log_2 Q(x).$$

This approach provides an alternative derivation of equation (3.25). For practical reasons, it is convenient to take the universal semi-measure as $m(x) = 2^{-H(x)}$.

The Shannon coding theorem (3.16) shows that for a given distribution $P(x)$, a binary self-delimiting code can be constructed that, on average, generates a code for string $x$ that is close to $\log_2 P(x)$ in length and this is optimal for that probability distribution. However, such a code is not universal for all probability distributions. In contrast, the algorithmic coding theorem shows that there is a universal code for any enumerable distribution (i.e. one that can be specified to a given number of significant figures). This codeword for $x$ is the shortest algorithm that generates $x$. Its length is $H(x)$ or $\log_2 Q(x)$ to within an additive constant $c_p$ independent of $x$.

The universal enumerable semi-measure $m(x)$ is a measure of maximum ignorance about a situation. It assigns maximal probability to all objects (as it dominates other distributions up to a multiplicative constant) and is in effect a universal distribution. As a universal distribution, the universal semi-measure provides insight into defining a typical member of a set and provides a basis for induction based on Bayesian principles, as is outlined in the next section.

### 3.9.1 Inference and and the universal distribution

Laplace developed the concept known as the principle of indifference, or the principle of insufficient reason, from an idea first articulated by Jakob Bernoulli. This concept provides a tool to cope with situations where a particular outcome might have several possible causes. Because there is no reason to favour one cause over any other, the principle states that they all should be treated as equally probable. That is, in the absence of any evidence that a tossed coin is biased, this principle would give equal probability to a head or a tail[2].

The principle leads to Bayes' theorem which determines how likely a particular hypothesis $\mathcal{H}_i$ is, given data $D$. That is, the probability of the hypothesis given the data is

$$P(\mathcal{H}_i|D) = P(D|\mathcal{H}_i)P(\mathcal{H}_i)/P(D). \tag{3.28}$$

This rule, which is little more than a rewrite of the definition of conditional probability, provides a basis for inference. If $\mathcal{H}_i$ represents a member of the set of hypotheses or models that might explain the data $D$, then the inferred probability or

---

[2] Of course, this approach does not take into account the cost of a mistake in assuming no bias. While each cause can be assumed to be equally likely, one would need a betting or insurance strategy to cover hidden biases, as is discussed later in section 6.2.3.

posterior probability is defined as $P(\mathcal{H}_i|D)$. This is the probability of that particular hypothesis given the data. If the probability $P(\mathcal{H}_i|D)$ of one particular hypothesis $\mathcal{H}_i$ is significantly greater than the alternatives, there is some confidence that the hypothesis $\mathcal{H}_i$ is to be preferred. That is, after seeing data $D$, $P(\mathcal{H}_i|D)$ gives a measure of how consistent the data is with the hypothesis. However, the Bayes' approach would seem to be of little value unless $P(\mathcal{H}_i)$, the probability that $\mathcal{H}_i$ is the correct hypothesis, is known for all possibilities. That is, one would need an accurate measure of the $P(\mathcal{H}_i)$ for every possible hypothesis and ensure that $\sum_i P(\mathcal{H}_i) = 1$.

Nevertheless, if there exists some estimate of the prior probability of a hypothesis $P(\mathcal{H}_i)$ in the absence of any data, that estimate can give a measure of how consistent the particular hypothesis is, given the data, by using Bayes' theorem. When the prior probability is not known, one can use the principle of indifference, mentioned above, to assume all causes are equally likely. Assuming the principle of indifference, one can estimate $P(\mathcal{H}_i|D)$ for each hypothesis. The results may favour one possible cause over another. These estimates of $P(\mathcal{H}_i|D)$ can be used as a revised set of prior probabilities. If new data $D'$ becomes available, an iterative process can provide another estimate of $P(\mathcal{H}_i|D')$. In which case, the evidence may more strongly favour one hypothesis over others. Thus, this process of inference makes as much use of the available data as is possible. However, there is a major difficulty that statisticians from a frequentist perspective have with this approach. In the frequentist framework, a large sample of outcomes is needed to infer a probability measure. There is no place for assigning probabilities for one-off events, whether these be based on the principle of indifference, or based on estimates of likely causes. Despite this, Bayesian statistics is now commonly used and Jaynes has encapsulated this principle in his idea of maximum entropy (section 5.3.4).

Nevertheless, it emerges that, if one considers hypotheses that can be represented as sets of binary strings of finite lengths, the universal semi-measure $m(\mathcal{H}_i) = 2^{-H(\mathcal{H}_i)}$, provides the best estimate of the prior probability $P(\mathcal{H}_i)$. In simple terms, where $P(\mathcal{H}_i)$ is not known, $2^{-H(\mathcal{H}_i)}$ can be taken to be the prior probability as a best guess. Here, $H(\mathcal{H}_i)$ is the algorithmic entropy of the string that encapsulates the hypothesis. Furthermore, Vitányi and Li [15] argue that optimal compression is almost always the best strategy for identifying an hypothesis. The arguments above are taken further in section 5.3 where what is called the minimum description length (MDL) approach is applied to model fitting.

*The universal semi-measure and inference*
Originally, Solomonoff [2], in dealing with a similar inference problem, developed what in effect was the algorithmic approach. Solomonoff argued that a series of measurements, together with the experimental methodology, provided the set of data to feed into Bayes' rule in order to give the best estimate of the next data point. Solomonoff came up with the concept of the universal distribution to use as the Bayesian prior; the initial probability estimate. However, Solomonoff's initial approach ran into problems as he did not use self-delimiting or codes from a prefix-free set. Levin [6], by defining the universal distribution in terms of a self-delimiting algorithm, resolved that problem. As a consequence, the universal

distribution of section 3.9 can be taken as the universal prior for a discrete sample space. Levin has argued that the universal distribution gives the largest probability amongst all distributions, and it can be approximated to from below. Effectively, the universal distribution $m(x)$ maximises ignorance or encapsulates the principle of indifference, and so is the least biased approach to assigning priors. Gács [30] using $2^{-H(x)}$ as the universal distribution (see section 6.2) has demonstrated the remarkable property that the randomness test $d(x|m)$ for $x$, given the universal semi-measure, shows all outcomes random with respect to the universal distribution (see discussion on randomness in section 6.2). If the true distribution is $\mu(x)$, it follows that $m(x)$ and $\mu(x)$ are sufficiently close to each other for $m(x)$ to be used instead of $\mu(x)$ for hypothesis testing even though the true distribution is unknown. In other words, the universal distribution as a prior is almost as good as the exact distribution. This justifies the use of the universal distribution as the prior to be used in Bayes' rule, provided that the true distribution over all hypotheses is computable. Effectively, as Li and Vitányi [10] point out on p 323, this process satisfies both Occam's razor and Epicurus' principle.

Occam's razor states that entities should not be multiplied beyond necessity, effectively saying that simpler explanations are best. On the other hand, Epicurus had the view that if several theories are consistent with the data they should all be kept [10] (p 315). Because any hypothesis with probability greater than zero is included in the universal distribution as a prior and the approach gives greater weight to the simplest explanation, the approach satisfies both Occam and Epicurus.

Solomonoff's prime interest was in predicting the next member of a possibly infinite sequence (see Li and Vitányi [10] for a reference to the underlying history). However, infinite sequences require a modified approach, which will be schematically outlined here for completeness. Nevertheless, first time readers might find it convenient to ignore the following paragraphs.

In the infinite case, an output is not just $x$, but rather the output of all infinite sequences that start with $x$. This set of all such sequences starting with $x$ is called the cylinder set (see 2.3.1) and is denoted by $\Gamma_x$. In contrast to the discrete case, as a UTM that outputs the start sequence $x$ with a particular programme may not eventually halt, possible non-halting programmes must also be included in the summation defining the semi-measure. As a consequence, the UTM must be a monotone machine, i.e. defined as a UTM that has one way input and output tapes (as well as work tapes). The universal semi-measure for the continuous case is given by

$$M_U(x) = \sum_{U(p)=x^*} 2^{-|p|} \tag{3.29}$$

where $M_U$ denotes that a monotone machine is to be used. Here, $x^*$ indicates that all programmes that output a string starting with $x$ are included. However, while the programme initially outputs $x^*$, the computation might not halt, but might continue outputting more bits indefinitely. This equation defines $M_U(x)$ as the probability that a sequence starting with $x$ will be the output of a programme $p$ generated by the toss of a coin. The continuous universal semi-measure $M$ has similar but not identical properties to the discrete case. Furthermore,

$$-\log_2 M(x) = H(x) - O(1) = K_M(x) - O(1),$$

where $K_M(x)$ is the monotone algorithmic complexity—i.e. the length of the shortest programme run on a monotone machine that outputs a string starting with $x$. For example, if the start of a sequence is the string $x$, the approach would imply that characters in the sequences are distributed according to a computable measure $\mu$. In which case, the probability $\mu$ that the next element is a $y$ is

$$\mu(y|x) = \mu(x, y)/\mu(x).$$

The estimate based on the continuous universal semi-measure $M(x)$ is of the same form, namely

$$M(y|x) = M(x, y)/M(x).$$

This converges rapidly to the equation immediately above, and Solomonoff has shown [31] that after $n$ predictions, the expected error by using $M(x)$ instead of $\mu(x)$ falls faster than $1/n$.

# References

[1] Chaitin G J 1974 Information-theoretic limitations of formal systems *J. ACM* **21** 403–24
[2] Solomonoff R J 1964 A formal theory of inductive inference: Part 1 and Part 2 *Inf. Control.* **7** 224–54
[3] Kolmogorov K 1965 Three approaches to the quantitative definition of information *Prob. Info. Trans.* **1** 1–7
[4] Chaitin G 1966 On the length of programs for computing finite binary sequences *J. ACM* **13** 547–69
[5] Levin L A 1973 On the notion of a random sequence *Sov. Math. Dokl.* **14** 1413–6
[6] Levin L A 1974 Laws of information (nongrowth) and aspects of the foundation of probability theory *Probl. Inf. Transm.* **10** 206–10
[7] Gács P 1974 On the symmetry of algorithmic information *Sov. Math. Dokl.* **15** 1477–780
[8] Chaitin G 1975 A theory of program size formally identical to information theory *J. ACM* **22** 329–40
[9] Calude C 2002 *Information and Randomness: An Algorithmic perspective* 2nd edn (New York: Springer)
[10] Li M and Vitányi P M B 2008 *An Introduction to Kolmogorov Complexity and Its Applications* 3rd edn (New York: Springer)
[11] Feldman D 1998 Computational Mechanics of Classical Spin Systems *PhD Thesis* University of California, Davis
[12] Shalizi C R and Crutchfield P 2001 Computational mechanics pattern and prediction, structure and simplicity *J. Stat. Phys.* **104** 819–81
[13] Bennett C H 1988 Logical depth and physical complexity *The Universal Turing Machine–A Half-Century Survey* ed R Herken (Oxford: Oxford University Press) pp 227–57
[14] Buhrman H, Tromp J and Vitanyi P 2001 Time and space bounds for reversible simulation *J. Phys. A: Math. Gen.* **34-35** 6821–30

[15] Vitányi P M B and Li M 2000 Minimum description length induction, Bayesianism, and Kolmogorov complexity *IEEE Trans. Inform. Theory* **46** 446–64

[16] Crutchfield D 1994 The calculi of emergence: Computational, dynamics, and induction *Physica* D **75** 11–54

[17] Crutchfield J P and Young K 1989 Inferring statistical complexity *Phys. Rev. Lett.* **63** 105–8

[18] Rissanen J 1976 Generalized Kraft inequality and arithmetic coding *IBM J. Res. Dev.* **20** 198–203

[19] Chaitin G J 1982 Algorithmic information theory *Encyclopedia of Statistical Sciences* ed N L Johnson and S Kotz vol 1 (New York: Wiley) pp 38–41

[20] Chaitin G 1979 Toward a mathematical definition of 'life' *The Maximum Entropy formalism* ed R D Levine and M Tribus (Cambridge, MA: MIT Press) pp 477–98

[21] Zurek W H 1989 Algorithmic randomness and physical entropy *Phys. Rev.* A **40** 4731–51

[22] Calude C, Dinneen M J and Shu C K 2002 Computing a glimpse of randomness *Exp. Math.* **11** 361–70

[23] Chaitin G J 1994 Randomness and complexity in pure mathematics *Int. J. Bifurcation Chaos* **4** 3–15

[24] Chaitin G J 2005 *Meta Math! The Quest for Omega* (New York: Pantheon)

[25] Kvaalen E 2008 Has the Riemann hypothesis finally been proven? *New Sci.* **197** 40–1

[26] Barrow J D 1999 *Impossibility: The Limits of Science and the Science of Limits* (London: Random House)

[27] Feferman S 2009 Gödel, Nagel, minds, and machines: Ernest Nagel lecture, Columbia University, Sept. 27, 2007 *J. Philos.* **106** 201–19

[28] Calude C, Campbell D I, Svozil K and Stefanescu D 1995 Strong determinism versus computability *The Foundational Debate, Complexity and Constructivity in Mathematics and Physics* ed W Depauli-Schimanovich, E Koehler and F Stadler (Dordrecht: Kluwer) pp 115–31

[29] Hutter M 2005 On generalized computable universal priors and their convergence (http://arxiv.org/PS_cache/cs/pdf/0503/0503026v1.pdf)

[30] Gács P 1988 *Lecture notes on descriptional complexity and randomness* (Boston University Computer Science Department) http://www.cs.bu.edu/gacs/papers/ait-notes.pdf

[31] Solomonoff R J 1978 Complexity-based induction systems: Comparisons and convergence theorems *IEEE Trans. Information Theory* **IT-24** 422–32

**IOP** Publishing

# Algorithmic Information Theory for Physicists and Natural Scientists

**Sean D Devine**

# Chapter 4

# The algorithmic entropy of strings with structure and variation

This chapter deals with the algorithmic approach to structures, such as a noisy image on a screen, that exhibit both order and randomness. It is shown that the algorithm that generates a noisy string needs to specify the pattern or structure common to the set of all similar strings, coupled with an algorithm that, given this set, picks out the particular variation. All strings in the same set will have the same algorithmic entropy which is here called the provisional entropy. The provisional entropy approach is formally equivalent to Kolmogorov's algorithmic minimal sufficient statistic 4.3.1 and is aligned with the ideal form of the minimal description length. These approaches provide a basis for Zurek's intuitive concept of physical entropy 7.2.3.

The particles in a Boltzmann gas enclosed in a container might undergo a rare fluctuation where all particles appear for an instant on one half of a container. Such improbable fluctuations are often termed fluctuations from equilibrium. However, when this happens in an isolated system, the provisional entropy is unchanged, as the algorithmic description of the momentum states increases to compensate. Here, to avoid confusion, such fluctuations are said to be distant from the most probable set of states, rather than distant from equilibrium.

In a natural system the algorithm that generates a particular configuration must first define the thermodynamic macrostate containing that particular configuration. It is shown in section 4.5, using the example of a Boltzmann gas, how the algorithmic entropy aligns with changes in the thermodynamic macrostate changes. Initially, there is a free expansion of a gas on one side of a container, a fluctuation to an improbable configuration and an isothermal compression to the original state. Both the algorithmic entropy and thermodynamic entropies are tracked through

doi:10.1088/978-0-7503-2640-7ch4

each of these processes to show directly that the thermodynamic entropy corresponds to the algorithmic entropy multiplied by $k_B \ln 2$.

However, there is a critical distinction between the algorithmic approach and the thermodynamic approach. The algorithmic approach specifies the entropy of a particular microstate or configuration in the system. The thermodynamic entropy is a property of the macrostate that contains the set of all compatible microstates. In other words, in an isolated macrostate, each microstate has the same algorithmic entropy which corresponds to the thermodynamic entropy of the macrostate.

## 4.1 Identical algorithmic approaches to strings with variation

The algorithmic entropy of a configuration representing a microstate in the natural world is the length of the shortest algorithm that exactly defines the string specifying the microstate. However, such a configuration may exhibit both structure and randomness. If the algorithmic description is to provide insights into natural systems, it must be able to consistently deal with different strings having the same structure, but which also exhibit variations of the structure. Previously, it was thought that the random components would dominate the length of the generating algorithm obscuring any pattern [1]. However, the provisional entropy approach, discussed in this chapter, avoids this apparent problem, but more importantly also allows the algorithmic entropy to be aligned with the thermodynamic entropy for an isolated system (see discussion in section 7.2).

For example, a noisy image on a screen will have some pixels that capture the image and which are common to all variations of that image. The exact description of a particular variation of the image relies on an algorithm to specify the common structure, and a routine to identify the particular variation of the structure that appear as noise. However, in the image case, all the configurations refer to noisy variations of the same image, whereas in the thermodynamic case, all the configurations are variations of the essential characteristics of the thermodynamic macrostate, in terms of the constants of motion and molecular species. In this case, the algorithmic entropy is seen to consist of a term defining the structure of the set of microstates, i.e. the pattern or common characteristics of all strings in the macrostate, followed by a routine that identifies the particular string of interest. This last routine, which captures the variation or noise has a length equal to the Shannon entropy, implied by the uncertainty in identifying a particular string (see the next section). Three equivalent approaches not only resolve the problem of strings that exhibit random variations of a structure, i.e. noisy strings, but also link the algorithmic approach more clearly to that of Shannon's information theory, and statistical mechanics. These three equivalent formulations, which also align with Zurek's physical entropy [2] and the Gács entropy [3, 4], are known as:
- the provisional entropy approach;
- the algorithmic minimal sufficient statistics approach; and
- the ideal form of the minimal description length.

The first two are discussed below, while the third is discussed in more detail in section 5.3. Furthermore, Zurek's physical entropy [2], which is a mix of the algorithmic entropy and the Shannon entropy, returns the same value as the three equivalent formulations above, although conceptually it is somewhat different.

## 4.2 The provisional entropy

Devine [5] has shown that where a particular string (for example one representing the configuration of a real-world system) exhibits both structure, and randomness or variation of the structure, there is an implicit reference to the set containing all similar strings exhibiting the pattern. As this set will be recursively enumerable, all variations of the string that exhibit this pattern can be generated by an algorithm that consists of two routines. The first routine enumerates the set of strings $S$ exhibiting the common pattern or structure, and which contains the string of interest, while the second routine identifies the string of interest, given the information that defines the set. The algorithmic measure of the particular string $x_i$ in the set will be termed 'the provisional algorithmic entropy' denoted by $H_{prov}(x_i)$. While originally the phrase 'revealed entropy' was used [5], the term 'provisional entropy' seems preferable [6]. This is because the observed pattern may not comprehensively account for all the structure in the string. The measure is provisional only. It is the best estimate of the algorithmic entropy given the available information, recognising that a deeper, unobserved pattern might well exist. In which case, the two-part description then becomes

$$H_{prov}(x_i) = H_{algo}(S) + H_{algo}(x_i|S) + O(1). \tag{4.1}$$

Here, $H_{algo}(S)$ is the length of the shortest self-delimiting programme that specifies the set $S$ with its characteristic pattern, while $H_{algo}(x_i|S)$ is the length of the shortest self-delimiting programme that picks out $x_i$ in the set. The contribution of the second term to the algorithmic entropy is in practice the same as the Shannon entropy, $H_{sh}$, of the set. That is, if there are $\Omega_S$ elements in the set, and all members are equally likely, each string can be identified by an algorithm of length $|\Omega_S|$. In this case, the length of the algorithm generating string $x_i$ is $H_{algo}(x_i|S) = \log_2 \Omega_s = H_{sh}$, and the provisional entropy becomes

$$H_{prov}(x_i) = H_{algo}(S) + H_{sh} + O(1). \tag{4.2}$$

Here, the information required to specify the size of $H_{sh}$ required for self-delimiting coding of $H_{sh}$ can be part of the specification of the set.

As has been mentioned for an isolated thermodynamic system, all allowable configurations have the same energy and, in many cases, the same number of particles. In the case of a macrostate with water, hydrogen and oxygen, the total particles mass is conserved. As each microstate in this situation is equally likely, all the strings within the set will have the same provisional entropy given by

In effect;

$$H_{\text{prov}}(x_i) = H_{\text{algo}}(\text{description of the set's structure})$$
$$+ H_{\text{algo}}(\text{identifying the string in the set}). \tag{4.3}$$

Even if all the structure of a typical string has been identified, there may be a few highly ordered non-typical strings that might show more structure. But if the system in the natural world is isolated, structural ordering in one part will be compensated for by disordering elsewhere. In which case, there can be no shorter algorithm.

However, there are conceptual issues involved in establishing the algorithmic entropy of an isolated physical system. The algorithmic entropy is associated with an actual microstate of the system and, in an isolated system, all states in the macrostate have the same algorithmic entropy. This makes sense as the thermodynamic entropy is a property of the macrostate. Within an isolated system this implies that, when there appears to be an ordered fluctuation away from the most probable set of states, bits are transferred elsewhere, but overall, energy and bits are conserved. As this is important, it is discussed further in section 4.3.4.

For example, a fluctuation, where the temperature drops as energy is transferred to electronic states, involves bits being transferred from the momentum degrees of freedom to specify both the electronic degrees of freedom and the programme bits. Again, as is discussed in detail in section 4.5; all the particles in a Boltzmann gas might accidentally appear on one side of a container. When this happens, the number of bits specifying position degrees of freedom drops, but the number specifying the momentum states increases, leading to an increase in temperature as is outlined in detail below in section 4.5.

Strictly one should say that, for an isolated system, such a fluctuation is a fluctuation within equilibrium, but away from the most probable set of states where the energy is associated with the momentum states. As section 4.5 reiterates, one tends to say that such a fluctuation is an ordered fluctuation. For an isolated system, such a fluctuation is ordered in the sense that it is a highly improbable state, but as discussed later the algorithmic entropy is the same for all microstates in the set. Here, instead of the commonly used word 'equilibrium' to define the end point of the second law of thermodynamics, it is conceptually safer to use the term 'most probable set of states' or the term 'equilibrium set' to refer the set of microstates that the system settles in over a long period of time.

This is discussed further in chapter 9.

## 4.3 The specification by a probability distribution

The provisional entropy approach outlined above, specified the algorithmic entropy in terms of the length of the shortest algorithm that described the optimal set containing the string of interest, together with the length of the algorithm that specified the string in that set. This is appropriate where all members of the set are equally likely, as is the case for a string representing a noisy black and white image on a screen, or a particular microstate in the macrostate of an isolated thermodynamic system.

Rather than all variations being equally likely, in many situations the variation from the standard pattern follows a probability distribution. An observation two standard deviations away from the central point of normal distribution is much less likely to be observed than an observation one standard deviation away. Given a set with specific characteristics, where a probability distribution is used to identify a particular variation of a string in the set, the most efficient method of identifying the variation is to use 'Shannon's noiseless coding theorem' (section 3.9), as strings that are less likely will have a longer code. This ensures that, within the set of possible outcomes, each string is optimally coded. However, for this to work, the probability distribution needs to be enumerable, which means in practice an algorithm must be able to calculate a point on the distribution to an agreed level of precision.

An example of this situation is in a thermodynamic system at equilibrium with a heat bath at temperature $T$. This corresponds to the Gibbs' canonical ensemble. The probability of an instantaneous configuration with total energy $E_i$ occurring depends on $e^{-E_i/(k_BT)}/Z$, where $Z$ is the partition function. Let a particular configuration $x_i$ exist with probability $P(x_i)$. The most efficient way of identifying or specifying the particular configuration is to use Shannon's coding theorem (section 3.9). From this theorem, the optimum code for a particular configuration has length $-\log_2 P(x_i)$ bits, rounded up to the nearest integer. In this case, given the probability distribution $P$, $H_{algo}(x_i|P) = -\log_2 P(x_i)$. In the case of configuration in the Gibbs' canonical ensemble, the length of the optimum code to specify a configuration with energy $E_i$ is $E_i/(k_BT)\log_2 e + \log_2 Z$.

In formal terms, let $H(P)$ represent the length of the shortest programme that computes the discrete probability distribution on the reference UTM to an agreed level of precision. The algorithmic entropy of a particular string $x_i$ that belongs to the distribution can now be specified by a two-part code. The first part identifies the set of possible strings by the probability $P$, while the second part identifies the actual string, given the probability distribution. Hence, for most strings,

$$H(x_i) = H(P) + H(x_i|P^*) + O(1). \tag{4.4}$$

Or

$$H(x_i) = H(P) - \log_2 P(x_i) + O(1). \tag{4.5}$$

The right-hand side of this equation corresponds to the provisional entropy, and also the algorithmic minimal sufficient statistic for the string discussed next in section 4.3.1. Note the $O(1)$ includes any decoding routine if it is not explicit in the algorithm. An equals sign in equation (4.4) holds for the overwhelming majority of strings in the distribution, but a few non-typical strings could have a shorter description. In which case, such strings actually belong to a different probability distribution and can be compressed further than that implied by equation (4.4). The critical point is that the *expected* value of the algorithmic entropy defined through a probability distribution corresponds to the Gibbs entropy for a canonical ensemble or the Shannon entropy for the set of strings, allowing for units. The expectation value of $H(x_i)$, i.e. $\langle H_{algo}(x_i)\rangle$ is found by multiplying each term in equation (4.5) by the probability of $x_i$ and summing over all states. In which case, the expectation value of $-\langle \log_2 P(x_i) \rangle = \Sigma_i P(x_i) \log_2(P(x_i) = H_{sh}$. As a consequence,

$$\langle H_{\text{algo}}(x_i) \rangle = H_{sh}(\text{set of all states}) + H(P) + O(1). \tag{4.6}$$

The above argument follows Zurek [2] (equation (4.17)) and Bennett [7] (equation (2)). As $H(P)$ is trivially small relative to the number of microstates in the system, these authors argue that the algorithmic entropy for a thermodynamic ensemble is virtually that of the Shannon entropy. The expected code length is close the Shannon entropy, $H_{sh}$. (This is discussed in more detail in section 7.2.) The decoding process to generate the actual string of interest involves finding $P(x_i)$ from $-\log_2 P(x_i) = |code(x_i)|$. The decoding procedure steps through all the strings with the same probabilities in order, until the $x_i$ associated with the correct code is reached. The more strings there are from a given probability, the greater is the coding length and therefore the greater the number of available codes.

### 4.3.1 The algorithmic minimal sufficient statistics approach to the provisional entropy

As has been discussed, the provisional entropy is the algorithmic entropy of a typical string in a set of similar strings. Earlier, Kolmogorov introduced the algorithmic equivalent of Fisher's minimal sufficient statistic concept, known as the Kolmogorov minimal sufficient statistic, or the algorithmic minimal sufficient statistic (AMSS). The AMSS for a string in a set of strings turns out to be identical to the provisional entropy. The approach, which is implicit in section 2.1.1 in Li and Vitányi [8], seeks the smallest set in which the string of interest is a typical member. The length of the algorithm that identifies the string in the smallest set is the provisional entropy. However, with both the AMSS or the provisional entropy approaches, one can never be sure that the minimal set has been found.

The AMSS is a minimal statistic as, for a typical member of the set, all the information has been captured and no further pattern is detectable in the string. If the smallest set captures all the regularity in the string, the shortest algorithmic description of the set, together with the algorithm that identifies the string in the set, corresponds to its algorithmic entropy. This set could be the set of microstates in a thermodynamic macrostate, or the set of configurations that specify a noisy image. Effectively, equation (4.3) provides the AMMS description of the string.

Prior to the work of Devine [5] on the entropy of patterned noisy sets, Vereshchagin and Vitányi [9] developed the AMSS approach to specify the shortest description of a string from the perspective of finding the optimal Turing machine (TM). In this approach, the TM is a function that specifies the structure, while the programme $p$ picks out the actual string of interest, given the structure in $S$. Here, $|p|$ corresponds to the term $H_{\text{algo}}(x_i|S)$ in equation (4.1). In this case, the combination of the TM and the programme given the TM needed to specify the string of interest is optimised (see equation (3.14)) to give

$$H(x) = \min_{i,p}\{H(T_i) + |p|\} + O(1). \tag{4.7}$$

There are many TMs or functions that can generate a string $x$. In order to describe a string with randomness and structure, there is a trade-off between a TM that has a short description, but which requires a longer programme $|p|$, and a machine with a short programme and a long description. If the description of the model is too sophisticated, it will overfit the data, but the reduction in the code length given by $|p|$ is insufficient to compensate for the increase in the length of the model description. Alternatively, if the model is too simple, the size of the code length $|p|$ will need to increase to provide the detailed corrections. The optimum occurs when all the pattern or structure is included in the specification of the machine $T_i$ and only the variation or random part is captured by $p$, which in this context is a code to identify a particular string, given the structure.

The result is identical to that of the provisional entropy or AMSS, but in the TM formulation the set is defined by the instructions specifying the TM, while the particular variation is defined by the programme $p$ run on the TM. In this case, $|p|$ corresponds to the Shannon term. That is, for a given $x$, the optimum is the same as that given by (4.8) or equation (4.1).

The algorithmic complexity of string $x_i$ is [9]

$$H(x_i) \leqslant H(S) + H(x_i|S) + O(1). \tag{4.8}$$

In other words, when the equals sign applies, $H(x_i) = H_{AMSS}(x_i) = H_{\mathrm{prov}}(x_i)$.

This represents the minimal statistic, as for a typical member of the set, all the information has been captured, and no further pattern is detectable in the string.

While the main mathematical discussion in the literature uses the term AMSS to define the optimum set in order to define the shortest algorithm, here the word provisional entropy will be used, because the measure is closely aligned with the thermodynamic entropy of a natural system.

### 4.3.2 Summing up

The upper measure of the algorithmic entropy, given the available information, is the provisional entropy, or as discussed above, the algorithmic minimal sufficient statistic. The provisional entropy is the best estimate of the actual entropy of a particular variation of a common structure. If all the structure is identified, the provisional algorithmic entropy will correspond to the true algorithmic entropy, resolving the problem raised in section 3.2.1. But as there may be no certainty that all the structure has been identified, the minimal description $H(x_i) \leqslant H_{\mathrm{prov}}(x_i)$. The algorithm exactly specifies a particular string, the variation or noise does not swamp the algorithm but the name 'provisional' indicates that the unrecognised structure may exist.

### 4.3.3 A simple example of the provisional entropy

The following provides a simple illustration of the way a particular string in a set of similar strings can be identified (Devine [5]). Consider the process of specifying the algorithmic entropy of a string of length $N$, with $R$ 1's and $N - R$ zeros. If the string represents a physical system where a 1 is a higher energy state than a zero, the number of 1's is a constant of the motion as energy is conserved. There are $\Omega_S = N!/[(N - R)!R!]$ members of the set of strings satisfying the requirement. The algorithm that defines a particular member of this set of strings must first specify $N$ and $R$, and given these must step through all strings of length $N$ and find those with just $R$ 1's.

Let the simple procedure defined as $COUNT(S)$ count the number of 1's in the string. If $COUNT(S) \neq R$, the string $S$ is not a member of the patterned set. The following procedure '$CRITERION$' determines if $S$ is a member of the set.

> $CRITERION$
>
> $IF\ COUNT(S) \neq R$, (*I. e. does not have the desired number of 1's*)    (4.9)
>
> $NO,\ ELSE\ YES$.

$R$ and $N$ are specified in the definition of the set or the corresponding macrostate. Self-delimiting coding specifies $N$ and $R$ by $\log_2 N + H(|\log_2 N|) + \log_2 R + H(|\log_2 R|)$ bits as previously discussed.

Given the macrostate or the properties of the set, the Shannon term, corresponding to $\log_2 \Omega_S = \log_2(N!/[(N - R)!R!])$ bits, is needed to identify say the $i$th string in the macrostate. Combining these, and including $H(\log_2 N)$. to allow for self-delimiting coding, the provisional entropy of each microstate is;

$$H_{\mathrm{prov}} = \log_2 N + \log_2 R + H(\log_2 N) + H(\log_2 R) + \log_2 \Omega_S + |COUNT| + |IF|.$$

Here the '$COUNT$' and '$If$' subroutines can be considered as common information, or if not, will nevertheless contain few bits relative to the other terms. Using Stirling's approximation $\log_2 \Omega_S$ is close to $-N(q \log_2 q + (1 - q)\log_2(1 - q))$, where $q = R/N$. For the situation where $R/N$ is 0.8, this becomes $0.72N$ impying that there are $2^{0.72N}$ members in the reduced set compared with $2^N$ for all strings of length $N$.

### 4.3.4 Hidden structure and the term 'provisional'

The AMSS or provisional entropy approach just discussed provides the shortest algorithm for only the typical member of the set of similar strings. While the typical member is random relative to the set of similar strings, if there is hidden structure, the string is a non-typical member, and a shorter algorithmic description is possible. A typical string of length 100 but with $R$ 1's is of the form $10110011...01100$. But the particular string where the initial segment is $R$ 1's followed by $100 - R$ zeros (of the form $1111...0000$) is not typical. In the latter case, there are only two members in the non-typical set of strings; the one just given and its reflection, i.e. $0000...1111$. This corresponds to an initial sequence of $100 - R$ zeros followed by $R$ 1's. As a consequence, $H(1111...0000) \ll H(10110011...01100)$.

Take as another example, the set of noisy period-2 binary strings. This is the set of random sequences of '10' and '11' of length $N$. The sequences are of the form $s_i = 1y1y1y1...1y1y...1y$ (where $y$ is randomly 0 or 1). For this situation, at least $N/2 + H(N/2)$ bits are needed to specify a typical string in the original set. But there are strings such as the string $s_i' = 101010...10$ that are non-typical, and this simple period-2 string can be specified by an algorithm of the form 'REPEAT 10 $N/2$

TIMES'. The algorithmic entropy of this string is much shorter than a typical one, and is given by $H_{\text{algo}}(s_i') \simeq H(N/2) \simeq |N/2| + H(|N/2|)$.

Here, the $H(|N/2|)$ bits are needed to account for the extra code length for self-delimiting coding. In other words, for this non-typical member of the set, $H_{\text{algo}}(s_i') = H_{\text{prov}}(s_i) - N/2$. The provisional entropy approach is not valid as the non-typical string belongs to a smaller set. But it becomes valid if the smaller set is used to determine a new provisional entropy. Nevertheless, as is discussed further below, in many physical situations, such as that representing an isolated thermodynamic macrostate, all members of the set will be typical.

Just to reiterate, as equation (4.3) indicates, the algorithmic entropy of most strings in a patterned set is given by the length of the algorithm that defines the set of all binary strings exhibiting the pattern, combined with the length of the algorithm that identifies the string of interest in the set.

### 4.3.5 Algorithmic entropy not critically dependent on detail

For large strings, the major contribution of the structural information of the algorithmic entropy is the same irrespective of whether the algorithm defines a string directly, or picks out the string after defining the set of similar strings first. This is because in most practical cases, the shortest algorithm that directly generates the string of interest implicitly, specifies the structure.

The example of the noisy 2-period string discussed earlier (where the first of every two characters is a 1, while the second is either a 1 or a 0) shows that estimates of the algorithmic entropy based on different algorithms are nearly identical, as the lengths are dominated by a few parameters. This can be seen in the examples below.

1. A direct method to specify a particular noisy period-2 binary string is to code the string by replacing each '11' by a '1' and each '10' by a '0'. For example, 11101011... becomes 1001... and the number of bits to do this is $N/2 + H(N/2)$. In which case, a short decoding routine needs to be appended to the code to generate the original string by scanning the coded string to replace a '1' by a '11', and a '0' by a '10'. The relevant algorithmic entropy based on this coding is

$$H(s_i) \simeq |code(s_i)| + |decoding\ routine| + O(1).$$

   $N/2 + H(N/2)$ bits are needed to specify $code(s_i)$ using self-delimiting coding. For large $N$, and ignoring the details of the short $O(1)$ decoding routine,

$$H(s_i) \simeq N/2 + H(N/2) + |1| + |0|. \tag{4.10}$$

2. An alternative algorithm can be found by recognising that the set of all such strings is recursively enumerable. As was discussed in section 4.2, each possible string in the set of period-2 strings of length $N/2$ can be generated by starting with the set of $N/2$ zeros. Then, by incrementing each string step through all the $N/2$ strings in turn. After each increment, a 1 can then be

interspersed between each binary digit so that each pair starts with a 1. The initial configuration of $N/2$ zeros requires $H(N/2)$ bits, while $N/2$ bits are needed to identify when the string $s_i$ is reached. The total algorithmic entropy must also include a short generating algorithm. In which case, the provisional entropy corresponds to $H_{\mathrm{prov}}(s_i) \simeq H(N/2) + N/2 + |1| + |0| +$ (*generating algorithm*).

For large strings with dominating parameters, it makes little difference as to which, of a number of algorithms, is used to specify the algorithmic entropy. The main differences lie in relatively short algorithms that specify stepping, checking or decoding routines. As shown in section 3.6, Chaitin has argued that there are a small cluster of short descriptions of similar length, and the dominant terms in these determine the algorithmic entropy.

## 4.4 How to specify noisy data

To recapitulate, the provisional entropy approach showed how a two-part algorithm is able to provide an algorithmically compressed specification of a particular string with recognisable structure, but also with variation of the structure. There are two different situations. One is where the first part of the algorithm specified the set of all strings with the same pattern or structure, and the other is where the set is generated by a probability distribution that captured all possible strings. The second part, given the set, or the probability distribution, specified the actual string of interest.

The points below explore the difference between these alternatives. The first is where the outcome itself is a structure but with noise imposed on the structure. The second is where the outcome is a spread of points defined by a distribution around a central point.

1. The first example is where a structure, e.g. a black circle is produced on a screen of black and white pixels, but where some pixels are randomly black or white adding noise to the ideal image. In other words, the image is a noisy black circle. According to the provisional entropy approach, the algorithm that defines the exact noisy image at a particular instant, must first define the black circle, which is the pattern common to all images. Once this is done, a second algorithm, with its length given by the Shannon entropy of all typical states, can specify the particular fluctuation from the exact image. Note here that the image must be a typical member of the set. A randomly produced image, where the screen is a nearly all black or a nearly all white, is not typical as it belongs to a different set.

2. The second is a different situation as the outcome string specifies the point of a distribution rather than a structure or image. For example, an outcome might be a black pixel on a white background that occurs according to a probability distribution such as the normal distribution. That is, the probability $P(r_i)$ is the distribution that specifies the probability that a point at distance $r_i$ from the centre will be a black pixel. In this case, a single outcome is one point, but many observations superimposed on each other

would generate a dense number of black pixels in the central region but with the density dropping the further from the centre.

This contrasts with the previous case where randomly black and white pixels were imposed randomly on an image or structure.

More generally, the distribution need not be about a central point but, could be about a straight line or some other model of the data. The setting of the pixels adjacent to the straight line is determined by a distribution that specifies the deviation from the line. In other words, the observation of a number of trials would see random black pixels scattered around the line that is meant to model the data. In this case, each pixel can be specified by using an algorithm to define the straight-line graph, which is like specifying the model, and then the deviation of a particular outcome from the model as specified by the probability distribution. This is outlined in detail later.

## 4.5 The non-typical state and the thermodynamic entropy

Both the provisional entropy (or equivalently the algorithmic minimal sufficient statistic (AMSS)), approach provides the shortest algorithm for the typical member of the set of similar strings. The typical member has no distinguishing features and is random relative to the set of similar strings. The discussion so far seems distant from thermodynamics. But there is a further important conceptual issue. In a natural system, the algorithm needed to define set of similar strings is invariably based on the requirements of a thermodynamic macrostate. In which case, for an isolated system, the set requirements implicitly include the specification of macroscopic parameters such as energy and entropy. This section explores a simple illustrative example to link the algorithmic entropy and the thermodynamic entropy. The questions being considered are: how does the algorithmic entropy change when heat flows into or out of a system as the volume and temperature changes? How do the algorithmic entropy changes relate to the changes of the thermodynamic entropy?

Consider a Boltzmann gas of $N$ non-interacting particles where the particles may be on the left side or the right side of a container. If a particle is on the left side denote the position by a 1; otherwise, a 0 for the right-hand side. This is, in effect, a very coarse resolution of the phase space, but it suffices to discuss the principles and is justified further below

The following five scenarios, illustrated in figure 4.1, identify the algorithmic and thermodynamic entropy changes for a macrostate of the Boltzmann gas where, except in the second and fifth cases, the system is isolated. The first scenario is the initial microstate where the $N$ particles in the isolated system are constrained to the left half of a container. The second scenario emerges when the constraint is removed and a free expansion occurs while the system is usually still considered isolated. Although from the AIT perspective this is not strictly so, as extra bits specifying position coordinates leak into the system. The resultant macrostate corresponds to a set of microstates where the particles are now randomly distributed over both sides of the container.

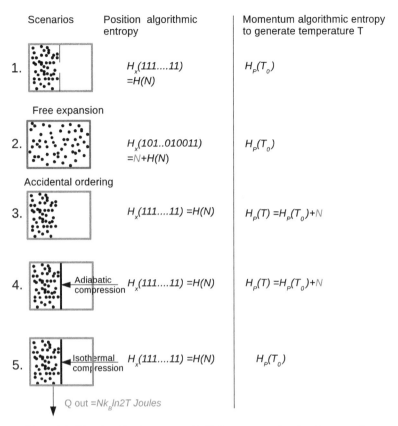

**Figure 4.1.** The algorithmic entropy of a Boltzmann gas showing five scenarios.

After the free expansion, the third situation occurs when, at a particular instant by chance a rare, natural fluctuation places all particles of the now completely isolated system on the left side of the container. While at first sight, this might seem identical to the initial situation in scenario 1, it is not. In this case, the gas is unconstrained. The fourth scenario is where the particles in the isolated system are forced into the left side of the container by compressing the gas. In the fifth scenario, the system is no longer isolated and an isothermal compression process returns the system in scenario 2 to the original state of scenario 1. It is shown that scenarios 2, 3 and 4 are variations of the same macrostate as the algorithmic entropy does not change, while scenarios 1 and 5 belong to a different macrostate with a different algorithmic and thermodynamic entropy.

Each of the five scenarios in the following outline corresponds to a scenario illustrated in figure 4.1. In the discussion, the momentum contribution to the algorithmic entropy will be denoted by $H_p(T)$ where, in each case, $T$ is the temperature that is consistent with the momentum contribution for that scenario.

    1. Consider the initial state where all the $N$ particles of the isolated system are constrained to the left-hand side of the container. The algorithmic entropy of the spatial coordinates corresponds to the number of bits that specify the

string representing the configuration $1^N$, i.e. a sequence of $N$ 1's corresponding to all particles being on the left-hand side of the container as in scenario 1 (figure 4.1). As outlined in section 3.4.1, the string $1^N$ can be represented using self-delimiting coding by $H(N) = |N| + H(|N|)$. As $|N| = \log_2 N$, and the momentum contribution at temperature is $T_0$ can be represented by $H_p(T_0)$ bits, it follows that

$$H(s_i) = H(N) = \log_2 N + H(|N|) + H_p(T_0). \tag{4.11}$$

2. Consider next a free expansion, or Joule expansion, where the constraint is removed resulting in scenario 2 in figure 4.1. The particles on the left-hand side freely expand to fill the whole volume without doing work. However, there is no change in temperature.

The thermodynamic argument for the free expansion considers the initial state as one where $N$ gas particles are confined to the left-hand side of a container with volume $V_0$, temperature $T_0$ and pressure $P_0$. Allowing a free expansion of the gas to fill both sides of the container expands the volume to $2V_0$. As the volume doubles, the pressure halves because the rate of collisions with the container walls drops, but the temperature remains constant, as the energy in the momentum degrees of freedom is unchanged. Nevertheless, with the increase in volume, the number of bits specifying spatial coordinates increases, but as the temperature is unchanged, the momentum contribution is still $H_p(T_0)$. While there is no heat flow, the system might be considered isolated. But as position or spatial degrees of freedom leak into the system, it is not strictly isolated. The process is irreversible and the thermodynamic increase in entropy is evaluated in the reverse process discussed in scenario 5.

From the algorithmic perspective, following the free expansion, the particles are randomly distributed over both halves of the container. In which case, each particle has two possible positions specified by a 1 or a 0. The total number of arrangements is now $2^N$ and the Shannon entropy is given by $N$, the uncertainty in identifying a particular microstate. Each of the $2^N$ strings can be coded with $N$ bits. But, as the coding for the algorithmic entropy must be self-delimiting, information on the size of $N$ is also required to allow the computation to read $N$. In which case, the algorithmic entropy of a microstate $s_i$ in this scenario $H(s_i) = N + H(N)$ bits as outlined in section 3.4.1.

The length of the representations of the microstate can be seen as a property of the macrostate of the system as all strings have the same algorithmic entropy. The energy, which is also a property of the macrostate, primarily constrains the momentum coordinates. However, it is unnecessary to specify the momentum states in detail. With this in mind, and expanding

$H(N)$ which is needed for self-delimiting coding, the algorithmic entropy of a typical state will be,

$$H(s_i) = N + |N| + H(|N|) + H_p(T_0)). \tag{4.12}$$

In this situation, the algorithmic entropy of the spatial degrees of freedom is $N$ bits greater than the situation of equation (4.11) where all particles were constrained. But, the algorithmic entropy of the momentum degrees of freedom is unchanged at $H_p(T_0)$. Where have these bits come from? The typical Boltzmann argument would be that the number of available states has increased. The algorithmic argument is that bits specifying external spatial degrees of freedom have leaked into the system as the gas expands. The leads to the next question; how does the algorithmic entropy of this situation relate to one where all the particles are accidentally found on one side of the container?

3. In the third scenario in figure 4.1, there is an extremely low, but finite, probability of $2^{-N}$ that the particles in the isolated gas system could all be found by chance on the left side of the container. From a traditional perspective, this is often termed a fluctuation from equilibrium as, when such a fluctuation occurs, the second law of thermodynamics drives the system back to a microstate in the most probable set of states.

   But, in contrast, the algorithmic perspective sees the entropy as associated with each microstate. This avoids some of the confusion around any discussion about whether a fluctuation is 'from equilibrium' or 'within equilibrium'. The algorithmic entropy of a so-called rare fluctuation is identical to that of a microstate in the equilibrium set. While the specification of the position coordinates denoted by $x$ need $N$ fewer bits than those given by equation (4.12), as the temperature fluctuates, spatial bits are shifted to the momentum states, increasing $H_p(T_0)$ to $H_p(T_0) + N$. As a consequence, the total algorithmic entropy of the fluctuation is the same as all other microstates in the isolated system. This is consistent. As the fluctuation is connected by a reversible path to the other states in the system, the algorithmic entropy cannot change. The critical point is that, as there is no heat flow from outside, the macrostate has not changed, either from an algorithmic perspective or a thermodynamic perspective. From the provisional entropy perspective just a different, but extremely unlikely, microstate has been picked out at an instant.

   But how does this relate to the fourth situation where the particles are compressed and constrained to be on the left side of the container?

4. In the fourth scenario of figure 4.1, the isolated gas is initially in scenario 2 after the earlier free expansion and is then compressed adiabatically, forcing all particles again to the left hand side of the container. The thermodynamic and algorithmic entropy are unchanged, once the algorithmic contribution to the momentum degrees of freedom $H_p(T_0) + N$ is taken into account. While the position states return to the initial situation corresponding to the

algorithmic entropy $H(N) = |N| + H(|N|)$, the gas compression does work on the system, raising the temperature and increasing the specification of the momentum states. However again, as there is no external heat flow, there is no thermodynamic entropy change from scenario 2. From an algorithmic perspective, there is also no change. Like the previous example of scenario 3, $N$ bits have shifted from specifying the position states to specifying the momentum states.

5. Scenario 5 considers a reversible process that can regenerate the initial state. This allows the change in entropy from the initial configuration and scenarios 2–4 to be determined. From an algorithmic point of view, scenario 1 differs from scenarios 2–4 by the $N$ bits that have entered the system as a consequence of the free expansion

The equivalent thermodynamic entropy change from scenario 2 to the initial state in scenario 1 can be determined by undertaking a slow, reversible, isothermal compression starting with the random distribution of the gas molecules of scenario 2 to reconstitute the initial state. The compression process does work to halve the volume and to return the pressure to its initial value. If heat is transferred to the environment in this slow reversible process, the end result is the initial state of scenario 1. The work done in halving the volume is $-\int_{2V_0}^{V_0} P dv$ while from the gas law, $PV = Nk_B T$. Here, $N$ is the number of particles and $T$ is the temperature. Substitution gives the work done as the integral $-Nk_B T \int_{2V_0}^{V_0} (1/V) dV = Nk_B \ln 2$. This shows that, during the isothermal compression, $Nk_B \ln 2T$ Joules of heat, corresponding to the work done on the gas, exit the system to return it to the initial state. The thermodynamic entropy loss returning the system to the initial state as in scenario 1 is $Nk_B \ln 2$.

From the algorithmic perspective, $N$ bits have been removed as heat in restoring scenarios 2–5 which is the same as scenario 1. Effectively, returning the system to the initial state by the isothermal compression process following the free expansion, requires a heat transfer of $k_b \ln 2T$ Joules per bit.

A number of key points follow from this illustration. The first is that the removal of one computational bit corresponds to a heat flow of $k_B \ln 2T$ Joules. This connection is a more straightforward demonstration than one relating a computational bit to the Shannon uncertainty and through statistical mechanics to the thermodynamic entropy. This connection is made more robust in section 8.3.

For an isolated thermodynamic macrostate, all microstates within the macrostate have the same algorithmic entropy as is discussed in section 9.3.2. The provisional entropy is the actual algorithmic entropy for each microstate. Only when bits enter or leave the system does the macrostate change. In which case, the set properties change. As already mentioned, conceptually the algorithmic approach finds it safer to use the term 'most probable set of states' rather that the term 'equilibrium'. In which case, a non-typical microstate in an isolated system is a fluctuation within an equilibrium system.

Another point of interest is that self-delimiting coding is needed to ensure that the algorithmic entropy changes align with the thermodynamic entropy changes. This is no surprise, as a natural computation is instantaneous and needs no end-markers.

The argument in the above discussion was simplified by specifying the position coordinate along the x-axis for a particle with a coarse resolution of the phase space by a 1 or a 0, depending on whether the particle was on the left-half of the $x$-axis line or not. Normally, the phase space coordinates specify the microstate for each particle in turn, where each significant figure increases the phase space resolution by a factor of 2. The specification when each particle of the gas is on the left-hand side of the container takes the form

$$1xxxxxx...xxx, \ 1xxxxxx...xxx, \ 1xxxxxx...xxx, \ .......$$

The first coordinate for each particle corresponds to splitting the position space into halves, which is 1, when the particle is on one side of the container, the second term for each particle corresponds to increasing the resolution of the position space by splitting each half into quarters. The third splits each quarter in one-eighths. Here, $x$ is randomly 0 or 1, for the situation of increasing resolution. For the situation where the particles are spread uniformly over both halves as in scenario 2, the initial 1 could be either a 1 or a 0.

But it is just valid to organise the string in terms of the most significant phase space coordinate first for each particle in turn and then the next significant for each particle and so on. In this specification, the representation where the particles are all on the left-hand side is $1^N xxxx...xxx$. As there are $N$ particles, the next $N$ characters denoted by $x$ will be a 0 or 1, depending whether the particle is on the left side or the right side of the next most significant position coordinate. The number of bits specifying the position states, after splitting the container into two halves, remains constant through the scenarios in figure 4.1. As a consequence, it is only the first $N$ values that are relevant to the discussion.

# References

[1] Shalizi C R and Crutchfield J P 2000 Pattern discovery and computational mechanics (arxiv.org/abs/cs/0001027)
[2] Zurek W H 1989 Algorithmic randomness and physical entropy *Phys. Rev.* A **40** 4731–51
[3] Gács P 1994 The Boltzmann entropy and randomness tests–Extended abstract In *Proc. Workshop on Physics and Computation* (Morristown, NJ: IEEE Computer Society Press) pp 209–16
[4] Gács P 1994 The Boltzmann entropy and random tests *Technical Report* Boston University Computer Science Department (http://www.cs.bu.edu/faculty/gacs/papers/ent-paper.pdf)
[5] Devine S D 2006 The application of algorithmic information theory to noisy patterned strings *Complexity* **12** 52–8
[6] Devine S D 2009 The insights of algorithmic entropy *Entropy* **11** 85–110
[7] Bennett C H 1982 Thermodynamics of computation—A review *Int. J. Theor. Phys.* **21** 905–40

[8] Li M and Vitányi P M B 2008 *An Introduction to Kolmogorov Complexity and Its Applications* 3rd edn (New York: Springer)

[9] Vereshchagin N K and Vitányi P M B 2004 Kolmogorov's structure functions and model selection *IEEE Trans. Inf. Theory* **50** 3265–90

**IOP** Publishing

Algorithmic Information Theory for Physicists and
Natural Scientists

Sean D Devine

# Chapter 5

## Modelling and the minimum description length

The provisional entropy and the equivalent, the algorithmic minimal sufficient statistic (AMSS) provide tools to model the real-world. Here, these approaches are seen to correspond to the modelling approach of the ideal form of the minimum description length.

An algorithm can specify a curve that fits noisy data, such as one that fits the Earth's position for every second of the year as it travels around the Sun. While Newton's laws capture the pattern of the trajectory, noise in each observed data point is covered by the provisional entropy or equivalently, the algorithmic minimal sufficient statistic. The approach minimises a two-part code, one describing the model in the form of Newton's law, and the other the actual data, given the model. The ideal form of the minimum description length (MDL) discussed in this chapter is effectively the same approach, except that it only explains the data and does not generate it. However, once a short decoding routine is appended to the minimum description algorithm, it can generate the data. Bayes' theorem, and the concept of the universal semi-measure, show that the ideal form of MDL identifies with the provisional entropy approach while Rissanen 5.3.3 has bypassed the computability limitations of the ideal algorithmic approach by introducing the stochastic complexity to replace the algorithmic complexity.

However, because the algorithmic entropy or algorithmic complexity is not computable, an independent process, such as a least-squares fitting procedure, is needed to establish the parameters for different models to find the shortest algorithm best fits the data. In simple terms, the aim is to find the shortest algorithm that specifies the model or structure and also the deviations from the structure. One can see that an algorithm that specifies a circle to generate the Earth's trajectory around the Sun will need to specify larger deviations to exactly fit the data, compared with an algorithm that specifies the trajectory as an ellipse. The ellipse algorithm is therefore the preferred model.

Interestingly, the maximum entry formulation by Jaynes (section 5.3.4) is shown to be consistent with the MDL approach, as minimising the description length is equivalent to establishing a probability distribution that maximises the Shannon entropy of the system.

## 5.1 Introduction

This chapter explores three identical approaches to algorithmic modelling. The first is modelling by finding the best description of a data set using the provisional entropy approach in section 4.2. The second is modelling by finding the algorithmic minimal sufficient statistic, outlined in section 4.3, while the third is modelling by finding the shortest description length of the data, by a process known as the ideal MDL. These are all equivalent, but will be discussed in turn, as each throws a different perspective on the modelling process. Following this, the stochastic approach known as practical MDL, will be outlined.

## 5.2 The algorithmic entropy approach to modelling

An example of using the algorithmic approach to specify a model and deviations from the model is the straight line model that optimally fits a noisy set of data described by the equation $y_i = ax_i + b + \text{noise} = y(x_i) + \text{noise}$. That is, given point $x_i$, what is the shortest algorithm that specifies the actually observed $y_i$? It is shown that the provisional entropy approach can be used to find the shortest description of the data, as the characteristics of the set of all strings is specified by the straight line model, and the deviations are specified by a probability term corresponding to the Shannon entropy of the variations. The following illustrates the principles.

The provisional entropy (section 4.2) for a particular string $y_i$, given $x_i$ is given by a two-part algorithm. In the noisy straight line model mentioned above, the first part is the length of the algorithm that defines the string from its equation and its associated enumerable probability distribution (i.e. $H[ax_i + b, P]$. The second part specifies the particular deviation from the straight line derived from the probability that such a deviation will be observed. Critically, if a point is observed several standard deviations from the straight line, it would be highly improbable, and an efficient coding methodology would require a longer code to specify such a large deviation from the ideal straight line. Given the model, the second part of the algorithm can be established by taking the deviation from the exact model due to the noise as $y_i - y(x_i)$ and specify the deviations by a probability distribution such as the normal distribution. From Shannon's coding theorem (section 3.9), the deviation can be optimally coded by a code of length $|code(y_i - y(x_i))| = -\log_2 P(y_i - y(x_i))$ rounded up. That is, given this code for the probability of the outcome, the actual deviation from the model can be calculated, as was outlined in section 4.3.

The two-part algorithm for each data point is

$$H_{\text{prov}}(y_i) = H[ax_i + b, P] - \log_2 P[y_i - y(x_i)] + |\text{decoding routine}| + O(1),$$

or, replacing the probability term by a code,

$$H_{\text{prov}}(y_i) = H[ax_i + b, P] + |code(y_i - y(x_i))| + |\text{decoding routine}| + O(1).$$

Here the decoding routine is specifically identified and the $O(1)$ term allows for short codes to join subroutines. The expectation value for the code term is the Shannon entropy of the deviations, i.e. $-\Sigma(P(y_i - y(x_i))\log_2 P(y_i - y(x_i))$. Selecting the optimum model corresponds to finding the provisional entropy or selecting the minimal set containing the string $y_i$ corresponding to the AMSS. The result is equivalent to the ideal MDL approach discussed later in the section 5.3.

The algorithm that generates point $y_i$ given point $x_i$, contains the probability based code, a decoding routine, the probability distribution needed to calculate the deviation from the model, and finally the specification of the model. The algorithm undertakes the following computational steps:
- takes the code for the deviation and knowing that $|code(y_i - y(x_i))| = -\log_2 P(y_i - y(x_i))$, generates the value of the probability for that string;
- calculates $y_i - y(x_i)$, the deviation due to the noise, from the probability values using the routine for generating $P$;
- generates $y(x_i)$ from $ax_i + b$; and
- the final computational step generates the point of interest by adding the two previous contributions to get $y_i = (y_i - y(x_i)) + y(x_i)$. This generates the straight line and the deviation from it for each point.

All the regularity is in the model while, the variation, which may be due to the limits of the model, noise, or experimental error, will appear as random deviations from the model. The model that best fits a series of data outcomes is the shortest algorithm that exactly specifies each $y_i$ by specifying first the model for the set of outcomes and then, for each outcome, the deviations from the model.

This again is the argument used to find the algorithmic minimal sufficient statistic for the data discussed in section 4.3.1. The model expresses the physical laws that would exactly describe the outcome if there were no variation. The variation is captured by the code that identifies the particular data string in the set of all strings defined by the model.

While the above discussion shows how data can be specified, the approach can be used to find the model that optimally fits the data. The approach highlights again the fact that the most compressed description of the set of observations $y^{(n)} = (y_1, y_2, y_3, \dots, y_n)$ is the model that best fits the set of observations with the deviations from the model minimised for each $y_i$ in the data string. Consider the situation where it is suspected that the straight line model, using the parameters $a$ and $b$ given above, is the best explanation of a data set. Here, the hypothesis is the straight line model, $y(x_i)$ but which also includes a probability distribution to cover the noise or variation. That is, the noise or deviation from the model for a particular data point $x_i$ is $y_i - y(x_i)$. However, the parameters $a$ and $b$, used to specify the straight line model, and the characteristics of the distribution, are not determined by the algorithmic approach. The parameters must arise by analysing the data trialling different models. In the simple straight line case, they might be determined by a fitting procedure such as one that minimises the sum of the squared deviations. In which case, the length of the description that optimally specifies the data depends on the following.

- The major contribution to the algorithmic entropy of a model usually is the number of bits needed to specify the model parameters, rather that the bits to specify model details. In which case, the number of bits in the parameters can be used to compare models.

  In general, a hypothesis or model, may be articulated as a physical law, a simple model (such as a straight line fit to the data), or be from a class of models such as a polynomial, Bernoulli, or Markov models. The approach outlined below does not establish the parameters of the possible models; rather, given the best fit obtained from a number of possible models, the approach establishes which of these best fits is preferred. For example, a trial fit of the data could use a straight line based on a standard fitting process such as least squares. Then a second degree polynomial could be trialled and so on. This process establishes the optimum parameters for each potential model. Given these models with their parameters, the chosen model is the one that provides the shortest algorithmic description of the data. The straight line model described above requires $2d$ bits to specify $a$ and $b$ to a precision $d$. If a second degree polynomial provides a better fit than the straight line, this would be because the increase in the model description to three parameters is offset by a reduction in the deviations from the model.

  In the three parameter case an extra $d$ bits are required for the algorithmic to specify the model ($3d$ bits in all) and this must be offset by a decrease in the deviation represented by the log probability term.

- The description of the deviation from the model, $y_i - y(x_i)$ is distributed according to a discrete probability model. According to Shannon's Coding theorem (section 3.9), the deviation can be optimally coded by a code of length $=-\log_2 P[y_i - y(x_i)]$. For a Gaussian discrete distribution, where each $x_i$ are specified to a given level of precision, the log probability term depends on $[y - y(x_i)]^2/(2\sigma)^2 - \log_2(\sigma\sqrt{2\pi}$ noting the standard deviation, $\sigma$ is determined from the data. If the outcome was not Gaussian or another symmetrical probability distribution, the implication is that hidden structure exists and the deviations would not be random. In which case, a more refined model would be needed.

- The limitations of the algorithmic approach can now be seen. The best parameters for each model and the associated probability distribution must first be determined before models can be compared. However, once the best model is found, by whatever means, the provisional algorithmic entropy based on the model is the best estimate of the algorithmic entropy of each string in the data set.

As is discussed further in section 5.3, the approach is only valid when the string, or strings, of interest are typical strings in the two-part description. They must be random in the set with no distinguishing features. If this were not so, as was discussed in section 4.3, hidden structure exists and another model would be better.

One further point, the model obtained by minimising the two-part description is the best explanation of the data, however, it is not necessarily the correct explanation.

### 5.2.1 A more general example

Instead of listing the Earth's position for every second of a year, Newton's laws can capture the motion in a set of equations. If the equations exactly described the Earth's motion around the Sun, the equations represent an extremely compressed version of the data. That is, given $x_i$ which will be taken to represent each second of the year, the model that best fits a series of data points for the motion of the Earth is the shortest algorithm that exactly specifies the observed outcome $y_i$ given $x_i$. However, in practice Newton's laws do not exactly specify the observational data, as variations occur. The variations from the model might be due to measurement error, perturbations from the Moon or a breakdown in the assumptions of simple spherical bodies. Where the deviations appear as noise, they can be represented by a probability distribution. In this situation the observational data can still be compressed by describing the data algorithmically—initially in terms of Newton's laws (which specifies the particular string should Newton's laws exactly predict the data point) and then by coding how the observed data point deviates from the simple predictions of Newton's laws.

The optimum compression of the data set is given by the provisional entropy or the AMSS as was discussed in section 4.3.1. A good model is one that maximally compresses the data. All the regularity is in the model while, the variation or randomness (which may be due hidden effects, to the limits of the model, noise, or experimental error) is captured by the code that identifies the particular data string given the laws. If later, a further cause or pattern in the variation is uncovered, as might occur by taking into account the Moon's effect, the compression can be improved.

### 5.2.2 The AMSS application to model selection

The previous section showed how to specify a string representing a data point given an understanding of the laws which generate the string and the deviation from the laws. Vereshchagin and Vitányi [1] developed an equivalent approach from a different perspective. Their approach sought the best model to describe a particular string or strings, using Kolmogorov's AMSS approach. In this version, as discussed earlier in section 4.3.1, the model is the Turing Machine (TM) that evaluates the function defined by the model.

These authors show, just as in the previous section, that for each credible model of the data, a two-part algorithm can be used to exactly define each string. The first part specifies the TM that might model the data, while the second part codes the deviation from the model to allow each point to be fitted exactly. The model with the shortest overall description is preferred. In other words, it is a short step from finding the shortest description of a string, to finding the best model for a set of strings by the processes outlined above. As previously discussed, one can try explaining the data with different models and select the one with that fits the data with the shortest algorithm as the best explanation. The shortest description of the data corresponds to the AMSS, as all the useful information is contained in the algorithm that defines the set or equivalently the TM that generates the function defining the set. The second algorithm picks out the string given the AMSS for the data set.

As Vereshchagin and Vitányi [1] explain; 'the main task for statistical inference and learning theory is to distil the meaningful information in the data'. And later, 'For every data item, and every complexity level, minimizing a two-part code, one part model description and one part data-to-model, over the class of models of at most given complexity, with certainty selects models that are in a rigorous sense are the best explanations of the data'.

## 5.3 The minimum description length approach

The MDL approach was developed by Rissanen [2, 3] (see also Barron *et al* [4]) as a practical method to find the best model to describe a sequence of data points. There are basically two forms of MDL.

The first form of MDL is a true algorithmic approach, that is identical to the provisional entropy or AMSS approaches to modelling. Known as ideal MDL [5], the approach seeks the shortest description of a data set by a two-part algorithm. The first algorithm captures the regularity of the data with a hypothesis or model. The second part is the algorithm that captures the deviation of the actual data from the regularity, given the model. If the model is too simple it may have a short description, but this will be more than offset by the longer description of the deviations from the regularity implied by the model. An optimum clearly exists and, as section 5.2 outlines, this optimum corresponds to the AMSS or provisional entropy approaches. However, while the ideal MDL approach finds the algorithm that best fits the data, it does not generate the actual outcome, rather it is a process that picks out the model parameters. The true algorithmic description requires the data item to be generated from the parameters and input data and so may require a decoding routine.

Just as for the approach discussed in section 5.2; the model captures the regularity of the set, and given the set, the string of interest is identified. Like the provisional entropy, the ideal approach also suffers from the fact that the algorithmic description is non-computable and there is no systematic procedure to decide whether the understanding embodied in the hypothesis or model is the best possible. Different models can be investigated, but the process is ad hoc.

Practical MDL, the second approach, addresses the non-computability problem by replacing the idea of algorithmic complexity with stochastic complexity. That is, rather than finding the length of the shortest actual algorithm, the stochastic complexity seeks the *minimum code length* for the data based on Shannon's Coding theorem (equation (3.17)). In practice, the code may be little different from that obtained from the true algorithmic approach. As is outlined later, practical MDL provides a tool for selecting the best model from a class of models by a systematic process. If the class is sufficiently broad, such as the class of polynomials, or the class of Markov models, the process identifies which model in the class describes the data with the fewest number of bits. Inevitably, the optimality is relative to the class or classes chosen. If this were not so, the approach could be used to determine all the laws of physics.

In what follows the ideal or algorithmic MDL for model selection will first be discussed. Section 5.3.3 briefly outlines the practical MDL approach. However, as the practical approach to MDL is a separate discipline in its own right, it is not the focus here. Rather, here the major focus will be on the algorithmic version and its alignment with the provisional entropy and the AMSS approaches.

### 5.3.1 Ideal MDL

The ideal MDL approach considers only hypotheses $\mathcal{H}_i$, corresponding to different models, that can be expressed as finite sets of binary strings of finite length [5]. In which case, the ideal MDL approach can be derived by taking the negative logarithm of Bayes' equation (3.28) above, to get

$$-\log_2 P(\mathcal{H}_i|D) = -\log_2 P(D|\mathcal{H}_i) - \log_2 P(\mathcal{H}_i) + \log_2 P(D). \tag{5.1}$$

Here, $D$ is the data that the model is to fit. The Bayes' approach selects the hypothesis that given the data, $D$ maximises the probability $P(\mathcal{H}_i|D)$. This is equivalent to choosing the hypothesis that minimises the right hand side of equation (5.1) and in so doing, provides the shortest description of the data. However, as $\log_2 P(D)$ is independent of the hypothesis or model, it is irrelevant and can be ignored. The Bayes' approach depends on assigning a probability to all the potential hypotheses $P(\mathcal{H}_i)$. Assigning this prior probability is usually ad hoc in the typical Bayes' approach. A simple assignment is to assume each hypothesis is equally likely. Where, as is usually the case, the prior probability is not known, as discussed in section 3.9.1 the universal distribution $m(\mathcal{H}_i)$ can be used as the prior to replace $P(\mathcal{H}_i)$. The universal distribution is the best estimate of the unknown probability. Furthermore, provided that the restrictions outlined below are satisfied, $m(D|\mathcal{H}_i)$ can also replace $P(D|\mathcal{H}_i)$ and the equation to be minimised to give:

$$-\log_2 m(D|\mathcal{H}_i) - \log_2 m(\mathcal{H}_i).$$

Because of the algorithmic version of Shannon's coding theorem (section 3.9), the universal distribution $m(.)$ is equivalent to $2^{-H(.)}$. Hence $H(\mathcal{H}_i)$, the shortest algorithmic description of the model hypothesis $\mathcal{H}_i$, such as the straight line model discussed above, can replace $-\log_2 m(\mathcal{H}_i)$ in the above equation. The hypothesis with the shortest algorithmic specification of all outcomes is seen to be the most probable. This is in effect favouring the simplest hypothesis from the perspective of Occam's razor. This leads to the equivalent expression of the above equation in algorithmic entropy terms That is, to within the $O(1)$ constant, the optimum model minimises:

$$H_{\text{algo}}(\mathcal{H}_i) + H_{\text{algo}}(D|\mathcal{H}_i).$$

This is equivalent to equation (4.2) that defines the provisional entropy of the hypothesis or model where

$$H_{\text{prov}}(D) = H_{\text{algo}}(\mathcal{H}_i) + H_{\text{algo}}(D|\mathcal{H}_i).$$

Here $\mathcal{H}_i$ specifies the optimal set containing the data. Such a set might be all strings of the form $ax_i + b$. Given the set, the actual data string is specified with $H_{alg}(D|\mathcal{H}_i)$ bits. That is, the best hypothesis is the one that minimises the provisional entropy, or selects the AMSS, as given by equations (4.2) or (4.8). If necessary, the approach can be generalised to include the probability distribution as outlined in section 4.3. If there is more than one possibility with the same minimisation, the hypothesis $\mathcal{H}_i$ chosen is the one with the shortest $H(\mathcal{H}_i)$. Effectively, the MDL argument is that the shortest algorithmic description, given the information available, is the preferred hypothesis.

Provided that the substitution of $H(D|\mathcal{H}_i)$ for $m(D|\mathcal{H}_i)$ is valid, for a finite set of hypotheses, the Bayesian approach coincides with the ideal MDL using $m(\mathcal{H}_i)$, as the prior probability. However, this substitution is only valid when the data string, represented by $D$ is a typical member of the data set implied by the hypothesis. To be typical, the string must be random with respect to the set. This requirement is identical to the set requirement discussed in section 5.2 for the provisional entropy or the AMSS approaches. The meaning of typicality in this context is discussed in the next section 5.3.2. These approaches are the same, but each provides a different perspective on model selection.

The ideal MDL approach provides a more formalised method for capturing data that links algorithmic information theory with model selection. As was mentioned in section 4.4 a model, in effect, is a way of compressing data. A good model is one that has a maximally compressed description of the data.

### 5.3.2 Example of a non-typical string in a set

The above argument for the MDL case requires the substitution of $\log_2 m(\mathcal{H}_i)$, or its equivalant $H(\mathcal{H}_i)$, for the logarithm of the probabilities in Baye's theorem. This section explores the situation where this is not valid.

Consider a model that describes a particular string as the outcome of process where the probability of a '1' is $P_1$ and that of a '0' is $P_0 = 1 - P_1$. If the hypothesis is that a 1 will occur with probability $P_1 = 0.8$, the approach will only work for the three approaches discussed if the outcome is a typical string in the set of strings satisfying the hypothesis. This hypothesis leads to the expectation that the process would generate a random string where 80% of the characters would be 1's and 20% would be 0's. However, a particular output could be the string of length 1000 that consists of 800 1's followed by 200 0's. But this output is not typical in the set of possible strings, as it shows more order or pattern than a typical member. In this case, if this string is observed as a particular datum, it is invalid to replace $m(D|\mathcal{H}_i)$ by $H(D|\mathcal{H}_i)$ to explain it. Such a surprise string would only be typical for a different model, as it is more ordered than expected. Just as in the AMSS case, a new hypothesis or model is needed. When the right hypothesis is found, and each member of the set is equally likely with respect to the new hypothesis then $\log_2[P(D|\mathcal{H}_i)] = -\log_2(1/\Omega)$ where $\Omega$ is the number of data strings in the restricted set. Similarly, in algorithmic terms, $H(D|\mathcal{H}_i) = \log_2\Omega$.

A more practical process to determine the optimum model to explain data but which overcomes the non-computability issues in ideal MDL, is discussed in the next section

### 5.3.3 Practical MDL

The practical MDL approach, developed by Rissanen, by-passes the computability problem inherent in the ideal MDL approach to model selection by defining the stochastic complexity to replace the algorithmic complexity [2, 3, 6]. The stochastic complexity is computable. It corresponds to the minimum description of the observed data string using the optimal codes based on probabilities, rather than on an exact algorithm (although at times the most efficient code might well be virtually the same as the shortest algorithm). Thus, the stochastic complexity is defined as the shortest description of the data, relative to a class of probabilistic models. Stochastic complexity was inspired by the AIT approach and Solomonoff's approach to induction (see section 3.9.1). Reviews can be found in Grünwald [7] and Hansen and Yu [8].

Shannon's coding theorem, which was discussed in section 3.4, shows that an optimal code can be found for a countable set of objects denoted by $y_i$, distributed according to a probability $P(y_i)$. These objects can be strings and, in this section these strings are considered to be derived from particular models. As section 3.4 points out, Shannon's noiseless coding theorem (equation (3.16), demonstrates that optimum codes from a prefix-free set can be chosen to virtually equal the probability rounded up, i.e.

$$|code(y_i)| = -\lceil \log_2(P(y_i)) \rceil.$$

The convention is to denote the code length by $-\log_2 P$ with the understanding it is to be an integer. One further point is that, where the probability model is expressed as a probability density, the variables $y_i$ are taken to a chosen level of precision such as eight significant binary characters. In this case, a probability $-\log_2 P(y_i)$ for each $y_i$ is replaced by $-\log_2[P(y_i)\delta]$, where $\delta$ represents the grid size determined by the resolution. As the $\delta$ is constant throughout the MDL optimisation procedures, it can be ignored.

Again, the principle behind the approach is that, the better the model of the observed data, the more compressed the description will be. But the question arises as to whether the process has advantages over other statistical methodologies that select hypotheses or models. In general, the practical MDL approach avoids over fitting, where there are too many parameters in the model relative to the data, as well as under fitting where the model is too simplistic. When there are too many parameters, the error term is small, but the overall description, including the model description, is longer. Under fitting the data gives rise to excessive variation in the data from the simplistic model's values, giving rise to a longer description of the deviation. For example, a data string of 20 points could be fitted by a simple straight line but the deviations might require a large contribution from the $-\log(P)$ term. However, a model with 20 parameters could give an exact fit but the model description might be too long. The best fit lies between these. In a practical sense, MDL satisfies Occam's razor.

The approach has some important differences from traditional data fitting, as there is no assumption that the process produces the true model or true parameters underlying the data. Rissanen points out [6] that the optimal model is not an approximation to anything; it just fits the data. The practical MDL approach can be derived from Bayes' theorem as outlined previously for ideal MDL. Alternatively, it can be argued that when the data is maximally compressed, all the useful information has been extracted. Minimising the stochastic complexity becomes, in effect, ensuring that the data is random relative to the class of models and that all pattern has been captured in the model in a manner similar to the AMSS approach.

Given a data set, the practical MDL approach seeks to find which member of a class of models provides the shortest description of the data. The argument is exactly the same as for the AMSS approach except that the stochastic complexity is used rather than an algorithm. The MDL model class under consideration is usually expressed in terms of the parameters that define the class. The class could be a set of linear regressions where the data $y$ is a linear function of several variables, say $x_1$ to $x_n$. In the non-linear regression case, a similar set of parameters $\alpha_1$ to $\alpha_{k+1}$ representing the coefficients of a polynomial of degree $k$ can be used. In this case, the model can be represented in terms of the parameter set $x$ and the model label $k$. A general Markov model is described by its order $k$, representing the length of the history required to define the future together, while in this class of models the parameter set becomes a set of probabilities $\hat{P}^{(k)}$. A Bernoulli model is the simplest Markov model with $k = 1$ and a probability $\hat{P}$. (Note here that $P(y)$ represents the probability of string $y$ in the set of strings, while $\hat{P}$ is the probability of the next character in string $y$ and characterises the model.) The non-predictive version [2] shows that in certain circumstances the minimum description of a string of length $n$ reduces to:

$$-\log_2 P(y|\hat{P}^{(k)}, k) + (k/2)\log_2 n + O(\log_2 n).$$

The second term, derived from the stochastic complexity, parameterises the model class, while the first term is a probability based code that, given the model specified by parameters $\hat{P}^k$ and $k$, codes for the data. Consider a data string with $r$ $1's$ in the string of length $n$ and a Bernoulli with $k = 1$ as a trial. The shortest description for large $n$ depends on $nh(\hat{P}) + (\log_2 n)/2$, where $h$ is the entropy rate—the entropy per symbol [9]. The maximum likelihood estimate of the probability gives $\hat{P} = r/n$. However, if a higher order Markov model is to be considered as a better explanation of the data, a larger $k$ value will add bits to the specification of the model. If this increase is more than offset by a decrease in the code length derived from the probability term, the latter model will be preferred. The optimum description is the one that minimises the total length over the whole class of models.

The practical MDL approach has evolved significantly since the early work of Rissanen [2, 3, 6]. Later versions use a normalised maximum likelihood model to provide better descriptions of the data.

### 5.3.4 Maximum entropy formulation

The 'maximum entropy' approach developed by Jaynes is an attempt to make the maximum use of information when modelling a system [10–12]. The approach, which has at its heart Laplace's principle of indifference, seems to work despite the scepticism of the traditional frequentist understanding of probability. Interestingly, as the following outlines, the MDL approach, can be used to justify the maximum entropy approach of Jaynes [13, 14]. In other words, minimising the description length is equivalent to maximising the Shannon entropy.

In an actual experimental situation, the true probability $\hat{P}_i$ of a particular outcome $i$ may not be known. If there are $n$ independent trials, and outcome $i$ occurs $n_i$ times, the probability of outcome $i$ given by $\hat{P}_i$ can be approximated by $n_i/n$. However, while $n_i$ may not actually be known, any information observed determines the constraints on the possible spread of outcomes. For example, one constraint should be that the total of the probability should be 1. That is, $\Sigma n_i/n = 1$. Similarly, for an energy distribution over a number of outcomes each with energy $E_i$ and total energy $E$, the average observed energy per state is constrained by $\Sigma E_i n_i/n = E$. These constraints limit the possible values of the probabilities for each outcome. In which case, the maximum entropy principle can identify the model that best fits the constraints by determining the probability distribution $\hat{P}_i'$ that maximises the entropy. If the Shannon entropy

$$H(\hat{P}_1, \ldots, \hat{P}_k) = -\Sigma_i \hat{P}_i \log_2 \hat{P}_i. \tag{5.2}$$

has a maximum when $\hat{P}_i = \hat{P}_i'$, the set of probabilities $\hat{P}_i'$ is the preferred distribution.

In the maximum entropy formulation, the Lagrangian multiplier is used to capture the information embodied in the constraints to find the value of $\hat{P}_i$ that maximises the entropy. Li and Vitányi [14] give the example of the so-called Brandeis dice problem (see also Jaynes [11]), where the average outcome of the throw of a dice indicates bias. The observed bias constrains the allowable probabilities. The set of probabilities $\hat{P}_i$ that maximises the entropy, given the constraints, is then found. The following outlines why minimising $-\log_2 P(x|\hat{P})$ is equivalent to maximising the Shannon entropy.

In general, the linearly independent constraints can be represented by a series of equations of the form: $\Sigma_j a_{i,j} n_j/n = x_i$, Where $x_i$ represents the observed value of a physical quantity (Rissanen [13]). There will be a set of possible distributions $\hat{P} = (\hat{P}_1, \hat{P}_2 \ldots \hat{P}_k)$ each of which satisfies the above constraints, and each will have an associated probability as a hypothesis for explaining the constraints. (Note that here the probability of the hypothesis $P$ representing a particular model, is to be distinguished from a particular set of probabilities $\hat{P}$ that satisfy the constraints $x$.) Any allowable probability distribution should fit the data, hence $P(x|\hat{P}) = 1$. In which case, the ideal code length associated with the model ought to be $-\log_2 P(x|\hat{P}) = 0$. Thus the best set of probabilities is the set that minimises $-\log_2 P(x|\hat{P})$. For large sequences of data, this is equivalent to maximising $n!/(n_1!...n_k!)$. This, given Stirling's approximation, is equivalent to maximising the entropy of equation (5.2) demonstrating the validity of the Jaynes' approach.

Interestingly too, Jaynes [12], appendix A argues that Kolmogorov's more general probability approach is consistent with his own.

## References

[1] Vereshchagin N K and Vitányi P M B 2004 Kolmogorov's structure functions and model selection *IEEE Trans. Inf. Theory* **50** 3265–90

[2] Rissanen J 1978 Modeling by the shortest data description *Automatica* **14** 465–71

[3] Rissanen J 1989 *Stochastic Complexity in Statistical Inquiry* (Singapore: World Scientific)

[4] Barron A R, Rissanen J and Yu B 1998 The MDL principle in modeling and coding *IEEE Trans. Inf. Theory* **44** 2743–60

[5] Vitányi P M B and Li M 2000 Minimum Description Length induction, Bayesianism, and Kolmogorov complexity *IEEE Trans. Inform. Theory* **46** 446–64

[6] Rissanen J 1987 Stochastic complexity *J. R. Stat. Soc.* **49B** 252–65

[7] Grünwald P D 2005 A tutorial introduction to the minimum description length principle *Advances in Minimum Description Length: Theory and Applications* ed P D Grünwald, I J Myung and M A Pitt (Cambridge, MA: MIT Press)

[8] Hansen M H and Yu B 2001 Model selection and the principle of minimum description length *J. Am. Stat. Assoc.* **96** 746–74

[9] Rissanen J 1986 Stochastic complexity and modeling *Ann. Stat.* **14** 1080–100

[10] Jaynes E T 1957 Information theory and statistical mechanics *Phys. Rev.* **106** 620–30

[11] Jaynes E T 1979 Where do we stand on maximum entropy *The Maximum Entropy formalism* ed R D Levine and M Tribus (Cambridge, MA: MIT Press) 15–118

[12] Jaynes E T and Bretthorst G L 2003 *Probability Theory: The Logic of Science* (New York: Cambridge University Press)

[13] Rissanen J 1983 A universal prior for integers and estimation by minimum description length *Ann. Stat.* **11** 416–31

[14] Li M and Vitányi P M B 2008 *An Introduction to Kolmogorov Complexity and Its Applications* 3rd edn (New York: Springer)

**IOP** Publishing

# Algorithmic Information Theory for Physicists and Natural Scientists

### Sean D Devine

# Chapter 6

# The non-typical string and randomness

The algorithmic approach resolves the mathematical problem of randomness. If a string is random, it must show no structure or pattern and therefore cannot be specified by an algorithm shorter than the length of the string. The lack of randomness, or Kolmogorov's 'deficiency in randomness' as it is called, is a measure of how much a string can be compressed given its length. This leads to the Martin-Löf test of randomness and it is shown that the deficiency of randomness provides a universal Martin-Löf test of randomness. No test of randomness can do any better than a Martin-Löf universal test.

An alternative universal test is the sum $P$-test which is somewhat easier to grasp. The idea is that if you place a bet on the outcome that is supposed to be random, a non-random outcome will be a surprise and with a judicious bet, this surprise will provide a significant payoff.

Universal constructs are extremely useful as the term 'universal' indicates the optimal test for randomness, the optimal Turing computer, or the optimal semi-measure to use as a probability.

## 6.1 Outline on perspectives on randomness

Mathematicians have had great difficulty in defining randomness in a robust manner. For example, Von Mises [1] attempted to define a randomness test for an infinite sequence by requiring that relative frequencies converge for all sub-sequences. While intuitively this would seem to be reasonable, mathematicians have identified weaknesses with the approach. However, algorithmic information theory provides a number of different perspectives on randomness that ultimately lead to a more robust approach. From an AIT point of view, most strings are random in the sense that they cannot be generated by a shorter algorithm. As they show no pattern or structure, they are not compressible. However, while the sequence '111 ...11' of length 100 is just as likely to occur by chance as any other string of the same length, we do not see it as random. The reason is that we recognise that '111 ...11' has pattern and for that reason is compressible, i.e. it can be specified by an algorithm that is shorter than the string of 1's. Such a string is not a typical member of the set of all strings of length 100.

Typicality is related to the equilibrium concept in statistical mechanics. Section 7.2.2 shows that the different possible configurations of a gas in phase space (position-momentum space) can be represented by a series of 1's and 0's. The overwhelming majority of strings existing in the most probable set of states are typical as they have no distinguishing features. However, where strings are not typical they can be algorithmically compressed. As these can be described by a shorter algorithm than that describing a typical string, they are said to be ordered. Such an example is the configuration in phase space represented by '111 ...11100000 ...000', a string of repeated ones and repeated zeros. While such a highly ordered string can occur by chance, this is very unlikely.

Martin-Löf, a colleague of Kolmogorov, recognised that randomness is to do with typicality and the idea of incompressibility. He developed the randomness test known by his name. Chaitin developed the equivalent concept of $m$-randomness which is probably simpler to grasp. The following outlines the key AIT perspectives on randomness. However, as the different perspectives can be a bit overwhelming they are summarised first and will be discussed in more detail in the following sections:

- most strings are algorithmically random. As is discussed below, only 1 in 1024 strings of any length (greater than 10) can be algorithmically compressed by 10 bits or more;
- Kolmogorov developed a measure he called the 'deficiency in randomness' (or 'randomness deficiency') of a string; i.e. the more ordered a string is, the more it is deficient in randomness. Hence deficiency in randomness defines order;
- Martin-Löf [2] defined a universal $P$-test for randomness that is as good as every conceivable valid randomness test. If a string is deemed random at a particular level by a universal test, no valid test of randomness can do any better. Randomness deficiency can be used as a universal test of randomness;
- Chaitin's measure of $m$-randomness, where $m$ is the number of characters the string can be compressed algorithmically, is equivalent to a Martin-Löf universal test of randomness allowing for the fact that in the Chaitin case self-delimiting codes (i.e. codes from a prefix-free set) are used;
- an alternative test is the sum $P$-test of Levin and Gács [3]. The idea behind this is that a judicious betting process can turn a profit if the string is claimed to be random but is actually ordered. The outcome of the sum $P$-test is virtually identical to the Martin-Löf $P$-test based on deficiency in randomness, except that, again the sum $P$-test requires the computation to be restricted to a self-delimiting set of computational instructions;
- algorithmic information theory makes considerable use of universal concepts; i.e. those that dominate all others members in the class. In this sense the

concept of a universal test for randomness is analogous to the concept of a universal computer (additively dominates) and the concept of a universal semi-measure (multiplicatively dominates).

Before looking at the different perspectives in detail, the concept of randomness deficiency will first be outlined. AIT recognises that most real numbers of a given length are algorithmically random. This can be seen, as there are $2^n - 1$ binary strings with lengths less than a given $n$. Ignoring the 1, this means that there are just under $2^n$ strings shorter than $n$. If one wishes to find the number of these strings that can be generated by an algorithm shorter than $n - m$, only $2^{n-m}$ shorter algorithms are available. For example, if $n = 100$ and $m = 10$, there are $1.27 \times 10^{30}$ strings of length 100 but only $1.24 \times 10^{27}$ strings of length less than 90. Hence at most, only 1 in 1024 strings of length 100 can be algorithmically compressed by more than 10 bits or 10%. There are too few shorter strings available to provide the compressed description. In practice, there will be even fewer strings available, as many shorter possibilities will already have been used. For example, some of these short string will not be available as they are a compressed representation of strings longer than $n$; others will not be available as they themselves can be compressed further. As most strings cannot be significantly compressed, the algorithmic entropy of a string $x$ of length $n$ is most likely to be close to $n + |n|$; i.e. the string's actual length, and the size of the code for its length. Those strings that cannot be compressed to less than $n - m$ are called '$m$-random' (see, for example, Chaitin [4]).

Given the uniform distribution that corresponds to the situation where all outcomes are equally likely, Kolmogorov's randomness deficiency provides a measure of how non-random a string is. The less random the string, as it can be compressed, the greater is its randomness deficiency. For a string of length $n$ the randomness deficiency $d(x|n)$ is defined by

$$d(x|n) = n - C(x|n). \tag{6.1}$$

This definition uses $C(x|n)$, the plain algorithmic complexity of string $x$ given its length $|x| = n$. While the definition could be in terms of the algorithmic entropy $H(x|n)$ as self-delimiting coding is used, the discussion using $C(x|n)$, is more straightforward for simple examples. However, as is discussed below, the outcome of a randomness test known as the sum $P$-test that uses self-delimiting coding, or coding from a prefix-free set, will differ slightly from the $P$-test that uses plain coding.

For most strings of a given length, $C(x|n) = n$, as most cannot be generated by an algorithm shorter than $n$, and knowing $n$ does not shorten the algorithm. In which case, $d(x|n) = 0$ and such strings are deemed random. The greater $d(x|n)$ is for a particular string $x$, the less random the string, or using Kolmogorov's term, the greater is its randomness deficiency. A highly ordered string, such as a string of $n$ repeated ones has $d(x|n) = n$ as, in this case, $C(1^n|n) = O(1)$.

Where $d(x|n)$ is large, the string is highly non-random as $C(x|n) \ll n$. Such a string is non-typical and its algorithmic complexity is much less than its length. For example, the string '11…1' of one hundred 1's in a row can be compressed to about

$\log_2 100$ bits, i.e. $C(x) = \log_2 100 + O(1)$ (equation (3.2)). As $C(x|100)$ is the complexity given the length of the string is 100, $C(x|100) = O(1)$, and the randomness deficiency is $100 - O(1)$. Clearly $111...1$ is a non-typical string in the set of strings of length $n = 100$. This approach resolves the intuitive problem that, while tossing a coin and obtaining one hundred heads in a row is just as likely as any other outcome, it is somehow completely unexpected.

Another way of viewing this is to divide a set of outcomes into two sets where the typical set contains those strings that can be compressed very little, and the non-typical set of those strings that can be significantly compressed. Most outcomes will fall into the typical set containing the more random outcomes. A significantly compressible, or a non-typical string, will only occur rarely in a coin toss (unless the coin is biased). It is seen that randomness deficiency is also a measure of how distant a configuration, representing a microstate in the natural world, is from random, or how distant it is from a typical microstate in the equilibrium set. As has been mentioned, this is analogous to the argument used in statistical mechanics that equilibrium (i.e. random) configurations are overwhelmingly the most likely. While an ordered configuration from the set of most probable states can be observed in principle, this will happen only as a rare fluctuation. In the natural world it is convenient to use the algorithmic entropy $H(s)$ rather than $C(s|n)$. In which case, $H(equilibrium) - H(s)$ measures the degree of order in a natural system in terms of its distance in bits of the ordered state from a typical state (section 8.6 and chapter 10).

A further point, which will later be seen to be significant, is to determine the fraction of strings that can be compressed a given amount. Consider the string $x$ of length $n$. There are $2^{n+1-m}$ strings able to be generated by an algorithm of length less than or equal to $n - m$. The fraction of such strings is $2^{1-m}$. This is the number of strings with $C(x|n)) \leqslant n - m$ or with the randomness deficiency, $d(x|n) \geqslant m$. For example, for $n = 100$ and $m = 10$ only 1 string in 512 can have $d(x|n) \geqslant 10$. This illustrates how $m$ can be used as a measure of randomness.

The previous discussion involved defining randomness for strings of a given length. This implies the uniform distribution. However, the measure of randomness deficiency can be extended to a string $x$, in a more general set of strings denoted by $S$.

While the number of elements in a set $S$ is often denoted by $|S|$, in this book the vertical lines are taken to refer to the length of the algorithmic specification. Hence, to avoid confusion, $\Omega_S$ will be used to denote the number of members of the set. For large sets, most strings will be typical and will be represented by a code of length close to $\log_2 \Omega_S$, i.e. the algorithmic entropy of a typical string is close to the Shannon entropy of the set.

The randomness deficiency for the string $x$ in a set $S$ is given by

$$d(x|S) = \log_2 \Omega_S - C(x|S). \tag{6.2}$$

If the string is ordered and can be compressed, its randomness deficiency will be high, as it is an non-typical member of the set. Consider the set $S$ of all strings of length $n$ with $r$ 1's and $(n - r)$ 0's. An example is the set of sequences of length 100 where there are 80 1's followed by 20 0's. This set of strings will be called the 80:20 set. In this case, the set has $\Omega_S = 100!/(80!20!)$ members and the typical string can be compressed to $\log_2\Omega_S = 69$. Thus any member of the 80:20 set can be coded in a way that compresses the representation to no more than 69 characters. In contrast, a truly random string of length 100 would require 100 characters. So while the strings in the 80:20 set are ordered relative to all strings, the typical string in the set has $C(x|S) \approx 69$ which from equation (6.2) gives $d(x|S) = 0$[1]. However, there are non-typical strings in this set that can be compressed further. They can be deemed 'deficient in randomness' relative to the typical string in the 80:20 set.

A non-typical member is the string consisting of 80 1's followed by 20 0's, i.e. 111...11000...00. The algorithm that generates this string would be of the form '$OUTPUT$ 1, $(100 - 20)$ *times and* $OUTPUT$ 0, 20 *times*'. Given the length of the string is 100, as $\log_2 20 = 4.32$. Rounding up it is seen that 5 bits are needed to code the integer 20. As 80 can be derived from 100-20, $C(x|S) \approx 5 + O(1)$. Here, the $O(1)$ covers the specification of 0, and 1, and the calculation of 100-20.

As $C(x|S) \approx 69$ and $\log_2\Omega_S = 69$, the randomness deficiency of a typical string in the 80:20 set is $d(x|S) = 0$. However, for the ordered string of 80 1s, the randomness deficiency will be $d(x|S) \approx 69 - 5 - 0(1) = 65 - O(1)$. It can be seen form equation (6.2) that $d(x|S)$ for the set $S$ of all 80:20 strings of length 100 will range from around 0 for random strings where $C(x|S) = 69$ to $\log_2\Omega_S - O(1)$ for a highly ordered 80:20 string.

An extension to this approach is where the deficiency in randomness is defined relative to a recursively enumerable probability distribution $P$. In which case, a typical member of the set will be coded by its probability in the set. According to Shannon's noiseless coding theorem, the optimum code length for such a string will be the integral value of $-\log_2 P$. In this case, a typical member is one where the length of the algorithmic description fits the logarithm of its probability in the set. Most strings can be compressed to a code of length $-\log_2 P$. However, an ordered string or one that is non-typical relative to the probability can be compressed by more, and the deficiency in randomness becomes $d(x|P) = -\log_2 P - C(x|P)$, which is the same as the earlier definition of equation (6.1). For the simple case of the uniform distribution of all strings of length $n$ each of the $2^n$ strings is equally likely. Hence, $P = 2^{-n}$ and $d(x|P) = n - C(x|n)$.

The deficiency in randomness measures how much an ordered string can be compressed relative to a random string. As the following outlines, the deficiency in randomness provides a basis for a robust randomness test.

## 6.2 Martin-Löf test of randomness

Martin-Löf, who worked with Kolmogorov for a short period, developed a test for randomness now known as the Martin-Löf test [2]. However, before discussing the test in detail, the idea will be explored. A string of length, say, 100, consisting of a mix of 50 1's and 50 0's would be probably be considered random unless there was an obvious pattern such as the 50 1's forming the initial sequence. But what about a

---

[1] For large strings Stirling's approximation can be used to show that $\log_2\Omega_s = nh$ where $h$ is what is called the entropy rate.

mix of 49 1's and 51 0's, or 40 1's and 60 0's? In other words, how much variation from the 50:50 ratio would correspond to a non-random string?

Martin- Löf recognised that, while each string in the set might be equally likely, it is possible to divide the set of strings into regions based on some quantifiable feature of the strings. If this can be done, and one of these regions has fewer strings than the other, the probability of a string falling in the region with fewer strings, will be lower than the typical string which falls in the larger region. Randomness is always relative to an implicit or explicit set of strings. For example, a string with a sequence of 100 1's in the set of all strings with length 100, would intuitively seem less random than any string where there is a roughly even mix of 1's and 0's. The trick is to define the feature that puts the string of 100 1's in a region which has few strings. Because strings in this region are non-typical there is a low probability of any string falling in this region. While all strings are equally likely to be observed, the probability of observing a string that falls into a region with appropriate features, or character-istics, can differ markedly from one falling in the typical region. In a thermodynamic system in the natural world, this is, in effect, finding a process to distinguish a highly improbable microstate from one in the most probable set of strings.

Even though there is no absolute cut off between typical and non-typical, the boundary between the typical and non-typical regions can be set at a significance level defined by a positive integer $m$. The process is to find a test function that defines whether the string belongs to a region of low probability. If the chance of finding a string in the $m$ region is $\epsilon = 2^{-m}$, then typical strings belong to the majority region of $1 - 2^{-m}$. However, to be consistent, the test function cannot assign more than a fraction of $2^{-m}$ strings in the low probability region.

Using the test function, a succession of typical/non-typical regions can be characterised by halving $\epsilon$ at each increment of $m$. As $m$ increases, the typical region expands and fewer strings will be deemed non-typical or ordered, and more strings will be typical or random. In other words, the requirement to categorise a string as non-typical becomes more restrictive as $m$ increases.

As can be seen in figure 6.1, at $m = 0$, i.e. $\epsilon = 1$, no strings are typical, which is not very helpful. But at $m = 1$ half the strings will fall in the typical region as the value of $m$ implies the cut off is $\epsilon = 2^{-1}$. At $m = 2$, 75% of strings will fall in the typical region and be deemed random at this level, while 25% will be deemed non-typical and will be seen to be more ordered. As can be seen in figure 6.1, the typical region of the majority at level $m + 1$ includes the typical region at level $m, m - 1, m - 2$, etc.

The Martin-Löf test for the randomness of a string, effectively uses a test function to determine whether string $x$ lies outside the majority or typical region at the significance level $m$. If so, it can be rejected as being random at that level $m$. Such a test must be enumerable and lower semicomputable to be able to be implemented. The test does not show whether a string is random, rather it determines the basis on which a string is non-typical and can be rejected as being random. As mentioned, the fraction of strings in the non-typical region defined by $m$ can be no more than $2^{-m}$. That is, if $m = 2$, no more than 25% of the strings can fall in the non-typical region; otherwise, the test would be inconsistent.

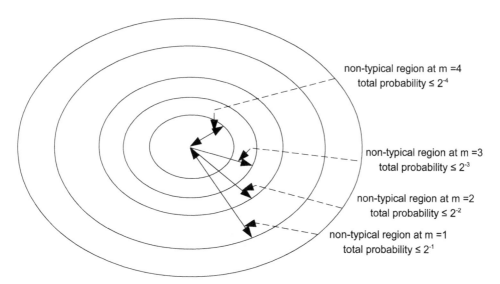

**Figure 6.1.** $Test(x) \geqslant m$ defines string $x$ as non-typical or non-random in the region $m$ where the total probability is $\leqslant 2^{-m}$.

There are therefore two aspects to the test. The first is to ensure that, under the test, the total probability of all strings in the reject or non-typical region is no more than the $2^{-m}$, and the second is to have a test procedure to determine whether a particular string belongs to the reject region. This test procedure defined by $Test(x)$ determines where $Test(x) \geqslant m$ for string $x$. If the total probability is less than $2^{-m}$ for $Test(x) \geqslant m$, then $x$ falls on the non-typical side of the typical/non-typical boundary at significance level $m$ and therefore $x$ can be rejected as being random. The mathematical formulation of this, when given the set of relevant strings characterised by a recursive (computable for all $x$) probability measure $P(x)$, becomes [5]:

$$\{\Sigma P(x): \text{Test}(x) \geqslant m\} \leqslant 2^{-m}. \tag{6.3}$$

In words, the above test states that one identifies all the strings where the test has a value $\geqslant m$. A string can be rejected as random and deemed ordered at the level $m$, provided the accumulated probability of all strings in the region $\leqslant 2^{-m}$. If this requirement is satisfied, a string can be consistently assigned to the reject or non-typical region for the given value of $m$ and is therefore non-random at that $m$ value. Any test for randomness that satisfies this assignment is a Martin-Löf $P$-test of randomness.

If there are $2^n$ strings in the set, an equivalent definition, can be based on the number of strings (denoted by $\#(x)$) that satisfy the criterion that $Test(x) \geqslant m$. That is, in this case the definition becomes:

$$\{\#(x) \text{ where Test}(x) \geqslant m\} \leqslant 2^{n-m}.$$

The test is valid if the number of strings that give a test result $\geqslant m$ is less than $2^{n-m}$.

**Martin-Löf test examples**

The Martin-Löf process can test whether a sequence, produced by tossing a possibly biased coin is random or not. Or to be more precise, at what level would the observed sequence be deemed non-random. Let $f(x)$ be the number of 1's in the string $x$ representing the outcome of $n$ tosses of a coin that might be biased. One might expect $f(x)$ to be about $n/2$ if the outcome is random. But how far from $n/2$ can the number of 1's be if the string is still considered to be random? The procedure is to devise a test of the form of equation (6.3) that involves $f(x)$. For example, Cover *et al* [6] use Chebyshev's inequality to develop a test function $\text{Test}(x) = \log_2\{2n^{-1/2}|f(x) - n/2|\}$. As there are $2^{n-2m}$ strings that satisfy $\text{Test}(x) \geqslant m$, the test is valid because $2^{n-2m} < 2^{n-m}$, satisfying the requirement.

An alternative test is to use the entropy rate $h$, the Shannon entropy per symbol in a string, mentioned above in section 6.1. Again let the number of 1's in a string of length $n$ be $f(x)$ and define $\hat{p} = f(x)/n$ so that $(1 - \hat{p}) = [(n - f(x)]/n$. In which case for large $n$, $h(x) = -\hat{p}\log_2\hat{p} - (1 - \hat{p})\log_2(1 - \hat{p})$. With appropriate coding, a string of length $n$ can be compressed to at least $nh(x)$. That means the string can in principle be shortened by an integer $m$, where $n(1 - h(x)) \geqslant m$. For example, a string with 75% of 1's can be compressed to $0.811n$. Such a string of length 100 can be compressed by at least $m = 18$ characters. Let a Martin-Löf test be $\text{Test}(x) = n(1 - h(x))$. $\text{Test}(x)$ effectively measures the amount the string $x$ can be compressed. On this basis $\text{Test}(x)$ is a valid test, as the accumulated probability of all strings satisfying $\text{Test}(x) \geqslant m$ is $\leqslant 2^{-m}$.

The entropy rate test can be demonstrated by considering a string of length 170. This length is chosen as it is sufficiently long that the entropy rate is meaningful, but not too long that 170!, which is needed to calculate accumulated probabilities, cannot be evaluated on an Excel spreadsheet. Consider the ratio 75:95 1's to 0's. At what level of $\epsilon$ would this string be rejected as random? In this case, $\text{Test}(x) = 1.701 > 1$. The accumulated probability of all strings in the region with $m > 1$ is 0.2499 which is less than $2^{-1}$. Thus the 75:95 string would only be rejected as random at the $m = 1$ cut-off level, i.e. 50% level. It is still reasonably random. On the other hand, a 70:100 string has $\text{Test}(x) = 3.8 > 3$. Taking $m = 3$, the cumulative probability of a string being in the region is $<2^{-3} = 0.038$. This is the region where $\epsilon < 0.125$. The 70:100 string can be rejected as random or considered ordered at the level of $m = 3$ or $\epsilon = 0.125$. On the other hand, the 70:100 string would not be considered ordered at $m = 4$.

The illustration shows that randomness is not absolute but related to an agreed level to define the boundary between random and non-random. But for a thermodynamic state, the most probable set of states is sharply peaked, relative to states outside the set.

### 6.2.1 Randomness deficiency as a Martin-Löf test

The randomness deficiency $d(x|P)$ in section 6.1 can be made into a test. For a set of strings defined to be an enumerable probability distribution $P$, the test function is[2]

$$\delta_0(x|P) = d(x|P) - 1.$$

For the particular case of the uniform distribution as $P = 1/n$, the randomness deficiency test assigns strings of length $n$ to a region using $\delta_0(x|P) = n - C(x|n) - 1$. As the number of strings where plain Kolmogorov complexity $C(x|n) \leqslant n - m - 1$ is $\leqslant 2^{n-m}$, the number of strings where $\delta_0(x|P) \geqslant m$ must be $\leqslant 2^{n-m}$. Putting this in probability terms by dividing by the number of strings, the result is:

$$\{\Sigma P(x) : \delta_0(x|P) \geqslant m\} \leqslant 2^{-m}.$$

This clearly satisfies the criteria of the test, but more importantly, as the next section shows, this is a universal test for randomness.

### 6.2.2 The Martin-Löf universal $P$-test of randomness

It can be shown that there are universal tests of randomness that dominate all other tests of randomness as was mentioned in an earlier bullet point. The argument, which is given in detail in Li and Vitányi [5] (p 131), shows that all effective tests of randomness can be listed by a systematic procedure. If $\delta_y(x)$ is the $y$th test, then the universal test $\delta_0(x|P)$ with respect to a set with probability distribution $P$ can be chosen to be

$$\delta_0(x|P) = max\{\delta_y(x) - y\},$$

where $y$ is an integer. Hence the universal test,

$$\delta_0(x|P) \geqslant \delta(x|P) - c$$

for all such tests. The universal test is as good as (allowing for the constant) any other conceivable or even inconceivable enumerable test. However, some understanding of 'as good as' is called for in this context. If the ordinary Martin-Löf test implies that $\delta(x|P) \geqslant m$, and $x$ is in the reject region at level $m$, the universal test has $\delta_0(x|P) \geqslant m - c$. The test $\delta_0(x|P)$ assigns more strings to the non- random region defined by $m$, as for a string to belong to the region in a universal test $\delta_0(x|P)$ need only be $\geqslant m - c$. If a test is not universal, its discrimination between random and non-random is more coarse. However, there is no one unique universal $P$-test. Rather there is a number such that each of the universal tests can additively dominate any other.

The masterstroke in the argument is that the test based on randomness deficiency, i.e. the test $\delta_0(x|P) = d(x|P) - 1$, is a universal test. What is more, it is consistent with the definition of $m$-randomness outlined in section 6.1. That is, Chaitin [7] has defined randomness as a string $x$ for which $H(x)$ is approximately equal to

---

[2] Readers will note that as $C(x|n) < n - m$, the '$-1$' is needed to ensure the relationship is $\leqslant$ rather than just $<$.

$|x| + H(|x|)$ or $H(x|n)$ is close to $n$. To be specific, a string of length $n$ is Chaitin $m$-random if it can be compressed to a string with length $n - m$, i.e. $H(x|n) > n - m$. This also applies to an infinite string $\alpha$ where the test is applied to sequences of the infinite string, i.e. provided that $\exists m$ for all lengths $n$ in the sequence, s.t. $H(\alpha_n) > n - m$. It is seen [8] that this definition is equivalent to the Martin-Löf definition of randomness at significance level $m$ allowing for the fact the Chaitin definition uses prefix-free complexity rather than plain algorithmic complexity.

Evaluating $\delta_0(x|P)$ and concluding that $x$ is random using a universal test is equivalent to establishing that the string satisfies all computable randomness tests including any not yet devised. However, unfortunately, $\delta_0(x|P)$ is not computable.

### 6.2.3 The sum $P$-test

Another way of looking at randomness is attributed to L A Levin by Gács in his 1988 lecture notes on descriptional complexity and randomnesss [9]. The approach, based on Levin's maximal uniform test of randomness [3], uses the level of payoff for a fair bet as a procedure to recognise a non-typical member of a set of outcomes (see the outline in Li and Vitányi [5]). Highly non-random outcomes are a surprise and ought to generate a high payoff if a bet is placed on such a surprise outcome occurring. For example, if a coin is tossed 100 times, the hypothesis is that all outcomes are equally likely. However, if the supposed fair coin happens to be biased 3:1 in favour of heads, in all likelihood there will be three times as many heads as tails. If each outcome is supposed to be equally likely, the occurrence of such a surprise outcome should be able to generate a return with a suitably cunning bet. The critical point is that surprise outcomes will be more algorithmically compressed than typical outcomes and therefore can be identified.

In order to illustrate the idea, let $H(x)$ be the algorithmic entropy for each outcome $x$. Make a \$1 bet with the agreement that the payoff for the outcome of a (possibly biased) coin tossed 100 times is to be $2^{100-H(x)}$. If the outcome is random, the payoff would be small, as $H(x)$ for such an outcome would be close to 100, the algorithmic description length of a typical string. But if $H(x)$ is small for the actual outcome, the measure of surprise is the amount of payoff the outcome produces. This payoff in effect takes $2^{-H(x)}$ as the universal probability distribution $m(x)$ (section 3.9)

The idea can be quantified. If all outcomes from tossing a coin 100 times are equally likely the probability for each is $p(x) = 2^{-100}$. The expected payoff for an unbiased outcome $x$ becomes

$$\sum_{|x| = 100} 2^{-100} 2^{100-H(x)} \leqslant 1.$$

As the expected return for the bet based on tossing a coin 100 times is no more than the stake, the bet is fair. This is because the Kraft inequality ensures $\sum_{|x| = 100} 2^{-H(x)} \leqslant 1$. However, if the coin is biased, or cheating is taking place, the returns become significant. For example, for the particular case of complete bias, where the outcome is *hhh...hh*, i.e. 100 heads, and noting that

$H(hhhh...hh) \sim \log_2 100 = 6$. The return of $2^{100-H(x)}$ for a 1 dollar bet is close to $2 \times 10^{28}$; a significant sum.

For the less unexpected case, where a coin is biased 3:1 in favour of heads, the outcome of 100 tosses of the coin is still far from random. Something like 75 heads will occur in the 100 tosses. The algorithmic entropy of an outcome in the set of biased strings is close to $\log_2 \Omega_s$ where $\Omega_s$ is the number of members in the set of all strings exhibiting this ratio. As there are $2 \times 10^{23} = 2^{78}$ members in the set, $H(x) = 78$. In the 3:1 case, the expected return is $\$2^{100-78}$. If an outcome improbably falls in this restricted set, the return is \$4.2 million, which is also not insignificant. It can be seen that the degree of surprise, corresponding to a non-random outcome, is related to the payoff

While it is unlikely that the person providing the coin would accept a bet where the payoff depended on how algorithmic compressible the outcome was, the idea can be formalised to define a randomness test. This payoff test is called the sum $P$-test [3, 9]. Conceptually, the approach is to see whether an apparently random string, is actually random or not by whether a judicious betting procedure will generate a positive return. If it is possible to define a fair betting regime that generates a positive return for certain outcomes, there must be hidden structure or pattern in the outcome string. On the other hand, for a truly random outcome, no fair betting regime will return an expected payoff higher than the stake. Not only does the payoff understanding of randomness intuitively make sense, within the sum $P$-test framework it becomes mathematically robust.

In order to generalise the approach, define $\delta(x)$ as a sum $P$-test where $P$ again is a recursive or computable probability. In the illustration above, $\delta(x) = 100 - H(x)$. This is the degree of order (chapter 10) and, as mentioned, is a variant of the deficiency in randomness. In general, for the sum $P$-test, $\delta(x)$ must satisfy the payoff requirement (mentioned above) that the expected return is less than one. That is,

$$\sum P(x)2^{\delta(x)} \leqslant 1.$$

It can be shown that if $\delta(x)$ is a sum $P$-test it is also a Martin-Löf $P$ test [5] (p 257), but the sum $P$-test is slightly stronger, as the above equation implies $\delta(x)$ uses self-delimiting coding and therefore satisfies the Kraft–Chaitin inequality (3.3). As a consequence, an ordinary $P$-test, denoted by $d(x)$ will differ from the sum $P$-test by a term less than $2 \log_2 d(x)$. This is due to the difference between simple coding and self-delimiting coding.

Similarly, a universal sum $P$-test exists for any recursive probability distribution $P$, not just the simple distribution in the illustration. Let $\kappa_0(x|P) = \log_2[m(x)/P(x)] = \log_2[2^{-H(x)}/P(x)]$ as the universal distribution $m(x)$ is equivalent to $2^{-H(x)}$ (section 3.9). The expected return for a bet with the payoff $2^{\kappa_0(x|P)}$ is $\sum P(x)2^{\kappa_0(x|P)}$. This is $\leqslant 1$ as $\sum 2^{-H(x)} \leqslant 1$. If the actual return for such a bet is significantly $>1$ then the string $x$ cannot be random.

Just as $\log_2 m(x)$ additively dominates all other semi measures, $\kappa_0(x|P)$ additively dominates all other sum $P$-tests. For example, the uniform distribution $L_n$ of a string of length $n$ has $\kappa_0(x|L_n) = n - H(x|n)$. Note that this differs slightly from the $P$-test based on the randomness deficiency because:

- the sum $P$-test uses self-delimiting coding to provide the entropy measure $H(x|n)$; and
- the extra $-1$ in the deficiency in randomness is not included. That is, if $\kappa_0(x|L_n)$ is defined using a prefix-free UTM, it differs by no more than $2\log_2 C(x|n)$ from the randomness deficiency test $\delta_0(x|L_n) = n - C(x|n) - 1$.

This shows that the distance from the most probable set of state is a robust Martin-Löf measure of order or the lack of randomness of a specific configuration in the natural world. This has implications in the discussion as to whether the order in the natural world indicates design or not [10].

The Levin or Gács' sum $P$-test is intuitively appealing, as it implies that if one can win money by a judicious betting procedure on a set of apparently random outcomes, the outcomes cannot be random. In this case, the degree of order is related to the return on a fair bet.

### 6.2.4 The use of universal concepts

AIT makes use of universal concepts. These are measures that either additively or multiplicatively dominate other measures (see the discussion on measure theory (section 2.3)). In the case of additive dominance, a universal measure gives the same result as any another universal measure but the zero level is shifted by a constant. For example, a universal computer can simulate any other computer and the length of an algorithm on a universal computer differs only by a constant from any other computer. That is, a universal Turing machine (UTM) additively dominates all other computers. Other than the setting of the zero point, all universal computers are as good as each other (although in practice the measures are more transparent if a simple UTM with a few core instructions is used). Again, the universal semi-measure $m(x)$ was defined to multiplicatively dominate all other semi measures—it is as good as any alternative. This is equivalent to the logarithm of the measure additively dominating all other semi-measure logarithms. As $\log_2 m(x)$ additively dominates all measures of algorithmic complexity, this allows one to substitute $-H(x)$ for $\log_2 m(x)$ and vice versa. Importantly, as was discussed in section 3.9.1, $m(x)$, even though a defective probability, can be used to replace an unknown prior probability in Bayes' theorem.

Similarly, for randomness tests, there is a test that additively dominates all other randomness tests—it is as good as the best. If one test assigns one string to region $m$ and another string to $m + 5$, the order is preserved with a universal test. However, the randomness labels may be shifted by a constant in comparing different universal tests. As a consequence, the simple deficiency in randomness provides a randomness measure that is consistent with all other universal randomness tests. In the same way, the self-delimiting equivalent of the deficiency in randomness is $\log_2[m(x)/P(x)]$, which is equivalent to $-\log_2 P - H(x|P)$, and can also be taken to be a universal randomness test. These show that high probability outcomes have low randomness deficiency, whereas low probability outcomes are non-typical.

As has been mentioned, physicists will recognise that the randomness arguments apply to a so-called equilibrium configuration in statistical mechanics. A typical string from the most probable set of states would be expected to pass all randomness tests. However, there are many non-typical configurations in the set of possible equilibrium states depending on whether the system is isolated or not (as was discussed in section 4.5). For example, all the atoms in an isolated Boltzmann gas could by chance find themselves on one side of the container, the ordering of the position degrees of freedom is balanced by the disordering in the momentum degrees of freedom. However, if the gas system was not isolated, heat would pass to the environment, leaving the specification of the momentum degrees of freedom unchanged. But, as the position coordinates become more non-random, the system becomes more ordered.

# References

[1] von Mises R 1919 Grundlagen der wahrscheinlichkeitsrechnung *Math. Z.* **5** 52
[2] Martin-Löf P 1966 The definition of random sequences *Inf. Control* **9** 602–19
[3] Gács P 1980 Exact expressions for some randomness tests *Z. Math. Logik Grundlagen Math.* **26** 385–94
[4] Chaitin G 1979 Toward a mathematical definition of 'life' *The Maximum Entropy formalism* ed R D Levine and M Tribus (Cambridge, MA: MIT Press) 477–98
[5] Li M and Vitányi P M B 2008 *An Introduction to Kolmogorov Complexity and Its Applications* 3rd edn (New York: Springer)
[6] Cover T M, Gács P and Gray R M 1989 Kolmogorov's contributions to information theory and algorithmic complexity *Ann. Probab.* **17** 840–65
[7] Chaitin G 1975 A theory of program size formally identical to information theory *J. ACM* **22** 329–40
[8] Schnorr C P 1973 Process complexity and effective random tests *J. Comput. Syst. Sci.* **7** 376–88
[9] Gács P 1988 *Lecture Notes on Descriptional Complexity and Randomness* (Boston University Computer Science Department) (http://www.cs.bu.edu/gacs/papers/ait-notes.pdf).
[10] Devine S D 2014 An algorithmic information theory challenge to intelligent design *Zygon* **49** 42–65

**IOP** Publishing

# Algorithmic Information Theory for Physicists and Natural Scientists

**Sean D Devine**

# Chapter 7

# Order and entropy

Order can be recognised when a short algorithm can generate a long string. A tree is more ordered than the minerals and gases that it becomes, once death and decay destroy the order. However, there is no way of knowing whether a short algorithm representing a structure exists. The order must be recognized first, or found by trial and error.

There are different ways to represent a structure algorithmically. A tree can be defined by the algorithm embodied in the DNA of a seed and given the inputs, such as resources, light, etc, the tree in principle can be generated. It is argued that, once all degrees of freedom are adequately tracked, the algorithm that generates a living structure such as a tree is shorter than any other.

The relationship between the algorithmic entropy, the Boltzmann, Gibbs and Shannon entropies are discussed. While the algorithmic entropy is the number of bits needed to specify the instantaneous microstate of a system, the expected value of the algorithmic entropy, allowing for units, aligns with the traditional entropies. Also, the provisional entropy of each microstate in a thermodynamic macrostate aligns with the traditional entropy of the macrostate. However, because the algorithmic entropy requires by the definition of the actual system to be specified, the algorithmic approach may need to include additional information not needed for the traditional entropies. For example, the resolution of the phase space is explicit in the algorithmic approach. In which case, it is simpler to take the limiting resolution of the phase space for the algorithmic entropy to be that required by the uncertainty principle.

A continuum version of the algorithmic entropy, called the Gäcs entropy has been developed by Gäcs as outlined in Li and Vitanyi [1], chapter 8.

It is shown that the provisional entropy approach is a full algorithmic alternative to Zurek's intuitive idea of physical entropy.

The chapter closes by a preliminary exploration of the issues that might apply for the algorithmic entropy to be consistent with the thermodynamic entropy.

## 7.1 The meaning of order

In principle it is possible to extract work from two separable subsystems of one physical system, if they are not in equilibrium with each other. One subsystem may be at a lower temperature, or equivalently, be at a lower pressure than the other, or embody more stored energy. On the other hand, it is impossible to extract work from two parts of a system that are equally disordered where the whole system has settled in the region corresponding to the most probable set of states. Clearly, if it is known that one subsystem has a lower algorithmic entropy than another, i.e. it is more ordered, work can be extracted by harnessing the forces driving the composite system towards the most probable set of states. Extracting work short circuits the path to the most probable set of states.

In general, it is only where members of a subset exhibit a common pattern that the order can be recognised and described. To an alien, one string of human DNA would show no obvious pattern, as the chemical sequence would be seen as just one of the myriad possibilities. While an intelligent alien might have the capability to undertake a randomness test (section 6.2.3) to determine whether the discovered DNA string does show order, this is unlikely to work as the DNA string may be maximally compressed. The surest way for the alien to identify a pattern is by observing the set of DNA from a variety of mammals noting there is much in common.

As section 6.2 argues, there is no computational process to ascertain the degree of order, or the lack of randomness. Nevertheless, an ordered sequence can be recognised as exhibiting a pattern because our minds, like that of the alien, perceive that the sequence belongs to a subset of similar patterned sequences. Our minds identify the subset as different from the full set of apparently ordinary or random strings. Once such a pattern is determined empirically, by observation or some trial process, the fact that no computational procedure exists to determine the pattern is not critical. If the pattern is recognised in a sequence $s$ that is a subset of a larger set, the algorithmic specification of the sequence can at least be partially compressed, i.e. be described by an algorithm much shorter than the sequence length. Thus, any common pattern implies that an algorithm $s^*$ exists which can specify the patterned string and for which $|s^*| \ll |s|$.

A simple example, discussed in more detail in section 4.3.4, illustrates the argument. Consider the set of all strings of length $N$ of the form $1y1y1y...1y1y$ where $y$ is randomly either '0' or '1'. As the set has a recognisable pattern, a sequence from the set is able to be compressed into a shorter description of somewhat more than $N/2$ bits. This contrasts with a general sequence $s$ of length $N$, where no order is discernible, and there is no certainty that any order exists. In the latter case, the shortest algorithm $s^*$ able to specify the sequence is given by $|s^*| \geqslant N$, the length of the string. In more formal terms, any patterned set is a subset of all possible strings.

Living structures exhibit order. For example, a particular plant at an instant of time is specified by an algorithm based on its DNA, and the instruction set encoding the physical and biochemical laws (as is discussed in more detail in chapter 9). The inputs to the algorithm are the accessible nutrients and the impacts of the external environment that determine the plant's growth trajectory. The algorithmic entropy describing the plant's configuration at an instant of time is generated by an algorithm that is deemed to halt at that instant. As time flows, the same algorithm, halting at a later time, generates a more biologically complex pattern. The halt requirement determines how many bits from outside the system are allowed to enter for the plant to grow. The core algorithm that generates the plant growth is in the DNA of each cell, but the core algorithm must access natural routines in the resources from the soil, the Sun with carbon dioxide and oxygen from the air. The set of all cells in a plant or animal has an underlying pattern, but with variations of the pattern. While a cell in an eye is different from one in a muscle, it is specified by the same DNA and differs only because environmental triggers switch on different genes. The switching depends on the chemical outputs of the neighbouring cells, neighbouring structures, and the external environment with the influences of gravity, light and temperature.

A biological cluster of cells would appear to be something like an attractor in a state space appropriate to an extremely complicated non-linear system, as section 10.4 outlines. The components of this cluster maintain homeostasis as the whole is maintained in a stable region by balancing interactions between the cells. Where homeostasis cannot be maintained, the algorithm terminates, causing death; perhaps because of an external input shock; perhaps because the algorithm gets corrupted by repeated copying; or perhaps because resource or physical limits constrain the continued reproduction of the cellular algorithm.

A question arises as to whether the shortest algorithm to specify a living structure consisting of different cell types is the algorithm that generates the structure from the DNA in each cell accessing bits from external resources, or an algorithm that copies each cell allowing for variation. In section 9.3.2 it is argued that, once everything is taken into account, the shortest algorithm is the one that generates the plant from the seed. Nevertheless, whichever approach gives the shorter algorithm, AIT can be used to investigate any biologically complex system (i.e. an organised complex system) at different levels of scale and, at each nested level, only the relevant patterned set needs to be explained. This approach is expanded in chapter 10 and tied into Chaitin's concept of d-diameter complexity [2].

Such an approach would be consistent with the top-down approach of Beer's viable systems model [3, 4] which is a framework for probing organised systems in terms of nested subsystems.

## 7.2 Algorithmic entropy and the traditional entropy

### 7.2.1 Specification of the state space

Before discussing different understandings of entropy, one needs to define how to specify a string that represents a configuration in the natural world. Such a configuration, which represents an instantaneous microstate of the system, can be specified by a string that captures the position, momentum, binding states and electronic states of all the species in the natural system. The space of coordinates specifying the system is termed the state space. As much of the discussion on microstates involves specifying position and momentum coordinates of each species along the $x$, $y$, $z$ axes, the term phase space is specifically used for this sub-space of the full state space. For $N$ species, the phase space is a $6N$-dimensional space known as $\Gamma$ space.

The state space approach allows a microstate, which corresponds to a particular configuration of a thermodynamic system, to be expressed as a string of binary characters. Where the specification of, say, the position or the momentum of the phase space coordinates is not discrete, it is necessary to specify the coordinates to an agreed degree of precision in binary notation. This in effect imposes a grain size or grid on the phase space that is physically realistic within certain limits. Because the Boltzmann entropy is based on the number of states, as discussed below, its value depends on the phase space resolution. However, in practice, as only entropy differences have physical significance, the phase space resolution only introduces a constant into the entropy value. Nevertheless, if the limiting resolution is considered to be determined by the uncertainty principle, the limiting volume of each cell in phase space can be taken to be $h^3$ where $h$ is Plank's constant.

There are several ways of specifying the phase space for $n$ particles. The most general is to start with particle 1 and specify its position coordinate along the $x$ to the agreed degree of precision, followed by the same process for the $y$ and the $z$ axes. The momentum coordinates of each particle are similarly expressed in turn. The string specifying a configuration $s_i$ in the $6N$-dimensional $\Gamma$ space, looks like

$$s_i = x_1, y_1, z_1, x_2, y_2, z_2 \ldots x_n, y_n, z_{,n}, p_{x1}, p_{y1}, p_{z1}, p_{x2}, p_{y2}, p_{z2}, \ldots\ldots p_{zn}$$

Here $x_1$ is the $x$ coordinate of atom 1, etc, while $p_{x1}$ is its momentum coordinate in the $x$ direction to the agreed degree of precision converted to binary format. Doubling the resolution by doubling the number of bits specifying each coordinate, increases the number of cells in the $\Gamma$ space by $2^{6N}$. While the Gibbs' entropy phase space corresponds to $\Gamma$ space, Boltzmann specifies the number of particles in each cell of 6-dimensional phase space.

On the other hand, Zurek, in discussing algorithmic information theory, uses an alternative approach to define the microstate as a string [5]. He divides the $6N$-dimensional $\Gamma$ space into cells and then argues that the cell size is chosen to be sufficiently fine for cell to either contain one particle or no particles. The configuration of a particular microstate can be specified by systematically listing the cells in order and denoting an empty cell by a 0 and an occupied cell by a 1. It makes no real difference in which way a microstate is specified, provided a simple short routine exists to convert one specification to another. This can be done for the approaches just outlined.

### 7.2.2 Boltzmann, Gibbs, Shannon and algorithmic entropy

Boltzmann, Gibbs and Shannon have different approaches to specifying an entropy that can be aligned with that of a thermodynamic system.

#### 7.2.2.1 The Boltzmann entropy

For non-interacting systems, and a fine grid of cells, the Boltzmann entropy is equivalent to $S_B = -k_B \ln \Delta\Gamma$, where $\Delta\Gamma$ is the volume occupied by the equilibrium microstate. That is, the set of most probable microstates, in the $6N$-dimensional $\Gamma$ space.

Boltzmann, recognised that a given macrostate of a gas specified in terms of temperature, pressure, and volume, will encompass a myriad of possible microstates. Boltzmann defined what is known as the Boltzmann entropy. This reduces to $S_B = k_B \ln \Omega$, where $\Omega$ is the number of available microstates states or possible configurations. Given the specification of the cell resolution in phase space, which adds a constant to the entropy measure, $\Omega$ can be established by dividing the 6-dimensional phase space into cells with $N_j$ particles in the $j$th cell. The number of microstates is given by $\Omega = N!/(N_1!N_2!...N_m!)$. Using Stirling's approximation this becomes the familiar $S_B = -k_B N \sum_j \hat{P}_j \ln \hat{P}_j$. Here, $\hat{P}_j$ represents the probability that a single particle is in cell $j$. However, note that $\hat{P}_i$ is not the same probability as used in the Gibb's approach outlined in the next section.

#### 7.2.2.2 The Gibbs entropy

On the other hand, the Gibbs' approach envisages an ensemble of replicas of the instantaneous microstate of a system where each replica is able to exchange energy. This allows a measure of the distribution of microstates consistent with Hamilton dynamics to be used to define the entropy. Each microstate of a system with $N$ particles can be specified by $6N$ position-momentum coordinates in the system's $\Gamma$ space. That is, the microstate $s = q_{1x}, q_{1y}, q_{1z}...q_{nx}, q_{ny}, q_{nz}, p_{1x}...p_{nz}$, where the $q_{1x}, p_{1x}$ are the position and the momentum coordinates, while the subscript $x$ denotes the $x$ component of the position or momentum vector of particle 1 etc. This contrasts with the Boltzmann measure where the probability measure specifies the probability that a *particle* is in a cell labelled $i$, in 3D phase space not, as in the Gibbs case, a microstate in $6ND$ $\Gamma$ space. In which case, the Gibbs entropy can be expressed as an integral rather than a sum, i.e.

$$S_G = -k_B \int \rho(X)\ln[\rho(X)]dX,$$

where $\rho$ represents the probability density of the states $s$.

There is a conceptual difficulty with this approach as the probability density behaves as an incompressible fluid, forcing the Gibbs' entropy to be constant over time. This would seem to undermine the second law of thermodynamics. However, it is usually argued that, at the initial time, the Gibbs entropy is based on a fine-grained probability distribution, but the observer averages probabilities densities over coarse-grained cells in $\Gamma$ space of size $\Delta$. In this case, the equation becomes a sum over all the coarse-grained cells, i.e. $S_\Delta = -k_B \Sigma_i \hat{P}_\Delta(i) \ln \hat{P}_\Delta(i)$. Here, $\hat{P}_\Delta(i)$ is the average probability that the *microstate* is in cell $i$. In other words, there is a blurring of the distribution of points in $\Gamma$ space and the blurring increases over time, either because of the lack of precise information, or because of the graininess of the Universe due to quantization. As the system evolves, the region of $\Gamma$ space increases, leading to an increase in the coarse-grained entropy.

However, for a large system of non-interacting particles in equilibrium, the Gibbs measure of entropy is the same as the Boltzmann measure.

### 7.2.2.3 The Shannon entropy

The Shannon entropy, which has been discussed in more detail in section 4.2, is a measure of the uncertainty in determining a particular message in a set of messages. From a thermodynamic perspective, a message corresponds to a microstate and, as a consequence, the uncertainty in identifying a particular microstate of a system can be determined by the Shannon approach. The Shannon entropy corresponds to the number of yes/no questions needed to identify that microstate. Where microstates occur with a probability $P_i$, $H_{sh} = \Sigma P_i \log_2 P_i$. As the Shannon entropy of a Boltzmann system of equally probable states is $\log_2\Omega$ bits, the Boltzmann entropy $S_B$ is related to the Shannon entropy by $S_B = k_B \ln 2 H_{\text{Shannon}}$. Here, the $\ln 2$ is the factor needed to convert the base-2 logarithm of the Shannon entropy to the natural logarithm required for the Boltzmann entropy.

### 7.2.2.4 The algorithmic entropy

The algorithmic entropy for the instantaneous microstate in a thermodynamic system is the length of the shortest algorithm that specifies the microstate. Where there is no shorter algorithmic description of the microstate, as each binary digit needs to be explicitly specified, the algorithmic entropy is a little more than the length of the description. The extra bits are to do with the overheads of the computational system. If, as is discussed below in section 7.2.2.6; there are $\Omega$ states in the equilibrium set or most probable set of states, most states need slightly more than $\log_2\Omega$ bits to be specified.

However, just to reiterate, the algorithmic entropy measure is a measure of the microstate of the system; it is the shortest description of an actual state. Nevertheless, as is discussed in section 7.2.2.6, the *expected* value of the algorithmic entropy over the macrostate containing a set of microstates, is virtually the same as the Shannon entropy and therefore, apart from the units used, is equivalent to the entropy of statistical mechanics. The alignment is not exact as, in contrast to the other entropies, the algorithmic approach must specify the conditions of the system under study and also computational overheads. These conditions are taken as given in the traditional approaches, as there is no need to specify the system in detail, nor indicate which messages, or members, are to be included in the set of possible outcomes. Although, as was discussed in section 3.5, while the common information must be specified algorithmically, the zero point for the algorithmic entropy can be chosen to include the common information. In which case, the Shannon entropy is seen to be the particular case of the algorithmic entropy for a typical state in the most probable set.

### 7.2.2.5 Ambiguity of entropies because of the phase space grid resolution

Zurek [5] shows that the ambiguity in the Gibbs entropy, arising from the choice of coarse graining of the phase space, can be absorbed into the background algorithmic description of the system. In other words, the way the phase space or other continuous coordinates are divided into cells is encapsulated in the message about the system. Zurek [5] points out that the overall description must be minimal. Fanciful grid structures, which complicate the coarse graining concerns of the Gibbs' entropy, require long descriptions and become ineligible. Effectively, as Zurek points out, in the algorithmic approach the complications of the choice of the grid structure are absorbed into the choice of the Turing machine (TM) used to specify the system. Alternatively, from the provisional entropy perspective in section 4.2, this information is part of the specification of the overall system. In practical terms, because the critical physical parameter is the entropy difference between states, issues to do with the universal Turning machine (UTM) used, or the message about the system (i.e. the common information) only shift the algorithmic entropy zero and therefore can usually be ignored. As mentioned above, it is simpler to take the limiting resolution of the phase space for the algorithmic entropy, to be that required by the uncertainty principle.

### 7.2.2.6 The expectation value of the algorithmic entropy aligns with the Shannon entropy of an ensemble

Once the specification of the microstate is defined, the length of the shortest self-delimiting algorithm that computes the microstate in the state space coordinates is the algorithmic entropy. Nevertheless, there is an important conceptual difference between the algorithmic entropy and the Shannon entropy. The algorithmic entropy returns an entropy value for an actual state and has meaning for what is seen as a non-equilibrium configuration, i.e. a configuration outside the most probable set of states. On the other hand, the traditional entropies return a value for a set of states, which, in the thermodynamic case, is usually the most probable configurations. This distinction should not create difficulties as the behaviour of the algorithmic entropy is like energy. Energy is seen as a property of the macrostate, but it is recognised that the energy is stored in the microstate.

The provisional entropy approach discussed in section 4.2 shows that the provisional algorithmic entropy $H_{prov}(x_i)$, of a microstate existing in an isolated macrostate containing myriads of such microstates, is given by equation (4.2). That is,

$$H_{prov}(x_i) = H_{algo}(S) + H_{sh} + O(1). \tag{7.1}$$

Here $H(S)$ is the algorithmic specification of the macrostate that defines the set of microstates. Given the macrostate, the number of bits needed to specify a particular microstate is the algorithmic version of the Shannon entropy of the whole system.

One can argue that $H(S)$ is negligible relative to the number of bits defining a particular microstate and that therefore the provisional entropy is virtually that of the Shannon entropy. This can be seen to be so for a representative thermodynamic system. If the position and momentum coordinates are defined to 8 significant binary digits, this requires 16 bits for each of the $10^{23} = 2^{77}$ particles in a mole of gas. The total, corresponding to the Shannon entropy would be $2^{81}$ bits. On the other hand, $H(S)$ would be at the most a few thousand bits [6]. Nevertheless, the contribution of the bits defining the macrostate may need to be tracked if one is comparing bit transfers between two different macrostates, as discussed in section 8.5.1.

Section 4.5 applied the provisional entropy approach to a simple model of a Boltzmann gas. It was shown that the number of bits squeezed out of the system when the gas was isothermally compressed, corresponded to a thermodynamic entropy change of $k_B \ln 2$ per bit. Later, in chapter 8 and in particular section 8.4, it is shown that in general, a reversible transfer of one bit, between subsystems or whole systems, corresponds to a change of thermodynamic entropy by $k_B \ln 2$. However, bits specifying stored energy states, do not contribute to the thermodynamic entropy, but can be envisaged as a potential entropy. It is only when the system settles in the most probable set of states, that these bits become realised entropy.

### 7.2.2.7 The expected algorithmic entropy of an ensemble

The situation corresponding to the Gibbs canonical ensemble, where a system is in thermal equilibrium with a heat bath is different. In this case, the set of states is defined by a probability function which contributes $H(P)$ bits to the algorithmic entropy. The number of bits specifying a particular microstate from Shannon's coding theorem is determined by the logarithm of $P(x_i)$ of that microstate in the set of states. The result below is from equation (4.5), as discussed in chapter 9.

$$H(x_i) = H(P) - \log_2 P(x_i) + O(1).$$

In this case, the algorithmic entropy increases when, for an instant, the system settles in a highly improbable microstate as the $-\log_2 P(x_i)$ term is large. This is because the heat flow of $k_N B \ln 2T$ Joules per bit from the heat bath is needed to maintain the temperature when, for such a rare fluctuation, energy is transferred to electronic states.

However, the expected value of the provisional algorithmic entropy over all microstates as outlined in chapter 9, is found by multiplying the above equation by $P(x_i)$ and summing over all states $i$. The expected entropy is given by

$$\langle H_{\text{algo}}(x_i) \rangle = H_{sh}(\textit{set of all states}) + H(P) + O(1). \tag{7.2}$$

The argument follows Zurek [5] equation (4.17), and Bennett [6] equation (2). These authors argue that, as the term defining the set of states is trivially small relative to the number of microstates in the system, the expectation value of the algorithmic entropy for a thermodynamic ensemble is virtually that of the Shannon entropy of the ensemble. As a consequence, the expected algorithmic entropy for the ensemble $\mathcal{E}$ becomes $H_{sh}(\mathcal{E}) = -\sum P_i \log_2 P_i$.

But the statistical entropy $S$ is related to the Shannon entropy by $S = k_B \ln 2 H_{sh}(\mathcal{E})$. As this in turn is related to the macroscopic thermodynamic entropy, there is now a connection between the expected value of the algorithmic entropy and thermodynamic entropy

There is a simpler 'hand waving' argument to connect the expected value of the algorithmic entropy with the Shannon entropy. As most strings are random, the expectation value of the algorithmic entropy will be dominated by the value for the most probable set of strings. Let there be $N$ microstates in the ensemble, and let $s_i^*$ be the minimal programme that generates $s_i$, the $i$th string that occurs with probability $p_i$ in the ensemble. If the expected value of the algorithmic entropy of a string in the ensemble is $\langle |s_i^*| \rangle$, then $\langle |s_i^*| \rangle = \sum_i P_i |s_i^*|$. This sum can be rearranged in terms of lengths of algorithmic descriptions so that $\langle |s_i^*| \rangle = \sum_l P_l l$ where $P_l$ is the probability of an algorithmic description of length $l$. In a thermodynamic ensemble, the overwhelming majority of possible states belong to the most probable set of configurations with $l$ close to $N$. In which case, for the overwhelming majority of states $l \approx N$, $P_l$ is large while for $l \ll N$, $P_l$ is negligible and can be taken to be zero.

Zurek [5] has shown that the algorithmic entropy of a typical state in an ideal Boltzmann gas of $N$ indistinguishable particles is identical to the entropy provided by the Sackur–Tetrode equation, further demonstrating the consistency of the algorithmic entropy approach. In doing this, Zurek finds how many bits are needed to specify or give the address of a particular configuration among the $\Omega$ possible configurations. A typical value of the address is $\sim |\Omega|$. This requires a description of length about $\log_2 \Omega$ bits. Any configuration is a sequence of 0's and 1's. If there are $\mathcal{C}$ cells in the phase space, there will be $\mathcal{C}^N / N!$ distinct configurations. As the number of cells is given by $\mathcal{C} = (V/\Delta V)(\sqrt{mk_B T}/\Delta_p)^3$, the algorithmic specification leads to the Sackur–Tetrode equation. Here, $m$ is the particle mass, $\Delta V$ is the three-dimensional cell volume, and $\Delta_p$ is the cell volume in momentum space. This argument again shows that the algorithmic entropy of a typical state is the same as the entropy of statistical mechanics.

The previous sections have argued that the algorithmic entropy of a typical string, representing a configuration in the most probable set of states, is virtually identical to the Shannon entropy. Despite the conceptual difference, the relationship between the algorithmic entropy and the traditional entropies is sufficiently robust that one can slip between one description and the other, even though the algorithmic entropy is a measure for an actual microstate, provided that one recognises the system specification requirement of the algorithmic approach.

In addition, the concept of provisional entropy conclusively links the two frameworks. The provisional entropy is the shortest known description of a string representing an instantaneous configuration of a thermodynamic system in its state space, whether a typical state or not. A thermodynamic macrostate in an isolated system consists of a collection of microstates all with the same provisional algorithmic entropy. However, as was shown previously in section 4.5, and is shown later in section 9.3 the algorithmic entropy for each allowable microstate of an isolated system can be directly related to the thermodynamic entropy.

### 7.2.3 Zurek's physical entropy, missing information and the algorithmic description

When a microstate belongs to the equilibrium set of states, corresponding to the most probable set of states, the algorithmic description is random and, as the microstate is typical, work cannot be extracted from the system. In this situation, the energy is dispersed uniformly through the system and the temperature is uniform. Where two subsystems, which might be seen as two separate systems, are not at the same temperature, or where there is a pressure differential, or one component has more energy stored in chemical species, work can be extracted. This is possible as the composite system has one part more ordered, or less random than another. Work is a process that hastens the trend towards randomness, by short circuiting the natural progression to the most probable set of states.

Zurek developed the concept of the 'physical entropy' $S_d$ of a microstate to provide an understanding of reversibility and work extraction from such a system. $S_d$ is a combination of the algorithmic entropy that captures the regularity of the microstate of a physical system and the Shannon entropy that captures the uncertainty [5]. Gell-Mann and Lloyd [7] in equation (7) have called Zurek's physical entropy the 'total information' or 'augmented entropy', and have used the term 'effective complexity' to refer to structural or regularity contribution to the total information. Similarly, Fuentes [8]) discusses the emergence of physical properties from the effective complexity perspective.

However, it is now clear that there is no need for a special definition of physical entropy, as Zurek's physical entropy and Gell-Mann's total information, correspond to the provisional entropy, or the algorithmic minimal sufficient statistic (AMSS), discussed in chapter 4. That is, the physical entropy is the equivalent to the number of bits that defines the structure or pattern in the string, together with the number of bits of uncertainty in specifying the exact state. This can be seen as Zurek's definition for a string $s_i$ defining a microstate, given information $d$ is

$$S_d = H_{\text{algo}}(s_i|d) + H_{\text{Shannon}},$$

where $H_{\text{Shannon}}$ is the Shannon entropy. This is identical to the provisional entropy;

$$S_d = H_{\text{prov}} = H_{\text{algo}}(\text{description of pattern}) + H_{sh},$$

as $H_{\text{algo}}(s_i|d)$ is $H_{\text{algo}}(\text{description of pattern})$, the algorithmic description of the set of strings given the information about the system. As has been shown, $H_{\text{Shannon}}$, the measure of uncertainty has the same number of bits as the algorithmic equivalent, $H_{sh}$.

As a consequence, Zurek's argument can be expressed in terms of the provisional entropy, which is the best guess of the true algorithmic entropy based on the given information. If the actual state is a typical state, establishing more detail about its algorithmic description, will not shorten the description. However, if a particular state is not typical, further information reduces the uncertainty, allowing for a shorter overall description. Consider a particular microstate specified by a string of length $N$ in a set of states. If there is no information about the microstate, the best estimate is to recognise there are $2^N$ such microstates and the algorithmic Shannon term in the provisional entropy is $\log_2 2^N = N$. The provisional entropy will need to specify $N$ by the algorithmic entropy of the description of the set, denoted by $H$ (description). This will be $H(N)$, showing that the provisional entropy for a string in the absence of any information is $N + H(N)$. This is of course the algorithmic entropy of a typical string.

However, if further information shows that the string of interest has 80% 1's, the algorithm that generates the set of possible strings can be specified by an $H(N, 0.8)$. Given the algorithm that generates the set, the algorithmic Shannon term picks out the string of interest as in equation (4.2). For large $N$ and given Stirling's approximation the length of the algorithmic Shannon term is $-N(0.8 \log_2 0.8 + 0.2 \log_2 0.2) = 0.722N$. This implies there are $2^{0.722N}$ members of the set. This extra information has reduced the algorithmic Shannon term from $N$ to $0.722N$ while the description of the set has increased slightly.

However, further information might show that all the 1's occur in the first $0.8N$ characters and the rest are 0's. In which case, this string belongs to a very small set which includes itself and its converse, i.e. the string where the last $0.80N$ characters are a 1. The algorithmic Shannon term is then $\log_2 2 = 1$. Most of the bits now specify the set of just two strings, and the algorithm that does this is extremely short relative to $N + H(N)$. Readers will note that going through this process is equivalent to finding the set where this string is typical, corresponding to the algorithmic minimal sufficient statistic discussed in section 4.3.1.

In the thermodynamic situation, gathering more information to reduce the uncertainty, is equivalent to refining the requirements of the set that contains the string of interest. The more structure or pattern displayed by the string of interest, the fewer strings will be in the set. Given a likely set, when more information becomes available, and it is seen that the microstate of interest has more structure or pattern than a typical microstate in the set, the microstate belongs to a smaller set. Its algorithmic description is shorter. In this case, Zurek would argue the physical entropy is lower. From the perspective here, the set that defines the provisional entropy or the AMSS is smaller. As there is less uncertainty in defining the string of interest, the provisional entropy is lower.

A simple example might be finding the shortest string to capture a particular 10 megapixel black and white image on a screen. If no pattern is seen, as the black and white pixels seem to be completely random one must use $10^6$ bits to specify a particular image configuration. But perhaps there is a fuzzy circle in the image. In which case, the characteristics of the set should be refined to only include strings that specify something like a circle. As more structure is perceived, the characteristics of the set narrow down the allowable strings. Jpeg compression is a process that compresses the description of the string representing a photographic image. However, the Jpeg process is lossy and the requirement here is to specify the string exactly. In the current case, any noise, variation or randomness of the image corresponds to the Shannon uncertainty and must be part of the algorithm that generates the string. A more realistic process for a black and white image is to express the image as an expansion of Walsh functions. The series of Walsh functions are orthogonal and like a Fourier expansion, if taken far enough, can exactly express a two-dimensional black and white image. In practice, a finite set Walsh functions can be used to define the structure of the image, i.e. the characteristics of all strings with the desired structure. Once all the structure is defined, given the structure, the noise, or a particular variation of the structure an extra algorithm that picks out the exact variation will have the same number of bits as the Shannon entropy of all the valid variants. Page 575 in Wolfram [9] gives examples of images formed from a Walsh expansion. An algorithm that defines the image structure first and then the variation, as in the provisional entropy approach, is significantly shorter than $10^6$ bits.

Figure 7.1(b) shows that as more order is recognised, the description of the set of similar ordered structures increases slowly. But when this happens, the number of strings in the set decreases faster, and the algorithmic entropy drops. The overall description of the noisy image will be much shorter than the typical 10 megapixel image. However, if no order or structure exists, gathering more information does not

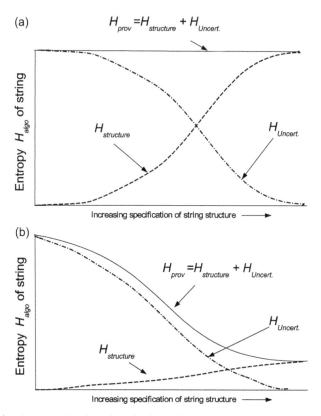

**Figure 7.1.** Provisional entropy. (a) where the string is a typical member of the set, increased information about the string does not shorten the specification. (b) Where the string is typical in a set that defines more ordered structure, further information shortens the description. Reproduced from [10]. © 2009 by the author. CC BY 3.0.

shorten the algorithmic description as in figure 7.1(a). The full $10^6$ megabits are needed to specify the random string. The critical point is that order, pattern or structure allows a shorter description. The use of an image as an illustration is helpful, but a microstate in the natural world belongs to a set which defines the thermodynamic microstate which contains the microstate of interest.

Figure 7.1 can also be used to illustrate the two situations for a thermodynamic macrostate, following the argument in figure 2 of Zurek's paper [5]. Here, however, the provisional entropy is used to replace the physical entropy. Where in equation (4.2), the provisional entropy is expressed in terms of the description of the set, in the diagram $H_{structure} = H_{algo}(S)$. Given the set with its structure, the Shannon related term captures the uncertainty. In the figure, the first in part (a) is where gathering further information does not reduce the total algorithmic entropy as the microstate is a typical one. The second part (b), is where the string is not typical. Hence once the set where this string is typical is found, the algorithmic Shannon related term decreases. In the figure, $H_{structure}$ refers to the specification of the set of all strings with a common structure. The following summarises the two situations:

a. figure 7.1 graphs the provisional entropy, when the microstate is in a typical or random state without any distinguishing features. As more information becomes available about the microstate, there is no net reduction in the provisional entropy. In effect, the AMSS for the particular state corresponds to the set of states where the state of interest looks random (see section 4.3.1).

b. figure 7.1(b) is the situation where the microstate is non-typical and has hidden order. Gathering extra information about the exact state leads to a reduction in the provisional entropy as the microstate is seen to belong to a restricted simpler set, indicating the microstate is more ordered. The approach is general for any noisy description where pattern, structure or order is revealed with more precise measurements. This process of more accurately determining the exact configuration of the system is also equivalent to refining the set or the model that contains the set of interest. The increased information that narrows down the uncertainty leads to a short specification of the algorithmic Shannon entropy.

### 7.2.4 The consistency of the provisional entropy

While the provisional entropy has the properties of a traditional entropy, the number of bits is independent of temperature. This raises the question as to how can a room temperature UTM simulate a real-world UTM at 100 °C?

But the thermodynamic entropy change, $\Delta S$ that flows into a system at temperature $T$ is given by $\Delta S = \Delta Q/T$ where $\Delta Q$ is the heat flow. Where heat flows into the system at a constant rate, as the temperature rises the associated entropy flow drops. Similarly, when bits flow into a system at a constant rate the temperature of the system also rises with the input of energy. As a consequence, the energy to set one bit must increase with the rise of $T$. Whether in the real-world, or on a laboratory computer operating at 100 °C, more energy is required to introduce one extra unit of information than a computer operating at room temperature. Both exhibit the same temperature dependence.

The definition of the algorithmic entropy requires that the algorithm halts once the state of interest is generated. However, real-world computations in general do not halt, as the configurations are continually changing. When bits are tracked properly as discussed in section 8.5.2 and section 8.5.1, these ongoing computations have the same number of bits in the system as when the algorithm halts. In practice, the halt requirement determines how many bits need to enter the system reversibly to define the state of interest. There is no inconsistency once it is recognised that a bit is a physical entity associated with energy. Where a system is isolated, and hence constrained to a particular macrostate, the ongoing computation generates micro-states with the same provisional entropy corresponding to that of the macrostate. Of particular interest is the situation where a system is maintained in microstate distant from the equilibrium set of states. Section 8.5.3 shows how, when bits are tracked entering and leaving the system, the outcome is consistent with the snapshot of the system in its halt state.

# References

[1] Li M and Vitányi P M B 2008 *An Introduction to Kolmogorov Complexity and Its Applications* 3rd edn (New York: Springer)
[2] Chaitin G 1979 Toward a mathematical definition of 'life' *The Maximum Entropy formalism* ed R D Levine and M Tribus (Cambridge, MA: MIT Press) 477–98
[3] Beer S 1981 *Brain of the Firm* 2nd edn (Chichester: Wiley)
[4] Beer S 1979 *The Heart of Enterprise* (Chichester: Wiley)
[5] Zurek W H 1989 Algorithmic randomness and physical entropy *Phys. Rev.* A **40** 4731–51
[6] Bennett C H 1982 Thermodynamics of computation–A review *Int. J. Theor. Phys.* **21** 905–40
[7] Gell-Mann M and Lloyd S 1996 Information measures, effective complexity and total information *Complexity* **2** 44–52
[8] Fuentes M A 2014 Complexity and the emergence of physical properties *Entropy* **16** 4480–96
[9] Wolfram S 2002 *A New Kind of Science* (Champaign, IL: Wolfram Media)
[10] Devine S D 2009 The insights of algorithmic entropy *Entropy* **11** 85–110

**IOP** Publishing

# Algorithmic Information Theory for Physicists and Natural Scientists

**Sean D Devine**

# Chapter 8

# Reversibility, and Landauer's principle

Landauer, as outlined in section 8.2, argues that both logical and thermodynamic irreversibility requires the loss of information as bits. Maxwell's demon is outwitted and the second law of thermodynamics still stands. Landauer's principle shows the entropy cost of removing or transferring a bit in a reversible system is $k_B \ln 2 T$ Joules. The implication is that for an irreversible universal Turing machine (UTM) to simulate a reversible real-world computation, the history of the computation must be kept to enable the computation to be reversed. Reversibility implies that the algorithmic entropy is a function of the state, not the path to reach the state. It is shown that when computational bits are tracked in a reversible computation, bits are conserved. The halt requirement for the algorithmic entropy on an irreversible machine is no longer necessary as number of bits in the halt requirement can be established by tracking bits already in the system and the bit flows into or out of the system.

From Landauer's principle, the net change in the thermodynamic entropy of a system, allowing for units, is identical to the bit flows through the system.

Later, chapter 10 explores how a living system can automatically regenerate an initial state and shows this autonomous process is critical to the maintenance of life, far from the decayed equilibrium or most probable set of states,

## 8.1 Introduction

A number of critical issues need to be explored to determine how to apply algorithmic information theory to a natural system. The first key point is that reversibility allows Landauer's principle to determine the energy needed to carry one computational bit during a reversible computational process. Following this, it is shown that, once programme or instruction bits are taken into account, bits in a natural isolated system are conserved, as these bits also need to be carried by energy.

Finally, it is shown that the algorithmic entropy of a system determined by an algorithm that halts, is identical to the algorithmic entropy determined by establishing the bits already in the system plus the bit flows in, less the bit flows out, provided everything is tracked to ensure reversibility.

## 8.2 Landauer's principle

This section explores how Landauer's principle [1] can relate the bit flows between two states evaluated by the algorithmic entropy to the thermodynamic entropy change. Landauer's principle arose out of the paradox of Maxwell's demon. The historical difficulty with the statistical approach to thermodynamics is illustrated by the thought experiment involving an informed agent. The agent, commonly known as Maxwell's demon, is able to extract work at no cost, by judiciously manipulating the particles of a gas in a container. One version of the thought experiment makes the argument that a container of gas can be divided into two halves, both at the same temperature. Maxwell's demon opens a trap door in the dividing wall to allow faster moving particles to collect on one side of the container and closes the door to stop the faster particles returning, thus keeping the slower moving particles on the other side. Over time, the side with the faster moving particles will be at a higher temperature than the side with the slower moving particles. It appears that work can then be extracted violating the second law of thermodynamics.

Prior to Landauer's insight, Szilard [2, 3] and later Brillouin [4, 5], in attempting to save the second law of thermodynamics from Maxwell's demon, argued that, as the demon needed to measure the position–momentum coordinates of a particle in order to know when to open the trap door, it was necessary for the demon to interact with the system under study. From this perspective, acquiring this information involved an entropy cost of at least $k_B \ln 2$ per bit. Landauer [1] showed that this explanation was not completely satisfactory as a thermodynamically reversible process cannot lead to an overall increase in entropy. As is discussed in detail in Devine [6], Landauer's approach resolves the paradox of Maxwell's demon—the intelligent interventionist who otherwise would be able to extract work for no cost. Landauer pointed out that that it was not the entropy or energy cost of acquiring a bit that was critical; it was rather the **irreversibility** of the process. Bennett [7–10] and Zurek [11] show that the demon cannot violate the second law of thermodynamics as the demon is a computational system. The demon must erase the information that was gained in making a measurement, in order to make room for the next measurement. This erasure, which implied logically irreversibility of the computation undertaken by the demon, meant the total system of the demon plus the gas was irreversible. The loss of information about a prior state, when information is discarded, or because there is more than one prior state, has an energy cost—the cost of erasure. The demon was foiled by having to pay $k_B \ln 2 T$ Joules for every bit that it needed to erase from its memory operating at temperature $T$ and would need a continuous supply of energy to flip new bits. If such a process is to continue, there will be an increase in the demon's temperature and heat needs to be passed elsewhere. The demon is in effect part of the total system and constrained by physical laws. As a consequence, when the equivalent computational process becomes logically irreversible, the system is no longer thermodynamically reversible.

Bennett (see also [11]) illustrates the argument with a gas of one particle and uses the demon to trap the particle on one side of a partition in order to extract work. The entropy loss occurs when the demon's memory is reset to allow the process to cycle. However, there are subtleties as Bennett [10] points out. Where information initially is random, the entropy of the system drops if the random information is erased, but the entropy of the environment still increases. One can envisage this erasure as setting all bits to zero, effectively ordering the system and transferring energy outside the system. It is only the reversible erasure of a bit that corresponds to $k_B \ln 2T$ Joules. As a bit is physical, the reversible erasure of a bit in the system by a natural process must create a corresponding bit in the environment. But irreversible erasure costs more, increasing the total thermodynamic entropy of the Universe. As Lloyd [12] puts it, 'Essentially, the one-to-one dynamics of Hamiltonian systems implies that when a bit is erased the information that it contains has to go somewhere. If the information goes into observable degrees of freedom of the computer, such as another bit, then it has not been erased but merely moved; but if it goes into unobservable degrees of freedom such as the microscopic motion of molecules it results in an increase of entropy of at least $k_B \ln 2$'. From a physical point of view in the natural world, erasure corresponds to a decrease in the number of states accessible to the system. If, for example, heat is removed from a system maintained at constant pressure by a piston, the volume must contract, as the number of position bits decreases. When the system is no longer reversible, the cost of removing a bit is at least $k_B \ln 2T$ Joules of heat.

However, readers should be aware that, while Landauer's principle is widely accepted, there is ongoing discussion on the underlying physics and philosophical issues, and there is criticism of its applicability. The key papers expressing the different interpretations of the Maxwell demon problem, and a discussion on the 'new resolution' involving erasure and logical irreversibility, are to be found in Leff and Rex [13, 14]. More recent criticisms involve concerns surrounding the operation of functioning computers and whether logical reversibility implies thermodynamic reversibility and vice versa [15]. Norton has introduced a 'no-go' principle' that sees fluctuations in a system as undermining reversibility, while del Rio *et al* [16] have considered the effect of quantum entanglement in the observer's memory. Ladyman and Robertson review some key issues [17] and the 'no-go' principle'. Irrespective of the philosophical issues, recent experimental evidence supporting Landauer's principle is strong [18–21]. In the approach here, the system is considered to be classical. Fluctuations are deterministic and not stochastic, and the 'no-go' argument is irrelevant, as are arguments about the practicalities that might arise in constructing reversible computers. Here, Landauer's principle follows directly from the conservation of bits in an isolated system, as discussed later in section 8.5.1.

## 8.3 Outline of Landauer's argument

However, before exploring the consequences of Landauer's approach, we need to be clear what, in this context, a bit is [6]. While a '0' or a '1' in a computer memory is often represented by the level of charge in a capacitive memory unit, a bit is distinct from its method of storage. Again, one might specify the ground state of an atom by the character '0' and the excited state by a '1' separated by $\epsilon$ Joules. However, these characters do not represent bits in the Shannon or computational sense.

Landauer's argument used a symmetrical bi-stable well as the storage device that carries one bit of information. The setting can be either a '0' if the left hand well is occupied or a '1', if the right hand side is occupied. The '0' and the '1' are separated by a potential barrier, but carry the same energy. Landauer used the term 'RESTORE TO ONE' to denote the process that manipulates the potential barrier and the relative depth of the wells to ensure the 'ZERO' well, if occupied, empties at the temperature $T$ into the '1' well. While the right-hand side of the system is occupied after this reset process, it becomes unclear whether the prior state was a '0' or a '1'; i.e. whether originally the right hand side or the left-hand side was occupied. The phase space of the system has been halved. No computational process can shift the bit settings to their previous state, as the end result is irreversible. Whichever side of the bi-stable well was originally occupied, according to Landauer, the process of resetting dissipates at least $k_B \ln 2 T$ Joules for a system at temperature $T$.

Another simple example is to measure a bit as a '0' or a '1', depending on which side of a box contains a gas particle. If the two sides are originally separated by a partition, the partition can be removed and the gas system compressed isothermally, ensuring the particle is constrained to the '1' side, the volume is halved. However, in doing so, it is unclear on which side the particle was originally. Information has been lost as isothermal compression has halved the phase space as was discussed in section 4.5. The loss of one bit of information carried by the $k_b \ln 2 T$ Joules is passed to the environment, increasing the entropy of the environment.

Scenario 5 captured in figure 4.1 in section 4.5 describes the generalised case where $N$ atoms are compressed to one side of a container. The entropy loss to the environment in this case is shown to be $N k_B \ln 2$. From Landauer's perspective, as it is no longer possible to determine which of the $N$ particles was initially on the right-hand side of the container, bits specifying this information are erased. The entropy of the environment increases through the heat flow of $N k_b \ln 2 T$ Joules.

The energy associated with a bit in the context of Landauer's principle refers to the energy required to move a bit relative to the background thermal noise. In a reversible system, the energy dissipated increases the number of bits in the momentum degrees of freedom. This temperature dependence of the energy associated with a bit can be understood in terms of Shannon's so-called 'ultimate limit'. This limit identifies the minimum average energy of $\ln 2 N_0$ Joules to send one bit through a communication channel at the channel capacity. $N_0$ is the noise spectral power density. As the noise power density can be taken to be $k_B T$ in a system at temperature $T$, for a bit to be recognised against the background noise, the energy per bit must be $\geqslant k_B \ln 2 T$ Joules. This is consistent with Landauer's principle suggesting that a real-world computer operates at the ultimate limit. The Shannon limit indicates why more energy must be associated with each bit when the temperature rises, as the bit needs to be identified above the thermal background. Even though the real-world does not know what temperature is, when physical laws drive the system from one state to another, for the observer, 'bit language' and temperature are useful constructs.

Consider an isolated system consisting of two subsystems. One of these is the subsystem of interest at temperature $T_0$, in contact with the other, which is the surrounding environment at temperature $T_1$ with $T_0 > T_1$. Reversible removal of one bit from the subsystem of interest adds one bit to the environmental subsystem corresponding to a transfer of $k_B \ln 2T_0$ Joules. Bits are conserved for a reversible transfer, however, as has been emphasised, if reversibility is lost, the energy cost is greater. Because the reversible path has not been tracked, while $k_B \ln 2T_0$ Joules of heat are transferred to the environment, the thermodynamic entropy transfer to the environment has increased to $k_B \ln 2T_0/T_1$.

The concept can be illustrated by a two-dimensional matrix of $\mathcal{N}$ randomly aligned magnetic spins or magnetic moments, with $2^{\mathcal{N}}$ possible microstates. Because $\mathcal{N}$ is the Shannon entropy of all the spin states, the unit of measure is clearly a bit, and not just an arbitrary binary representation. The spin-up and the spin-down states have the same energy. In this case, the erasure operation 'RESTORE TO ONE' can be achieved by applying a slight magnetic field to lower the potential energy of the spin-up state corresponding to 'ONE'. The dissipated energy goes to the momentum degrees of freedom. If the system temperature is below the Curie temperature, once a few spins align, coupling between spins can align all spins, in effect setting all spins to 'ONE'. In this case, the number of magnetic states reduces from $2^{\mathcal{N}}$ to 1. Because $\log_2 1 = 0$, the corresponding statistical entropy becomes 0. (Although the algorithmic entropy does not drop to zero but drops from $\mathcal{N} + H(\mathcal{N})$ to $H(\mathcal{N})$, that is, is close to $\log_2 \mathcal{N}$.) The bits in the magnetic system decrease, but bits increase in the momentum system when disorder, as latent heat is transferred to the momentum degrees of freedom. Provided the detailed computational path is kept, the information to provide reversibility still resides in the system, and there is no change in the system's algorithmic entropy and hence the thermodynamic entropy. If $k_B \ln 2T$ Joules are required to erase one bit, $k_B \ln 2T$ Joules can restore the system to the original microstate only if the reversible path is exactly followed. However, as Landauer showed, once heat has passed from the momentum subsystem to an external sink, degrees of freedom within the system are lost and all the information on the prior microstate has been erased from the system. At that point, the system's state space is compressed as bits have been erased, but the environmental state space expands. The entropy cost of restoring the system increases in thermodynamic terms.

As is discussed in more detail in section 8.5; the overall increase in the entropy of the total system plus the environment when bits exit the system is because the programme bits, normally ignored, dissipate as heat once reversibility is lost.

## 8.4 The simulation of a reversible real-world computation

This principle of Landauer has important implications, not only for reversibility, but because it provides an AIT perspective on the way natural processes can effectively regulate a system, maintaining it in a homeostatic set of states to counter the effects of the second law of thermodynamics. However, there is an important difference between a real-world computation and that on a typical reference computer. The generalised gates in the real-world computer (i.e. the atoms and molecules and computational elements that change their states under the computation, while passing information through the system) are reversible. In the laboratory computer, the computation that specifies how the system steps through its bit space is determined by the initial bit settings which includes the programme that manipulates the physical laws embedded in the gates [1, 22, 23]. However, in this case, the AND and OR gates of the typical reference UTM are irreversible.

Nevertheless, the simple ballistic computer of Fredkin and Toffli [24] illustrates in principle how physical processes can be structured to form a reversible computer. A more relevant example that illustrates the relationship between a physical or a chemical process and a computational process is the Brownian computer of Bennett [7, 9]. This is the computation embodied in the process by which RNA polymerase copies a complement of a DNA string. Reversibility is only attained at zero speeds as the computation randomly walks through possible computational paths. Indeed, because the process is driven forward by irreversible error correction routines that underpin natural DNA copying, the process is no longer strictly reversible.

Reversibility is hardwired into the computational process through the physical laws that determine the computational behaviour of the components such as atoms and molecules. The input string to the computation is stored in the initial states of the atoms or molecules at the start of the process. Given the initial state, the physical laws, which determine the interaction between the states of the species in the system, drive the trajectory of the system through its state space. Similarly, as Landauer [22] points out, any conventional UTM is itself constrained by physical laws and is also a real-world device. In this case, the input and the output are not the digits written on an input/output device such as a tape, but the initial configuration and the final configuration of bits stored within the computer at the start and finish of the computation.

While it is possible to construct reversible gates [24], in practice when an irreversible reference UTM is required to simulate a real-world UTM, the history of the computation needed for reversibility must be kept and tracked; otherwise, if these history bits are discarded, the entropy of the environment increases. The Landauer principle, outlined above, clarifies the essentials of a computing process undertaken by a physical system. The input string to the computation is stored in the states of the atoms and molecules at the start of the physical process. In an isolated computer system, bits are conserved, as energy is conserved. While the Hamiltonian dynamics of the system conserves information, whenever a process becomes irreversible, information is no longer conserved. In this case, $k_B \ln 2$ entropy units per degree of freedom must be transferred from the system, with at least a corresponding entropy increase in the environment. As was discussed above, Landauer showed it is not the cost of measurement of the information that is critical, but it is the energy cost that arises when information leaves the system by being transferred to the external environment. It is this that causes irreversibility. Bennett [7–10] and Zurek [11] take the argument further.

In a nutshell, the state space configurations of the real-world computer is encapsulated in what Landauer [22] and Bennett [10] call information-bearing degrees of freedom (IBDF). Reversibly discarding 1bit of information from the IBDF at a temperature $T$, contributes $k_B T \ln 2$ joules to the environment. Both logical and thermodynamic irreversibility follow if this information is no longer available. This leads to a reduction of entropy of the system matched by a greater increase of entropy in the Universe. Irreversibility can occur when heat is transferred out of the system or when material escapes, carrying bits in the material's 'information-bearing' degrees of freedom. Similarly, a transfer of information into the system also destroys reversibility, unless the transfer process retains reversibility. Chapter 8 of Li and Vitányi [25] review relevant issues related to reversibility and the thermodynamics of real-world computing.

The bit space configurations of the reference irreversible UTM must capture the same information as the real-world computer that it simulates. This can be achieved if the history information in the reference UTM is tracked properly. This is such an important point that it will be revisited throughout the book. In the next section 8.4.1; Bennett [9] lists the steps required to do this. Consider the example of oxygen and hydrogen igniting to form water increasing the system's temperature. If nothing escapes, this is a reversible process. Given the initial state of the system, the programme on the reference UTM that defines the algorithmic entropy of the final state of the system must also specify the final momentum states, not just the atomic and molecular species and track the history of the process. These momentum states and the history bits are needed for reversibility. If heat is lost irreversibly, lowering the temperature to form liquid water, the conventional computer must discard bits associated with these momentum states in order to simulate the final configuration of the real-world system.

Figure 8.1 is a schematic diagram of different regions of the bit space in a conventional computer. These regions are more or less distinct in a conventional computer, while in real-world computations the programme region, which expresses physical laws is not obvious, as the information is embodied in the interaction between the species in the system. In a conventional computer, the bit settings in the programme region under the programmer's control determine the trajectory of the system in bit space as the input moves to the output. Although once an input and the programme are encoded as 'on' and 'off' bits in a computer, the distinction between the programme and the input becomes arbitrary. A more rigorous argument that demonstrates this point for a simple UTM is shown in Chaitin [26].

For similar physical situations (as was outlined in section 1.4 bullet point 2), the zero of the algorithmic entropy can be chosen in a way that allows the common routines to be ignored. As only entropy differences are significant, the common routines capturing physical laws and the specification of the system, cancel. This is

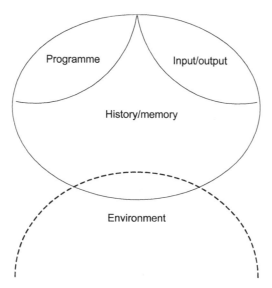

**Figure 8.1.** Schematic of a computational system.

extremely fortunate, as the specification of all the natural laws would be an impossible task. In effect one can set an entropy zero that takes most laws as given, and only considers those laws that are specifically needed to describe the changes of the states.

### 8.4.1 Maintaining reversibility in a laboratory UTM

Physical processes are in principle reversible and can map on to a logically reversible TM that operates on the input string (representing the initial state) to produce an output string (representing the final state). The computation takes place through the operation of the physical laws determining the trajectory of the system through its states. However, in practice most real-world systems are open systems and information and material may enter or leave the system. As is mentioned in the previous sections, when information is removed, either because energy is removed, or because species leave carrying information, the computational possibilities of the system are altered. The usual non-reversible UTM describes a non-reversible physical process when the history of the computation is lost. The minimal irreversible programme p* that generates the output from the input on the reference UTM is shorter than the reversible programme that generates the complete final state. However, reversibility can be retained in an irreversible computer simulating a real-world reversible computer, if the information needed for reversibility is stored in the computer memory and available. An algorithm that works in both the forward and the reverse direction can insert the information that otherwise would be lost at the irreversible computational steps [9, 27, 28]. An example is the heat produced when ice crystallises from water. If this heat is kept within the system, the process is reversible, but if it is passed to the environment reversibility is lost. Alternatively where the history information is kept, the initial state can be generated as Bennett [9] shows in detail. Broadly speaking, reversibility can be achieved in a laboratory UTM by the following process:

- generate the output from the input;
- copy the output;
- reverse the computation to regenerate the input from the accumulated history states.

The process is reversible as each computational step is reversible when information in the history states is accessed.

Section 8.5.1 shows how tracking the computation and its history from the perspective of a conventional UTM allows reversibility to be maintained.

A question arises as to how a catalyst might affect a real-world computation. The programme implicit in the Brownian computer described by Bennett [7, 9] may be able to be shortened if a path, originally involving a catalyst, is replaced by a more direct computing path. The speed of the process without the catalyst might be less, but the outcome would be the same as the bits in the catalyst are the same before and after the computation. Related to this, several authors [27, 29, 30] have considered the trade-off between computer storage and number of computing steps to reproduce a given output. The storage can be reduced if bits are lost to the environment, making the process more difficult to reverse.

The difference in algorithmic entropy between an input state $i$ and an output state $o$ is the number of bits that must enter or leave the system when $i$ shifts to $o$. This entropy difference is independent of the UTM used, as any simulation constant cancels between UTMs. If the system is to be restored by computing $i$ from $o$, the flow of bits must be reversed as discussed in more detail in section 8.6. The thermodynamic cost of maintaining order, or equivalently restoring a system to a previously more ordered state, when bits are added or discarded corresponds to $k_B \ln 2$ per bit from Landauer's principle [1], provided all bits are tracked to ensure reversibility. The consistency of the argument can be seen by considering the following examples.

- An adiabatic expansion of an ideal gas against a frictionless piston increases the spatial disorder. The movement of the piston in effect is like a programme, changing the computational trajectory of the components of the gas. The algorithmic entropy is derived from the shortest description of the instantaneous configuration of the gas in terms of the position and momentum coordinates of each gas particle. In algorithmic terms, while the contribution to the algorithmic entropy of the position coordinates increases through disordering, the algorithmic entropy of the momentum coordinates decreases to compensate. This decrease corresponds to a drop in the temperature. Adiabatic compression is the converse process. Adiabatic demagnetisation is analogous to an adiabatic expansion. The process of adiabatic demagnetization randomises a set of aligned spins as an external magnetic field is reduced. The consequential disordering of the spin states soaks up the entropy embodied in the thermal degrees of freedom, as energy is transferred to the magnetic degrees of freedom. As a consequence, the system's temperature drops. While a system remains isolated, no erasure of information, or total change in entropy occurs.

- On the other hand, an isothermal expansion of a gas against a piston can disorder or randomise a system, as heat enters to do work against the piston. In contrast to the adiabatic case, the algorithmic description of the system increases as heat flows in. As is shown in more detail later, the thermodynamic entropy increases by $k_B \ln 2$ for each extra bit needed in the algorithmic description, as shown in section 4.5. Conversely, isothermal compression orders the gas. For an isothermal magnetic system, the equivalent of isothermal compression is where external magnetic field is applied to aligns spins and in doing so passes $k_B T \ln 2$ joules per spin to the environment.

- In an open, real-world system, the computational processes that reset the states of the computational elements (i.e. the atoms, molecules, spins, etc) require energy to be expended or released. This may occur through electrical energy; through magnetic field gradients that align spins; through photons and molecular structures that enter or leave the system; through heat flows into or out of the system; and finally through work being done on, or by the system. Energy sources within the system can also be redistributed to reset the computational states as, for example, when hydrogen and oxygen are converted to water by these real-world computational processes. In the hydrogen–oxygen case, the energy released is passed to the kinetic energy states of the system and the bits carried by the energy increasing the length of the algorithmic description of the momentum states. Provided the system is isolated there is no entropy change. As one water molecule replaces two hydrogen atoms and an oxygen atom, the description of the species also changes. The physical (or computational) processes within the system disperse the entropy. When the system is no longer isolated, regions that are disordered relative to the environment, such as those where bits are embodied in the kinetic energy degrees of freedom, can then pass excess bits to the environment leaving the more ordered regions behind.

  While a subsystem can be ordered, by passing disorder elsewhere, ordering of the whole system only occurs when entropy is ejected—for example, when heat is passed to a low entropy sink in the environment, or high entropy molecular fragments escape the system. The programme on the reference UTM that specifies the states must capture the same information as the real-world UTM. When material enters or leaves a real-world system, expanding or contracting the state space, the corresponding process in the reference computer involves expanding or contracting the bit space. This could happen when bits passing to the computer memory area corresponding to the environment. Alternatively, it could occur through connecting or removing a memory device such as a memory stick. For example, when species enter a real-world system, altering the trajectory through its state space, the equivalent for the reference computer can be envisaged as a programme change brought about by adding programme bits via a memory device.

## 8.5 The algorithmic entropy as a function of state

The thermodynamic entropy is a function of state. That is, the value of the entropy depends on the details of the macrostate of a system, not the path to get there. This is why is it valid to establish the entropy of a particular macrostate by tracking heat flows that take place by a reversible path from a known state to the state of interest. But having determined the thermodynamic entropy of the state of interest, the path to that state is irrelevant. As is shown below, the algorithmic entropy in a reversible real-world system is also a state function. This leads to the following important properties of the algorithmic entropy:

- if the algorithmic entropy is a function of state, the path to constitute that state does not affect the algorithmic entropy of the state. A consequence of this is outlined below. The halting algorithm that defines the algorithmic entropy will have the same value as that obtained by tracking bits into and out of the system;
- The algorithmic entropy of different microstates in a reversible isolated system, is conserved just as energy is conserved. A corollary is that when bits flow into or out of a system from a wider system, and these bits flows are tracked, bits are also conserved.

### 8.5.1 When bits are tracked, bits are conserved

The computations in the natural world require reversibility to be maintained. As computations are driven by laws that define the rules of interaction between atoms and molecules, one can envisage these real-world species acting as generalised computational gates or computing automata. The real-world computation makes no distinction between the programme and the configuration of the natural system. However, care is needed in aligning real-world computations with those on a laboratory UTM. The laboratory machine is in effect a bit measuring device. From an observer perspective, the programme, specifying the interaction between the states in terms of physical laws, implemented on the laboratory reference computer, is defined separately from the bits representing the configurations of the system. If the real-world computation on UTM $W$, with its real-world gates, corresponds to $U_W(s_0) = s_h$, the simulation of this process on the laboratory UTM $U$ with programme $p_h$ is

$$U(p_h, s_0) = s_h.$$

The stored energy in the computational structures in $W$ carries bits that can be identified with the programme bits $p_h$. Given the initial state, $s_0$, and denoting the halt requirement by the suffix $h$, $p_h$ represents the programme bit settings that generate the halt state '$s_h$'. Strictly, from a real-world perspective, the full initial state is $(p_h s_0)$ as the programme instructions are embodied in real-world gates. When such a computation progresses in a real-world isolated system, bits that previously specified stored energy states, or bits that specified programme operations, remain in the system. Those specifying stored energy states are driven by second law processes to become bits specifying momentum states.

On the other hand, if the system is no longer isolated, programme bits carried by species that enter the system, change the computational trajectory just as would happen when a memory stick is plugged into a conventional computer.

The observer finds it convenient to separate bits entering the system as specifying configurations or species, from bits that act as programme instructions. But this separation may be somewhat arbitrary. The flow of these bits into the system increase its overall thermodynamic entropy, as the system would trend to a new set of most probable states. Order is only maintained if the history bits leave the system effectively eliminating reversibility. From Landauer's principle, this increases the overall entropy of the Universe. Erasure is the computing process by which these bits are transferred to the environment, increasing the temperature of the environment, and hence its entropy.

In the laboratory computer, the programmer, by understanding the behaviour of the computational gates, sets the initial bits to bring about the desired computation. If the laboratory UTM is to adequately map a real-world computation, as Zurek [11] points out, real-world computations are reversible, and the laboratory UTM simulating the real-world must keep the residual programme bits and the history of the computation to maintain reversibility [1, 7, 9].

As discussed earlier, in section 8.4.1, the history and the residual programme bits can be used to regenerate the initial state. From an algorithmic point of view, these bits, needed to reverse the computation, are part of the algorithmic entropy of the total system as outlined by Zurek [28] and Bennett [8, 9].

As a consequence, the halt state in the above computation is strictly $s_h = \hat{s}_h, g(p_h, s_0)$, where $\hat{s}_h$ is what the observer deems to be the halt state while $g(p_h, s_0)$, which hereafter will be denoted by $g_h$, is the history of the computation capturing the information required for reversibility. As $\hat{s}_h$ and $g_h$ are generated together, for the majority of states $H(s_h) = H(\hat{s}_h)$. The full history, $g_h$ is the reversible programme that reinstates the initial configuration [8, 9]. Once programme bits are tracked separately from state bits, $g_h = p_h^{-1} = p_h$, as $p_h$ is reversible.

As a consequence, the forward and reverse computations are related by

$$U(p_h, s_0) = \hat{s}_h, g_h,$$

and, because of reversibility,

$$U(g_h, \hat{s}_h) = p_h, s_0.$$

From a laboratory perspective, as the computation progresses, programme bits either become the bits to define $\hat{s}_h$, or remain as residual programme bits to retain reversibility as is discussed in more detail in chapter 9.

When the system is reversible and no entropy is lost to the environment, the process is logically and thermodynamically reversible [7, 9, 11]. Furthermore, as there is no alternative path to $s_h$ (other than the reverse computation from the successor state $s_{h+1}$), this must constitute the shortest reversible algorithm to generate the halt state and therefore an equals sign is appropriate in the following equation. As the trajectory through bit space reversibly generates the final state together with the history bits, the algorithmic entropy is conserved provided the history is kept. Hence,

$$H(\mathrm{p}_h, s_0) = H(s_h) = H(\hat{s}_h, g) = H(s_0) + H(s_h|s_0^*). \tag{8.1}$$

Once a full account is taken of all bits in the system, this leads to the following theorem.

**Theorem** *In an isolated, reversible, discrete system, the algorithmic entropy as the bits specifying the initial configuration and the programme with its halt instruction, must be conserved as the system moves through its computational trajectory. The bits involved appear in the algorithmic entropy of the computed final state, together with the algorithmic entropy embodied in the computational history.*

As is discussed, this has implications for understanding the second law of thermodynamics and relating the algorithmic entropy to the thermodynamic entropy.

The example of an isolated hydrogen–oxygen system, which from an observer perspective might be seen as ordered, illustrates the issues. Ignition initiates the computation undertaken by molecules of hydrogen and oxygen forming water. In the same process stored energy bits specifying the microstate of the system and programme instructions are turned into momentum bits, raising the temperature at each computational step. This is because, from the perspective of a natural world computation, the stored energy in the original gas system diffuses through the system, disordering the momentum states at each hypothetical stage. From a thermodynamic perspective, as stored energy is released, increasing the temperature, the thermodynamic entropy is said to increase as the system trends to the most probable set of states. However, the algorithmic entropy, as has been discussed, includes bits specifying the stored energy and programme states. The algorithmic entropy is conserved. As section 9.3.1 illustrates, what happens is that the stored energy bits, represent *potential* thermodynamic entropy. It is only when these bits are released as heat, to specify momentum states, that these bits represent the *realised* thermodynamic entropy.

While bits are conserved in an isolated thermodynamic system, particles such as hydrogen and oxygen may not be. Rather, when the number of bits specifying position states reduce as particles combine, bits from the programme states and stored energy bits are transferred to the momentum states to compensate.

On the other hand, when the system is not isolated, bits need to be tracked as discussed. Consider as an example the programme $\mathrm{p}_h$ embodied in the DNA of a seed that grows a tree but which also includes the nutrients and energy supply, needed to grow the tree. Alternatively, the resource string can be considered separately from the programme string during the growth trajectory. The initial configuration of the DNA molecules is the initial state of the system. The observer sees this state as separate from the instructions in the DNA, but the real-world does not. The programme specifying the tree at a particular instant halts if the resource supply is turned off. For the programme to continue to a later halt state, resource bits need to enter the system, increasing the number of bits needed to specify the later state of the tree. The history bits are embodied in the carbon dioxide, water and other products that ultimately exit the system. If these are taken into account the total entropy does not increase, but when these bits are eliminated from the system, the tree that is left is highly ordered, having a low algorithmic entropy. From a real-world perspective when bits are passed to the environment, the system becomes irreversible and the entropy of the environment increases[1].

### 8.5.2 Must the algorithm that specifies the provisional entropy halt?

Section 7.2.4 drew attention to the requirement that, by definition, the algorithm that determines the algorithmic entropy must halt if the entropy measure is to align with the thermodynamic entropy. It is shown here that the algorithmic entropy is a function of state and its value is independent of the path taken to reach that state. Hence, determining the number of bits in a system by tracking bit flows yields the same algorithmic entropy as that specified by a halting algorithm. The critical point is that in a real-world reversible system, bits are actual entities associated with energy.

However, it is customary to argue that, if the halting requirement is dropped, a shorter non-halting algorithm exists. For example, as discussed earlier, in section 1.6, an algorithm that generates all integers in turn on a laboratory computer is of the following form:

$$N = 0$$
$$A. \ \ N = N + 1; \ GO: T0 \ A$$

and is much shorter than one that generates a specific integer and then halts. It is seen that eventually, the above algorithm will compute, for example, the integer $1, 048, 576 = 2^{20}$ and continue forever without halting. On the other hand, the programme that halts when $2^{20}$ is reached, needs extra instructions of a length of about 20 bits ($=\log_2(2^{20})$) to add to the above algorithm to specify when to halt. It would seem that the halting programme must be 20 bits longer than the simple programme above.

While this is plausible for a laboratory computation, the argument does not apply to a reversible real-world computation. Firstly, replacing $N$ by $N + 1$ is not reversible and cannot represent a real-world computation, as information is thrown away each cycle. Secondly, a bit is not a '0' or a '1' on some printout, but a bit exists in the physical states of atoms and molecules and energy is required to create a new bit. Once the energy requirement to store a bit is taken into account, the number of

---

[1] H U W Price in his book *Time's Arrow and Archimedes' Point* [31] argues that scientists are muddled in their thinking about entropy and reversibility in statistical mechanics. The problem raised by Price would seem to be resolved, or at worst shifted elsewhere.

bits required to specify $N$ grows as $\log_2 N$ for an ongoing computation. This is identical to the number of bits needed to define the halt requirement, as discussed in section 1.6.1. The energy to create these bits must come from somewhere.

Indeed, most real-world computations do not halt, but are ongoing as the system moves from one configuration to another. But even if $\log_2 N$ grows slowly in the above equation, ultimately, for such an ongoing computation, there would be insufficient stored energy in the Universe to specify the latest integer. If bits are tracked properly and provided reversibility is kept, the number of bits to generate the $N$th integer is the same, whether the algorithm halts or continues indefinitely. The halt requirement in essence, is a process for counting the number of bits needed to define a particular state.

This is discussed in more detail in chapter 9.

### 8.5.3 Tracking bit flows in non-halting computations

A further point raises the question as to how the algorithmic entropy of an instantaneous configuration, measured as a snapshot at that particular instant, is related to the number of bits residing in the system as established by tracking net bit flows. The thermodynamic equivalent of this situation corresponds to answering the question: 'what is the thermodynamic entropy of a system where heat has been flowing in and flowing out, but where the heat flow has been stopped at a particular instant?'

In the thermodynamic case, given the thermodynamic entropy at the start of the process, the thermodynamic entropy at a later time consists of the start entropy plus the net entropy change of the system at that time when the system is deemed isolated. As the thermodynamic entropy is an exact differential, it is a function of state and the path to reach that state is irrelevant. This means that one can track entropy flows in and out of a system to determine entropy changes in going from one state to another.

Because it is not obvious that the algorithmic entropy is path independent, particularly as a complicated path might seem to introduce extra bits, an argument is needed to show that the algorithmic entropy, evaluated by tracking bit flows, is also path independent and is therefore a function of state. If this were not so, the algorithmic entropy could not align with the thermodynamic entropy.

The following theorem shows that, provided the path is reversible, for an ongoing computation, because the process does not halt in any intermediate state, a path connecting subroutines by tracking bit flows gives the same result as the shortest direct algorithmic description of the state. Indeed, most real-world computations do not halt, but are ongoing as the system moves from one microstate to another. It is shown later that this is of particular significance for a system that is maintained in a homeostatic or stable state by the inflow and outflow of bits to counter the degradation processes of the second law of thermodynamics.

**Theorem** *Given the initial algorithmic entropy, the algorithmic entropy established by tracking the bit flows in and out of a real system up to a given instant, is the same as the* *number of bits in the algorithm that generates the actual microstate at that instant and then halts.*

Following Devine [6], consider a system where the initial algorithmic entropy of state $s_0$ at time zero is specified by $H(s_0)$ configurational bits, and a programme p* that accesses a resource string $\sigma$ to generate a subsequent state $\epsilon_k$ from $s_0$ and then halts. The programme p* includes both the second law algorithm driving the system to the equilibrium set, such as the instructions to ignite hydrogen and oxygen to produce heat and water, as well as the instructions already in the system. The programme bits in p* that implement the natural laws defining interactions between species, as mentioned earlier, are distinct from the bits that specify the configurations $\sigma$ and $s_0$. However, when computational bits enter the system with the resource string $\sigma$, these are included as part of p*. Together, p*, $\sigma$ and $s_0$, make up the computational resources that are either in the system, or enter it, to generate $\epsilon_k$, the microstate of interest. In order to maintain the system, the process must eject the waste identified by the string $\zeta$. The real-world computation, which contains the reversibility information corresponds to

$$U(\text{p}^*, s_0, \sigma) = \epsilon_k, \zeta_l.$$

If no waste is ejected, no information is lost. The algorithmic entropy of the final microstate state at this instant must include the waste string $\zeta_l$ that contains the history and residual prgramme bits needed for reversibility. Here, because only algorithmic entropy differences are considered, there is no need for an $O(1)$ constant as the computations are UTM-independent. Furthermore, as the computations are ongoing, there is no need to include bits that link subroutines. With this in mind, the algorithmic entropy of the input equals that of the output, that is,

$$H(\epsilon_k, \zeta_l) = H(\sigma) + |\text{p}^*| + H(s_0).$$

As the strings $\epsilon_k$ and $\zeta_l$ have common information, $H(\epsilon, \zeta)$ cannot be separated into $H(\epsilon)$ and $H(\zeta)$. However, $H(\epsilon_k, \zeta_l)$ can be separated using $H(\epsilon_k, \zeta_l) = H(\epsilon_k) + H(\zeta_l|\epsilon_k^*)$. The requirement that the microstate $\epsilon_k$ can be sustained is that $H(\text{waste}) = H(\zeta_l|\epsilon_k^*)$ bits, must be ejected from the system as waste. In this case,

$$H(\epsilon_k) = H(\epsilon_k, \zeta_l) - H(\text{waste}) = H(\sigma) + |\text{p}^*| + H(s_0) - H(\text{waste}).$$

Or, the algorithmic entropy of the final state $\epsilon_k$ is given by

$$H(\epsilon_k) = H(\sigma) + |\text{p}^*| + H(s_0) - H(\text{waste}).$$

This demonstrates the theorem that the number of bits $H(\epsilon_k)$ in the halt state equals the bits in the initial state plus the number of bits that have entered the system, less the bits in the waste ejected at the halt instant. Here, $H(\text{waste})$ includes heat bits, programme bits embodied in species that leave, and bits specifying the position states of species that leave the system. The waste, partly as heat and as species, exits a real-world system because the external environment in effect undertakes a computation on the system. Heat is transferred when some bits specifying the momentum states in the system become bits specifying the momentum states in the environment. This can be visualised as an environmental cold wall surrounding the system absorbing energy by collisions, or by bits increasing the momentum states in the environment as radiation escapes through a transparent wall. Similarly, the computation can transfer both programme and state bits to the external environment when species escape, rather like removing bits in a conventional computer by unplugging a memory stick. The following conclusions summarise the above result.

1. Given the initial algorithmic entropy of the system, the algorithmic entropy of the final state at a particular instant, can be determined directly from the net bit flows, rather than by finding the algorithm that generates the final state and halts. One need not require the actual programme that generates a state to halt, but can instead determine the net number of bits in the system when the halt state is reached. The critical parameter is the number of bits that are in the system.

2. Tracking bit flows enables the net change to the bits in the system to be identified. Hence, if the algorithmic entropy is defined in terms of bit flows, in contrast to the situation where the halting algorithm is specified, bits that pass from one routine to another do not need the linking instruction outlined in section 3.3. That is, in an ongoing real-world computation, outputs of subroutines are placed in a position that they are directly accessible to other routines when needed. This allows heat and algorithmic entropy flows into and out of a system to be related to thermodynamic entropy flows, without the need to identify the shortest algorithm that halts to define the final state. If the system resides in a homeostatic set of states, all having the same algorithmic entropy $H(\epsilon_k)$, not only must the bits in and the bits out be equal to maintain homeostasis, but also the energy carried by the bits entering and leaving the system must balance.

3. Furthermore, given the start entropy, as is discussed in more detail in chapter 8, the net bit flows from Landauer's principle correspond to the net thermodynamic entropy change to the system. A simple thought experiment reinforces the connection between the algorithmic entropy and the thermodynamic entropy. Effectively, the difference in algorithmic entropy between two states is about the transfer of bits of information, whereas the thermodynamic entropy is about the transfer of heat energy at a given temperature.

When $\Delta H$ bits are transferred between two states in a computational system at a temperature $T$ the energy transfer is $\Delta Q = k_B T \ln 2 \Delta H$ from Landauer's principle [1] provided bits needed to maintain reversibility are tracked. The thermodynamic entropy change is $\Delta Q / T = k_B \ln 2 \Delta H$.

An example that illustrates the point is seen for the difference between a block of ice at 0 K and melted ice at the same temperature constrained to the same shape. Given the original ice configuration, the bits that need to enter the system to specify the melted configuration is $\Delta Q / (k_B T \ln 2)$. Allowing for units, the provisional entropy has meaning for off-equilibrium, or non-typical configurations.

4. The greater $H(\text{waste})$ is for a given input, the shorter the snapshot or halting algorithmic description and, as the system is further from equilibrium set, the more ordered it is. Interestingly, Schneider and Kay [32] have measured the energy dissipation for an ecology and have shown that the more biologically complex the ecology, the more effectively it processes inputs and, as a consequence, transforms more of the stored energy into heat. The waste is more degraded, in the sense that the bits originally specifying stored energy states, are more comprehensively transformed into bits specifying the momentum states and which can be ejected mainly as heat. Life hastens the trend to equilibrium.

## 8.6 External interventions to restore a degraded system

As has been mentioned, the degradation process driven by the second law of thermodynamics can be visualized as a computing process. The input string $i$ specifies the information in the system, the information in the nutrients and any source of concentrated energy. A programme string $p^*$ specifies the algorithm embodying the physical laws, which have not been made explicit, but which drive the system to a more disordered configuration. The output string $o$ is generated by the computation on computer $U$ where $U(p^*, i) = o$. If all the information is kept in the computation, i.e. nothing escapes the system, the process is thermodynamically and computationally reversible.

However, the process becomes irreversible when the system loses information through heat transfer, or through material carrying bits exiting the system. This information must be replaced if the system is to be restored to its original macrostate. It was shown in section 8.5.3 that the algorithmic entropy is a function of state. As a consequence, the bits specifying a particular microstate are path independent. The number of bits that leave a system when a state goes from $i$ to $o$, is given by $H(i) - H(o)$. The system can be restored to the initial state provided,

$$H(i) - H(o) = H(i|o^*), \qquad (8.2)$$

bits are returned to the system. Because this is an entropy difference, the number of bits is the same whether the computation is accomplished on a real-world computer or a laboratory simulation. However, the information in $o^*$ is equivalent to the number of bits in $o$ together with $H(o)$ [11]. If reversibility is lost, a further $|H(o)|$ are needed to compute $i$ from $o$. As a consequence, equation (8.2) is the least number of bits that must reversibly leave the system to generate $o$ and enter the system to regenerate $i$. If the system was initially ordered it can do work as happens when a heat input forces a gas to do work against a piston. Zurek [11, 28] argues that if one knew the exact description of these states, a cyclic process based on this information would be maximally efficient for extracting work.

In order to see how an external intervention can restore a system, consider a system that was originally in a microstate $\epsilon_i$ belonging to a stable set of states $\epsilon_i$, $\epsilon_j$, etc, all of which have the same provisional entropy, e.g. $H_{prov}(\epsilon_i)$. The disturbance $\delta$ switches the trajectory of the system to a new configuration $\eta_j$ outside the stable set. This is analogous to plugging a memory stick containing a computer virus into a computer. The corresponding computation $p_\delta^*$ effected by the disturbance or virus is $U(p_\delta^*, \epsilon_i^*) = \eta_j$. The number of bits that enter or leave the system due to the disturbance is

$$|p_\delta^*| = H(\eta_j) - H_{prov}(\epsilon_i).$$

Here, a positive sign represents an entropy inflow. The measure is an entropy difference and is the same whether on a real-world computer or a reference UTM. Applying the above argument over a cycle, at least $H_{prov}(\epsilon_i|\eta_j^*) = H_{prov}(\epsilon_i) - H(\eta_j)$ bits must be returned to the system to restore it to one of the states in the original stable set. This leads to the thermodynamic requirement from equation (8.2) that at least

$$k_B \ln 2 H(\epsilon_i|\eta_j^*) = k_B \ln 2[H_{prov}(\epsilon_i) - H(\eta_j)] \qquad (8.3)$$

Joules per degree must be introduced into the system to restore $\epsilon_i$. If reversibility is lost, or bits cannot be tracked, the real cost is higher.

Ashby [33] has argued that an open system must have the regulatory capability to adapt to a changing environment to maintain homeostasis. From a cybernetic point of view, an external regulator is required to maintain the system's variables within a viable region. This approach leads to Ashby's law of requisite variety, which states the regulation requirement of a system is that the Shannon entropy of the set of regulation states must at least equal the Shannon entropy of the set of disturbances [33, 34]. From a computational point of view, the argument above shows that where an external regulator passes information in and out of the system, a law similar to Ashby's law of requisite variety emerges. But here the law becomes: 'The change in algorithmic entropy introduced by the regulation process must be equal and opposite to the change in algorithmic entropy introduced by the disturbance'.

The point of view outlined here considers the disturbance and the regulator to be external to the system and both act on it. However, when a natural system is maintained distant from the most probable set of states, the second law processes that drive the system towards the equilibrium set act as the disturbance. This situation is different from that just discussed as the drivers *are part of the system*. Similarly, where a system self-regulates, the regulation process acts from within the system. For example, a forest can maintain itself distant from the equilibrium set of states off-setting decay, by utilising photons from the Sun without any external intervention. But if the light is blocked the forest will degrade to a local equilibrium. Section 10.4 generalises the argument discussed above for the situation of self-regulating systems that operate under second law degradation processes.

# References

[1] Landauer R 1961 Irreversibility and heat generation in the computing process *IBM J. Res. Dev.* **5** 183–91

[2] Szilard S 1929 Uber die entropieverminderung in einem thermodynamischen system bei eingriffen intelligenter wesen *Z. Phys.* **53** 840–56

[3] Szilard L 2003 On the decrease of entropy in a thermodynamic system by the intervention of intelligent beings *Maxwell's Demon 2: Classical and Quantum Information, Computing* ed H S Leff and A E Rex (Philadeplphia, PA: Institute of Physics Publishing) pp 110–9

[4] Brillouin L 1951 Maxwell's demon cannot operate: Information and entropy. I *J. Appl. Phys.* **22** 334–7

[5] Brillouin L 1962 *Science and Information Theory* 2nd edn (New York: Academic)

[6] Devine S 2018 Algorithmic entropy and Landauer's principle link microscopic system behaviour to the thermodynamic entropy *Entropy* **20** 798

[7] Bennett C H 1982 Thermodynamics of computation–A review *Int. J. Theor. Phys.* **21** 905–40

[8] Bennett C H 1988 Logical depth and physical complexity *The universal Turing Machine–A Half-Century Survey* ed R Herken (Oxford: Oxford University Press) pp 227–57

[9] Bennett C H 1973 Logical reversibility of computation *IBM J. Res. Dev* **17** 525–32

[10] Bennett C H 2003 Notes on Landauer's principle, reversible computation, and Maxwell's demon (http://xxx.lanl.gov/PS_cache/physics/pdf/0210/0210005.pdf)

[11] Zurek W H 1989 Thermodynamics of computation, algorithmic complexity and the information metric *Nature* **341** 119–24

[12] Lloyd S 2000 Ultimate physical limits to computation *Nature* **406** 1047–55

[13] Leff H S and Rex A F 1990 *Maxwellas Demon: Entropy, Information, computing* (Princeton: Princeton University Press)

[14] Rex A 2017 Maxwell's Demon—A historical review *Entropy* **19** 240

[15] Kish L B, Khatri S P, Granqvist C G and Smulko J M 2015 Critical remarks on Landauer's principle of erasure-dissipation: Including notes on Maxwell demons and Szilard engines *2015 Int. Conf. on Noise and Fluctuations (ICNF)* (Piscataway, NJ: IEEE)

[16] del Rio L, Aberg J, Renner R, Dahlsten O and Vlatko Vedra V 2011 The thermodynamic meaning of negative entropy (https://arxiv.org/pdf/1009.1630.pdf)

[17] Ladyman J and Robertson K 2014 Going round in circles: Landauer versus Norton on the thermodynamics of computation *Entropy* **16** 2278–90

[18] Bèrut A, Petrosyan A and Ciliberto S 2015 Information and thermodynamics: Experimental verification of Landauer's erasure principle *J. Stat. Mech.: Theory Exp.* P06015

[19] Jun Y, čilo Gavrilov M and Bechhoefer J 2014 High-precision test of Landauer's principle in a feedback trap *Phys. Rev. Lett.* **113** 190601

[20] Hong J, Lambson B, Dhuey S and Bokor J 2016 Experimental test of Landauer's principle in single-bit operations on nanomagnetic memory bits *Sci. Adv.* **2** e1501492

[21] Yan L L, Xiong T P, Rehan K, Zhou F, Liang D F, Chen L, Zhang J Q, Yang W L, Ma Z H and Feng M 2018 Single-atom demonstration of the quantum Landauer principle *Phys. Rev. Lett.* **120** 210601

[22] Landauer R 1992 Information is physical *Proceedings of PhysComp 1992 Los Alamitos* (Oxford: IEEE Computer Society Press) pp 1–4

[23] Toffoli T 1982 Physics and computation *Int. J. Theor. Phys.* **21** 165–75

[24] Fredkin E and Toffoli T 1982 Conservative logic *Int. J. Theor. Phys.* **21** 219–53

[25] Li M and Vitányi P M B 2008 *An Introduction to Kolmogorov Complexity and Its Applications* 3rd edn (New York: Springer)

[26] Chaitin G 1975 A theory of program size formally identical to information theory *J. ACM* **22** 329–40

[27] Li M and Vitányi P M B 1996 Reversibility and adiabatic computation: trading time and space for energy *Proc. R. Soc. Lond., Ser.* A **452** 769–89

[28] Zurek W H 1989 Algorithmic randomness and physical entropy *Phys. Rev.* A **40** 4731–51

[29] Buhrman H, Tromp J and Vitanyi P 2001 Time and space bounds for reversible simulation *J. Phys. A: Math. Gen.* **34-35** 6821–30

[30] Vitányi P M B 2005 Time space and energy in reversible computing *Proc. 2005 ACM Int. Conf. on Computing Frontiers, Ischia, Italy* 435–44

[31] Price H 1996 *Time's Arrow and Archimedes' Point: New Directions for the Physics of Time* (New York: Oxford University Press)

[32] Schneider E D and Kay J J 1994 Life as a manifestation of the second law of thermodynamics *Mathl. Comput. Modelling* **16** 25–48

[33] Ashby W R 1964 *Introduction to Cybernetics* (London: University Paperbacks)

[34] Casti J 1996 The great Ashby: Complexity, variety, and information *Complexity* **2** 7–9

IOP Publishing

# Algorithmic Information Theory for Physicists and Natural Scientists

Sean D Devine

# Chapter 9

# The algorithmic equivalent of the second law of thermodynamics

The second law of thermodynamics implies that overwhelmingly most of the time an isolated system settles in the most probable set of states. A rare fluctuation away from the most probable set of states occurs when bits specifying momentum states are transferred to bits specifying stored energy or programme states. What this shows is that both bits, and the energy that carries the bits, must come from somewhere. Bits either must be in the system and the type of energy that carries the bits changes, or bits must enter the system from outside, as programme instructions, stored energy states, or heat. When bits enter or leave the system, the transfer can be considered as taking place from a larger system that contains the system of interest.

Here it is shown that the thermodynamic entropy primarily recognises bits that specify the momentum and the position states. If an isolated reversible system is distant from the most probable set of states, bits in stored energy and programme states do not contribute to the thermodynamic entropy and can be thought of as representing potential thermodynamic entropy. The thermodynamic entropy increases when the second law of thermodynamics drives these potential entropy bits to become bits specifying the momentum states.

A simple model is used to highlight issues of accidental ordering where bits are conserved. A more sophisticated model that is rich enough to identify the practicalities of how the thermodynamic entropy increases, considers a three-atom system, with three units of stored energy per atom. All the possible configurations of the simple system can be identified, and the bits involved in specifying each microstate can be tracked.

The algorithm that generates an improbable state requires not just the specification of the electronic and momentum states, but requires a longer term where the bits correspond to the negative log(probability) contribution as a consequence of

Shannon's noiseless coding theorem. This probability-related contribution pads out the algorithmic entropy contribution of the momentum and stored energy states to ensure the total algorithmic entropy for each microstate in the three-atom system is the same. Where a system resides in a microstate in the most probable set of states, bits are primarily in the momentum states, whereas in an improbable microstate, most bits are captured by the log(probability) term.

This simple model is generalised to show that microstate in the most probable states has few bits stored as instructions, but most are stored in the momentum states. This leads to the concept of the degree of order of a particular state as the number of bits specifying the instructions that need to move to the momentum degrees of freedom to generate a typical state belonging to the most probable set.

It is shown that because of reversibility, stored energy bits are real bits with associated energy. Computational structures storing programme bits associated with energy emerge, when residual bits in the most probable set of states, drive the system backwards in time.

It is also shown that the shortest algorithm that specifies a real-world microstate is one that reaches the microstate by a reversible trajectory. Similarly, while a catalyst may provide a longer path to a particular microstate, the end result is path independent.

## 9.1 The meaning of 'equilibrium'

As has been mentioned, the algorithmic entropy is a measure for a particular microstate of a real-world system, whereas the thermodynamic entropy is a measure for a set of states within a defined macrostate. The two different concepts can be decisively related within a consistent understanding of the term 'equilibrium'. While this has been discussed previously, the discussion is expanded here.

That there is confusion in discussing equilibrium can be seen by considering an isolated system where the initial configuration is a mixture of hydrogen and oxygen molecules in the ratio of 2:1. Once ignition occurs, depending on the temperature and pressure, the system settles in the most probable set of states where the constituents are primarily water as steam, with residual amounts of molecular hydrogen and oxygen. As the whole system is already in chemical equilibrium, it is confusing to argue that the second law of thermodynamics drives the system to equilibrium where the entropy is maximum.

Again, because the hydrogen–oxygen system is isolated, there can be an extremely rare fluctuation from the most probable set of states, as might happen when water molecules dissociate into significant quantities of hydrogen and oxygen molecules. Yet such fluctuations are still valid states in the chemical equilibrium. The commonly used term 'fluctuation from equilibrium', to refer to these rare occurrences, is confusing. Where a microstate, or sets of microstates, are connected by a reversible path, as is the case for an isolated system, the entropy should not change. For example, If a Boltzmann gas is adiabatically and reversibly compressed to fill half the volume of a container, the entropy does not change. But, as discussed in section 4.5, if the same gas, which initially filled the whole container, underwent a random fluctuation generating a microstate where all the particles filled one half of the container, the microstate would be identical to that generated by compressing the gas adiabatically. In which case, the term 'fluctuation from equilibrium' is inappropriate, as the entropy must be unchanged. Here, to avoid confusion, the set of states with the maximum thermodynamic entropy will be termed the 'most probable set of states', or the 'equilibrium set', rather than equilibrium. Rare fluctuations from the most probable set of states will be termed 'fluctuations within equilibrium' rather than 'fluctuations from equilibrium'. From this perspective, the second law of thermodynamics implies that, for overwhelmingly most of the time, the system exists in the most probable set of states. This is particularly important from an algorithmic perspective as, for an isolated reversible system, the algorithmic entropy is the same for each microstate in the system, even those that might be termed 'ordered fluctuations'. With this in mind, it will be shown that a rare fluctuation from the most probable set of states shifts bits from momentum states to stored energy and programme states, but the algorithmic entropy of each microstate in the macrostate remains constant. This recognition is also consistent with the argument that the von Neumann entropy of an isolated system, described by a time-dependent Hamiltonian, is invariant over time [1].

In traditional thermodynamics, the Boltzmann entropy determined from the most probable set of states is virtually identical to that determined from all the states in the system. If $\log_2\Omega_{all}$ represents the Boltzmann entropy for all the states in the system, and $\log_2\Omega_{set}$ represents entropy for states in the most probable set, $\log_2\Omega_{all}$ is indistinguishable from $\log_2\Omega_{set}$. This is because the overwhelming majority of states are in the most probable set and it makes little difference which value is used in Boltzmann entropy formula, $k_B \ln 2 \log_2\Omega$. However, from the algorithmic perspective, as the entropy is associated with each microstate, the distinction between a microstate in the most probable set and one outside this set becomes important.

A further point is that, because natural laws are reversible, bits and the energy associated with the bits, must come from somewhere. As is discussed next, they may come from within the system, or from outside the system.

### 9.1.1 The source of bits in different scenarios

The first scenario is where the bits come from within the system. This can be illustrated by a simple model of atoms in an isolated gaseous system with an excited state and a ground state. If a laser excites all the atoms, and the system is then isolated, the excited states decay, transferring energy to the momentum degrees of freedom as the system moves to the most probable set of states. In so doing, the thermodynamic entropy increases. The initial configuration could just as easily be envisaged as an extremely rare fluctuation from the most probable set of states. This raises the question as to what happens to the bits specifying a microstate in the most probable set of states?

The second scenario is where energy and bits enter the system from outside because the system and its environment are connected, but are not in equilibrium. In this case, one can consider the system and its environment as a composite system of separate subsystems. Both bits and energy flow between the system and the environment, driving the composite system to the most probable set of states. Once this happens, there is no distinction between the two subsystems. An example might be where a system of aligned spins, below the Curie temperature is coupled to a higher temperature system. Such a composite system would be deemed distant from the most probable set of states. Bits flow from the momentum states in the high temperature system, disordering the spins, increasing the total number of states. If the flow of bits is stopped, e.g. by insulating the magnetic subsystem so that heat bits are not transferred, a halt configuration is produced. The halt requirement, in effect, determines how many bits enter the magnetic system for it to stabilise at a particular temperature. Generally, the flow of bits continues until the most probable set is reached. One can either determine the algorithmic entropy by tracking bit flows, or by treating the composite system as an isolated system distant from its most probable set of states, as was discussed in section 8.5.2.

A more complex example is where the DNA in a seed accesses external resources to grow a plant. The external resources are fed into the system through the programme specified by the structure of the DNA. When the resources are no longer available, e.g. the Sun is blocked, or necessary nutrients are no longer available to be consumed, the programme terminates. Generally, such computations are ongoing, as both resource inputs and the expulsion of decayed products are needed to maintain the system distant from the equilibrium set of states.

Another situation is the free expansion, or Joule expansion, of a gas where the number of states increases when the gas expands without doing work. From a Boltzmann perspective, the thermodynamic entropy increases as the number of available states increases when the gas expands into the available space as was illustrated with the example in section 4.5. From the algorithmic perspective, a free expansion corresponds to the situation where bits specifying position states, initially outside the system of interest, become part of it. In a sense these bits leak in from the wider external system.

The next sections explore the relationship between the algorithmic entropy of an isolated system and the increase in thermodynamic entropy as an isolated system trends to the most probable set of states.

## 9.2 The increase in thermodynamic entropy as a system trends to the most probable set of states

If the initial state of an isolated system is deemed to be highly ordered, in the sense that it belongs to a highly improbable microstate, it will inevitably follow a trajectory towards the most probable set of states under the actions of the second law of thermodynamics. Thereafter, for most of the time, the system will settle in the most probable set of states. However, even then, rare fluctuations from the most probable set of states will briefly occur until the system again trends towards a microstate in the most probable set.

Zurek, in an appendix [2], has shown how the algorithmic entropy in an ergodic or quasi ergodic system increases as the system moves from an initial ordered state to a disordered one. The Zurek argument assumes a finite, but large, discrete set of accessible states defined by choosing an appropriate degree of resolution in the system's phase space. Zurek envisages a reversible transformation where the state $t + 1$ is related to state $t$ by $s_{t+1} = U_z s_t$. $U_z$ is a describable transformation that takes the system reversibly through all its states.

In which case, the increase in algorithmic entropy from $s_0$ to $s_t$, corresponding to the length of the algorithm that implements the transformation $s_t = U_z^t s_0$. The number of bits involved depends on $\log_2 t$ as $H(U_z^t) = \log_2 t + H(\log_2 t) + H(U_z)$. $H(U_z)$, representing the bits specifying natural laws, is expected to be highly compressed as natural laws are simple compared with the number of steps required as $t$ grows. As a consequence,

$$H(s_t) = H(s_0) + H(U_z) + H(t), \tag{9.1}$$

where $H(t) = \log_2 t + H(\log_2 t)$ As the system is reversible, there is only one forward path to define $s_t$ and equation (9.1) has an equals sign. The dominant contribution to the algorithmic entropy from this perspective is $\log_2 t$, where $t$ is the number of computational steps to reach the halt state. In effect, $\log_2 t$ is counting how many extra bits are needed to reach this halt state. The most probable set of states will exist in the region of a typical string. Furthermore, as $\log_2 t$ dominates the algorithmic entropy, $H_{\text{typical}} \approx \log_2(t_{\text{typical}}) \approx \log_2 \Omega / 2$ where $\Omega$ is the total number of states in the system and $t_{\text{typical}}$, the number of computational steps taken to reach a microstate in the most probable set of states. In which case, the algorithmic entropy in the region of the most probable set of states will be $\approx \log_2(t_{\text{typical}}) \approx \log_2 \Omega$.

In other words, according to the Zurek argument, the algorithmic entropy in the region of the most probable set of states will correspond to the Shannon entropy and will align with the Boltzmann entropy of $k_B \ln 2 \log_2 \Omega$ [3]. For example, $\log_2 \Omega_{all}$ for a mole of a Boltzmann gas would be something like $2^{81}$ if there are $2^{77}$ particles and the position and momentum states of each of the particles are specified by 8 bits. Only 1 in 1000 states can be specified by 10 fewer bits. If we define a typical state as one that is described by an algorithm within 10 bits of $2^{81}$, the algorithmic entropy of a typical state, $H_{\text{typical}}$, is at least $2^{81} - 10$. This is indistinguishable from $\log_2 \Omega_{all}$.

While this may make sense to an external observer, the question is where do the bits that contribute to the increase in $\log_2 t$ come from? The observer's algorithm that simulates the system, usually does not take into account that bits are entities associated with energy. It will be shown that in the natural world, these extra bits actually reside in the system, either specifying the stored energy states or alternatively, reside in the structures that carry the programme information. As these bits are not specifying momentum states, they do not contribute to the thermodynamic entropy. Once the natural structures carrying instructions such as atoms, molecules and species are dismantled, under the dynamics that implements the second law, the instruction bits become bits that specify the momentum states so increasing the system's temperature and the thermodynamic entropy. However, while Zurek discusses fluctuations from the most likely value where $H(s_t) = H(s_{\text{typical}})$, his transformation $U_z$ does not adequately recognise that the trajectory from an ordered configuration to a most probable one, does not necessarily increase monotonically.

As the trajectory of a real-world computational system steps through the micro-states, stored energy may pass to the momentum states in one step and be returned to another stored energy configuration in the next step. As a consequence, the system's temperature, representing the number of bits in the momentum states, fluctuates. While the successor of a disordered configuration at a higher temperature could be a low temperature fluctuation, it is the overall trend towards the most probable set of states that leads to the increase in thermodynamic entropy. Even then, fluctuations from the most probable set still occur as part of the ongoing trajectory. Not only does the algorithmic entropy not increase monotonically in the trajectory, the Zurek approach does not take into account that the number of bits in an isolated macrostate must be conserved. While the implication is that programme bits, as captured by $\log_2 t$ term, enter the system it needs to be clear where these bits come from.

Rather than using the Zurek approach just outlined, a less restrictive approach, building on section 8.5.1 will be used. In that section it was argued that when the initial state $s_0$ follows a trajectory to the halt state $s_t = \hat{s}_t$, $g$, what the observer sees as the halt state $\hat{s}_t$ has a longer description than $s_0$. Both programme and stored energy bits have been shifted into $\hat{s}_t$. The real-world computer that shifts $s_0$ to $s_t = \hat{s}_t$, $g$ enacts physical laws embodied in atoms and molecules that behave as generalised gates, the natural equivalent of computational gates. In an isolated system, the general computation that generates the trajectory $s_0$ to $s_t$ on the UTM denoted by $U$ corresponds to

$$U(\mathrm{p}_t, s_0) = s_t = \hat{s}_t, g_t.$$

This highlights the need for $g_t$ to be tracked to provide reversibility as $U(g_t, \hat{s}_t) = \mathrm{p}_t s_0$. From this perspective as the initial state $s_0$ goes to $s_t$, the number of bits specifying the configuration increases with $t$, but if the programme or total bits in the system are counted, bits are conserved. Because of reversibility,

$$H(\mathrm{p}_t s_0) = H(s_t) = H(\hat{s}_t, g_t) \tag{9.2}$$

and

$$U(g_t, \hat{s}_t) = \mathrm{p}_0 s_0.$$

As the number of steps $t$ increases, the trend is for the number of bits in the momentum states to increase, when bits in stored energy states and programme bits become momentum bits. Even so, as previously discussed, when $t$ increases, bits can flow back against the trend, as happens when momentum states re-constitue stored energy states, or partially reconstitute the programme states. From an external perspective, the transfer of bits looks like an ordered fluctuation. As shown in section 9.3.2, $H(\hat{s}_t)$ is maximised in the most probable set of states, leaving only residual bits in $g_t$.

Any increase of the algorithmic entropy of $\hat{s}_t$ is compensated by a decrease in the residual programme bits and the history bits $g_t$, as bits are conserved. In the next section, it is shown by tracking bits that bits flows within an isolated system are consistent with bit conservation.

## 9.3 The relationship between algorithmic entropy and the thermodynamic entropy of a macrostate

The next step is to explore why the thermodynamic entropy increases as a trajectory that starts from what the observer sees as a highly ordered initial state, trends towards the most probable set of states. How this is related to the algorithmic entropy? To address this question, we will assume that a highly improbable microstate in a thermodynamic macrostate has been created prior to the system becoming isolated. This could be achieved by using an external laser to populate stored energy states within the system and, by so doing, create a microstate distant from the most probable set. In such a situation, the initial configuration is likely to be highly ordered from an external observer's perspective, as fewer bits are needed to specify the momentum states. But after the excitation, once the system is isolated it trends towards the most probable set of states, shifting bits to the momentum degrees of freedom.

Assume a finite but large discrete set of accessible states and that the trajectory of the system through the microstates is reversible. The macrostate contains myriads of microstates consistent with the requirement that all microstates have the same provisional entropy.

As has been discussed, the algorithmic entropy of the initial state on its own is $H(s_0)$ and the programme $p_t$ shifts $s_0$ to $s_t$ by enacting the physical laws embodied in the atoms and molecules. This reversible trajectory through the microstate can be tracked on the reversible laboratory UTM.

It is not obvious how a microstate in an isolated system can trend to the most probable set of states, increasing the thermodynamic entropy yet leaving the algorithmic entropy unchanged. Two simple models are used to illustrate the principle behind this, before the more general approach is outlined. While bits are conserved as shown in section 8.5.1, the models show how this is consistent with the thermodynamic entropy increase as a highly improbable microstate trends to a disordered microstate belonging to the most probable set. The following points arise.

- While the provisional entropy of each state in the isolated system is the same, the thermodynamic entropy, increases as bits move from specifying programme instructions and stored energy states to specify momentum states. The fewer bits in the momentum degrees of freedom, the further the initial configuration is from the most probable set of states.
- The first example below discusses the ordering of a binary string of length 1000, where 80% of the bits are a 1. However, the microstate specified by 800 1s in a row, is a highly improbable microsate. The bits needed to identify the surprise microstate in the set of possible states has a large contribution from the Shannon $-\log$(probability) term ensuring that bits are conserved, even for these surprise states.

- Another example is where the total energy in the system is constant, but because the stored energy states and the momentum states are not independent, there is mutual information between the stored energy states and the momentum states. The algorithmic entropy of the stored energy states and the momentum states are not additive, as the total number of allowable states is not the product of the number of stored energy states and the momentum states. Recognising of course that, as the volume of the system is assumed fixed, the contribution of the position states to the algorithmic entropy is constant.

- Where bits specify a highly improbable state, fewer bits are available to specify the stored energy and momentum states, as most of the bits are embodied in the programme settings. As outlined below, the bits associated with the probability contribution to the algorithmic entropy are real bits. The energy carrying these bits is stored as instruction bits in the programme states. It is the programme or probability bits that pad out the bits specifying a particular microstate ensuring that all microstates have the same provisional entropy.

### 9.3.1 Simple models illustrating isolated systems

*Specifying a simple string*

An example that illustrates how the strings that appear highly ordered can have the same algorithmic entropy as strings from the most probable set. Consider a binary string of length 1000, which can be envisaged as representing the macrostate of an isolated thermodynamic system. While there are $2^{1000}$ similar strings, we will assume the conservation of energy requires that 80% of the binary characters of the string specifying the system are to be a 1, and 20% are 0. That is, the conservation of energy for our model macrostate requires 800 1's. The Shannon entropy of the set of 80:20 strings, given by $-800(0.8 \log_2 0.8 + 0.2 \log_2 0.2)$, is found to be 722, implying there are $2^{722}$ potential strings satisfying the requirement. From an algorithmic perspective, each can be coded by 722 bits.

However, the simplest string in the set is 800 1's followed by 200 0's, and can be conveniently represented as $1^{800} 0^{200}$. This string, and its reflection $0^{200} 1^{800}$, can be expressed by a much shorter algorithm. The first 800 1's can be coded by about $\log_2(800) = 10$ bits, while the 200 0's can coded by 8 bits. Hence this highly ordered 80:20 string, and its reflection, can be coded with a little more than 18 bits, compared with 722 bits for the typical string.

This example clarifies the difference between the algorithmic minimal sufficient statistics (AMSS) and the provisional entropy approaches. In contrast to the provisional entropy approach of a natural system, the AMSS is not constrained by needing to specify where the bits come from, The AMSS approach asks, 'what is the appropriate set in which the particular string $1^{800} 0^{200}$ is typical? It cannot be typical in the full 800: 200 set as it can be specified with about 18 bits'. However, the provisional entropy approach specifies that a conservation law defining the macrostate applies to all allowed microstates with 800 1's, irrespective if some might seem more ordered. From this perspective all $2^{722}$ strings are equally probable given the requirement of the macrostate.

This raises the paradox that a typical string in the macrostate requires 722 bits to be specified, but the $1^{800}0^{200}$ and its reflection, belong to a set of two strings and only requires $\log_2 2$ bits to identify either of these, given the set.

The 721 extra bits do exist and are needed to specify the class within the macrostate that contains only two strings. This follows, as the probability of finding a string in this highly restricted class is $\log_2 2/2^{722}$. From Shannon's coding theorem, a string in this set requires 721 bits to specify the class and only one extra bit to specify which of the two strings is the string of interest. Equation (9.5) shows that the algorithmic entropy of this particular string in the set of all such strings will be $H(s_{ordered}) = 721 + \log_2 2$. This shows that even a highly improbable microstate is specified by the same number of bits as a microstate in the most probable set.

If the improbable $1^{800}0^{200}$ microstate is created in a system, it will trend to the equilibrium set and, as is demonstrated below, 721 bits must move from the programme states to generate a microstate in the most probable set.

The 721 bits pad out the description of the highly improbable state that can be defined by only 1 bit. The 721 bits also measures how distant the improbable state is from a typical state. If a fluctuation within equilibrium re-generates the highly improbable state, as is shown later, this corresponds to 721 bits being transferred from the momentum states back to the programme states of the system.

### A simple model with stored energy microstates

The above example assumed, in effect, all the energy was in the kinetic states of the system. Where stored energy states occur, the argument is more complex. In order to understand how bits are conserved in a system where stored energy states are allowed, we consider, as an illustration, a model consisting of three atoms.

This illustration helps to explain how the total algorithmic entropy is constant in an isolated system consisting of stored energy states and the momentum states. If $e_i$ is the string specifying all the stored energy or electronic states, and $p_i$ represents the momentum states of a microstate denoted by $\hat{s}_i$,

$$H(\hat{s}_i) = H(e_i, p_i) \leqslant H(e_i) + H(p_i). \tag{9.3}$$

The algorithmic entropy of a total system consisting of a stored energy subsystem and the momentum subsystem is not additive. However, it is shown below, using the simple model that, for a fixed distribution of energy between the electronic states and the momentum states, the two algorithmic contributions are additive. That is, the algorithmic entropy for the class of strings where $k$ units of energy are distributed among the momentum states, is the sum of the electronic and momentum contributions for that class.

Consider a system of three atoms where each atom will have four electronic states; a ground state and three excited states. Hence, 0, 1, 2, 3 units of energy can be stored in each atom. The electronic states of the three-atom-system store, at the most, 9 units of energy.

We will take the initial state to be one where the momentum states are characterised by the initial temperature $T_0$ and the electronic states are fully occupied by excitation with a laser. The energy embodied in the momentum states is $(p_1^2 + p_2^2 + p_3^2)/(2m)$, where $m$ is the mass of each atom. As the discussion here will focus on the energy associated with the momentum degrees of freedom, the initial background state of the three atoms in energy terms is $(0 + p_1^2/(2m), 0 + p_2^2/(2m), 0 + p_2^2/(2m)$, where here the 0 implies no energy has been transferred to the momentum states from the electronic states Once the system is isolated, energy will flow from the excited electronic states to the kinetic energy states corresponding to the momentum degrees of freedom. Once the initial state is formed, the system is isolated. Denoting the three excited electronic states as (3, 3, 3) and the kinetic energy states as (0, 0, 0) where here the background kinetic energy states or momentum states are ignored as their contribution to the algorithmic entropy will be constant through the discussion below. Similarly, the position states will be ignored as the contribution in bits to the total algorithmic entropy is also constant. In which case, the initial configuration will be (3, 3, 3)(0, 0, 0). Here, the first bracket represents the electronic energy in each of the three atoms, and the three zeros indicate no extra energy has yet been passed to the kinetic energy/momentum states of each atom.

As the initial state is a highly improbable in a closed system, over time, the second law of thermodynamics will redistribute the 9 units of energy from the electronic states to the kinetic energy/momentum states by transitions of the form

$$(3, 3, 3)(0, 0, 0) \rightarrow (2, 0, 1)(4, 1, 1),$$

as the system trends to the most probable set of states. It is important to note that while all 9 units of energy can be transferred to the kinetic energy/momentum states of one atom, only a maximum of 3 units of energy is allowed in the electronic state of an individual atom. That is, the configuration (0,0,0)(9,0,0) is allowed but (9,0,0) (0,0,0) is not. For simplicity, if we assume the boundary conditions for the atoms are those of a spherical container, the momentum of each atom is $p = \sqrt{(p_x^2 + p_y^2 + p_z^2)}$. From this viewpoint, the momentum phase space can be divided into spheres rather than into cartesian coordinates. If the energy moved from the stored energy states to the momentum states is $k$ where $k = 1, 2, 3, 4, 5, 6, 7, 8, 9$, the increase in the allowable momentum state lies on the surface of a concentric set of spheres with radii $\sqrt{2km}$. Hence if the kinetic energy state for the three atoms is (4,1,1), the value of the momentum specification for the first atom with $k = 4$ is $2\sqrt{(2m)}$.

By dividing the momentum phase space into radial units, each kinetic energy state aligns with one momentum state, simplifying the accounting of table 9.1 where each allowable microstate of the system is identified. One could increase the resolution by dividing the momentum phase space into increments of a rotation of the momentum vector, but this increases the complexity of the argument.

With this in mind, it is seen that the label $k$, going from 0 to 9, identifies the number of units of energy transferred to the kinetic energy or momentum states. As the table captures the energy distribution between stored energy states and kinetic

**Table 9.1.** Distribution of energy between electronic and kinetic states.

| Count $k$ | Allowable electronic configurations | Number of electronic states | Number of kinetic states | Total number of states |
|---|---|---|---|---|
| 0 | $(3, 3, 3)^1$ | 1 | 1 | 1 |
| 1 | $(3, 3, 2)^3$ | 3 | 3 | 9 |
| 2 | $(3, 2, 2)^3, (3, 3, 1)^3$ | 6 | 6 | 36 |
| 3 | $3, 2, 1)^6, (3, 3, 0)^3, (2, 2, 2)^1$ | 10 | 10 | 100 |
| 4 | $(3, 2, 0)^6, (3, 1, 1)^3, (2, 2, 1)^3$ | 12 | 15 | 180 |
| 5 | $3, 1, 0)^6, (2, 1, 1)^3, (2, 2, 0)^3$ | 12 | 21 | 252 |
| 6 | $(3, 0, 0)^3, (1, 1, 1)^1, (2, 1, 0)^6$ | 10 | 28 | 280 |
| 7 | $(2, 0, 0)^3, (1, 1, 0)^3$ | 6 | 36 | 216 |
| 8 | $1, 1, 0)^3$ | 3 | 45 | 135 |
| 9 | $(0, 0, 0)^1$ | 1 | 55 | 55 |
| Total | | 64 | 220 | 1264 |

energy states, the column identifying the momentum states is labelled by the equivalent kinetic energy. In the table, the notation $(3, 2, 0)^6$ indicates that there are six ways the stored energy states $(3,2,0)$ can be distributed amongst the three atoms.

For example, the table shows that where $k = 0$, there is only one stored energy state denoted by $(3, 3, 3, )$. If one unit of energy is shifted to the kinetic energy states, $k = 1$ and the possible stored energy states are $(2, 3, 3)^3$ and $(1, 0, 0)^3$ for the kinetic energy states. In this case, there are 9 states with $k = 1$. The number of kinetic energy states are simple to calculate as for each $k$, corresponding to $(k + 3 - 1)/(k!2!)$. That is, the number of ways $k$ units of kinetic energy can be arranged amongst the kinetic energy states of the 3 atoms. For each separate value of $k$, the number of electronic states can be found by counting the superscripts in states such as $(3, 2, 0)^6$. In contrast to the kinetic energy states, there is no obvious simple relationship for the number of electronic states, because of the restriction that each atom can carry no more than 3 units of stored energy. The numbers are best established by counting the actual states as outlined above and shown in table 9.1.

This simple model is rich enough to identify the practicalities of the way bits and energy move in an isolated system, and how the thermodynamic entropy increases as the system moves to the most probable set of states.

As we are using the row label $k$ to refer to the class of states where all the momentum states have the same kinetic energy, $e_i^{(k)}$ can be used to denote the string that specifies the $i$th electronic state in row $k$ and similarly $p_i^{(k)}$ is the string that specifies the $i$th momentum state in the row. Also, let $n_e^{(k)}$ be the number of electronic states and $n_p^{(k)}$ be the number of momentum states in class $k$ corresponding to the number of kinetic energy states. The total number of states in row $k$ is $n_e^{(k)} n_p^{(k)}$. But now, in contrast to equation (9.3), where the algorithmic contribution from the electronic and momentum states were not additive, for microstate $i$ in class $k$ the separate entropies are additive. That is, using $\hat{s}_i$ to represent the observed microstate, excluding programme and history states for class $k$,

$$H(\hat{s}_i^{(k)}) = H\left(e_i^{(k)}, p_i^{(k)}\right) = H(e_i^{(k)}) + H\left(p_i^{(k)}\right).$$

Table 9.2 is the extension of table 9.1 allowing the algorithmic entropy to be evaluated from the number of states in each class. For example, for $k = 4$ in the table, the number of electronic states $n_e^{(4)} = 12$ while the number of momentum states $n_p^{(4)} = 15$, giving the total number of states as $12 \times 15 = 180$. Hence for this row, each electronic state, according to Shannon's coding theorem, can be optimally coded by an algorithm of length $H(e_i^{(4)}) = \log_2 n_e^{(4)}$ bits, while the kinetic energy states by one of length $H(p_i^{(4)}) = \log_2 n_p^{(4)}$ bits. While this process determines the algorithmic entropy of string $\hat{s}_i^{(k)}$ to specify a particular string, the number of bits in the algorithm that picks out class $k$, class needs to be included. The probability of a string $P_k$ in class $k$ is the number of strings in the class divided by the total number of strings, i.e. $P_k = n_e^{(k)} n_p^{(k)}/1264$. According to Shannon's coding theorem the number of bits needed to specify class $k = 4$ is $-\log_2 P_4 = \log_2 n_e^{(4)} + \log_2 n_p^{(4)} - \log_2 1264$. Hence for a general $k$, as $\log_2 n_e^{(k)} = H(e_i^{(k)})$ and similarly for the momentum contribution,

$$\log_2 1264 = -\log_2 P_k + \log_2 n_e^{(k)} + \log_2 n_p^{(k)}$$
$$= -\log_2 P_k + H(e_i^{(k)}) + H\left(p_i^{(k)}\right).$$

The above equation shows that the algorithmic entropy of a state in class $k$ is the combination of the algorithmic entropy to specify the electronic state, and that to

**Table 9.2.** The algorithmic entropy for each class in the three-atom model system.

| count $k$ | electronic states | Kinetic states | total numb. states | $-\log_2 P_k$ | $\log_2 n_e^{(k)}$ $H(e_i^{(k)})$ | $\log_2 n_p^{(k)}$ $H(p_i^{(k)})$ |
|---|---|---|---|---|---|---|
| 0 | 1 | 1 | 1 | 10.304 | 0 | 0 |
| 1 | 3 | 3 | 9 | 7.134 | 1.585 | 1.585 |
| 2 | 6 | 6 | 36 | 5.134 | 2.585 | 2.585 |
| 3 | 10 | 10 | 100 | 3.660 | 3.322 | 3.322 |
| 4 | 12 | 15 | 180 | 2.812 | 3.585 | 3.907 |
| 5 | 12 | 21 | 252 | 2.327 | 3.585 | 4.392 |
| 6 | 10 | 28 | 280 | 2.174 | 3.322 | 4.807 |
| 7 | 6 | 36 | 216 | 2.549 | 2.585 | 5.170 |
| 8 | 3 | 45 | 135 | 3.227 | 1.584 | 5.492 |
| 9 | 1 | 55 | 55 | 4.522 | 0 | 5.7813 |
| Total | 64 | 220 | 1264 | | | |

specify the momentum state together with the algorithmic entropy needed to specify the class $k$. However, according to Shannon's coding theorem that, as each microstate is equally likely, with probability 1/1264, each microstate can be generated by a logarithm of the probability of length $\log_2(1/1264) = 10.304$ bits. This is consistent with the above equation and table 9.2 shows the last three terms in the table add to 10.304 bits for each row $k$.

However, rather than rounding the probabilities up for such small numbers, fractional bits are used to illustrate the principle in the table. A further point can be seen in the table. While the most probable set of states occurs when $k = 6$, the set of states $k = 5, 6$ and 7 are nearly as probable and, for that reason, should be included in a wider definition of the most probable set of states. If these are included, the length of the algorithm needed to represent a typical state in the most probable set is 9.5, making 10 bits rounded up. This is getting close to the 11 bits found from rounding up $\log_2 1264 = 10.304$. Of course, once a realistic number of states are included in a system, overwhelmingly most of the states will be in the most probable set, as the distribution with respect to $k$ is sharply peaked. In this case, as has already been discussed, it matters little whether the Shannon $\log_2 \Omega$ term is based on the most probable set, or the total number of states.

All strings in an isolated microstate have the same algorithmic entropy, which is identical to the Shannon entropy of $\log_2 \Omega = \log_2(1264)$. The thermodynamic entropy of the system is $k_B \ln 2 \log_2 \Omega$, showing the entropy per bit is $k_B \ln 2$. For a real system, with myriads of microstates, the algorithmic entropy of a microstate in the most probable set multiplied by $k_B \ln 2$ is the same as the thermodynamic entropy.

However, for a highly ordered, or improbable microstate, where few bits describe the actual configuration, the probability contribution to the bits at level $k$, adds to the algorithmic entropy of $\hat{s}_i^{(k)}$ ensuring all microstates in the isolated system have the same algorithmic entropy. For such strings, identified by a low value of $k$, such as $k = 1$, most of the bits come from $-\log_2 P_k$, which is large, and relatively few bits directly specify the improbable microstate. On the other hand, the contribution of $-\log_2 P_k$ for a string from the most probable set of states is relatively small. Most of the bits are needed to specify or identify a particular string from this large set.

So in summary, by separating the configurational strings into classes, depending on how much of the energy is in the momentum states, the algorithmic entropy that directly specifies the configuration, becomes the sum of the electronic and the momentum entropy contributions for each class plus the algorithmic entropy needed to specify the class. As is discussed in the next section, the contribution that specifies the class is equivalent to the programme bits residing in the system. When the system settles in the most probable set of states where $k$ is a maximum, the probability contribution is relatively small, as only a few programme bits are retained in the system. But these are still needed for reversibility or to step the microstate to another equivalent microstate in the most probable set.

One can say that for the ordered states, the algorithmic entropy represents the potential thermodynamic entropy, but for a microstate in the most probable set of states, the algorithmic entropy becomes realised as thermodynamic entropy.

### 9.3.2 General approach to specifying all states in an isolated system

The previous section gave two simple examples to show how the algorithmic entropy is related to the thermodynamic entropy in an isolated system. As was shown, when a system exists in an improbable configuration, what might be termed a fluctuation outside the most probable equilibrium set of microstates, the thermodynamic entropy is said to increase as the system trends to equilibrium. Here, the simple example in table 9.2 is generalised to provide a consistent understanding of what happens as the fluctuation trends to the most probable set of states. Even when the microstate moves from an ordered configuration to a disordered one in an isolated system, the algorithmic entropy does not change while the thermodynamic entropy does. Rather, as is shown below, bits specifying programme and stored energy states, become bits specifying the momentum degrees of freedom.

The discussion here follows [4] but rather than using the ratio of the bits in the stored energy states and the momentum states, the integer $k$ will be used. This is a simpler label that identifies the number of energy units that have transferred from stored energy states to the momentum states for different energy distributions. In which case, the transfer of bits between momentum degrees of freedom and stored energy degrees of freedom can be understood by defining the observed microstate $i$ as in equation (9.2) by the string $\hat{s}_i = e_i, p_i$, where $e_i$ represents the stored energy states, and $p_i$ the momentum states. Here, as the volume is assumed fixed, the bits needed to specify the positions of each atom can be ignored. But, as is discussed above, equation (9.3) reproduced below indicates that in general, the number of stored energy bits and momentum bits are not additive.

$$H(\hat{s}_i) = H(e_i, p_i) \leqslant H(e_i) + H(p_i)). \tag{9.4}$$

Rather

$$H(e_i, p_i) = H(e_i) + H(p_i | e_i^*).$$

But as the example above in table 9.2 showed, when the label $k$, representing the number of bits transferred to the momentum states, is used to categorise a class, or subset, of the microstates of the system, the bits are additive for that class. The total number of states in the class $k$ with the same distribution of energy between the stored energy states and the momentum states, is $n_e^{(k)} n_p^{(k)}$. As a consequence, for the category $k$, the stored energy and the momentum algorithmic entropies are separable and additive, i.e.

$$H(\hat{s}_i^{(k)}) = H\left(e_i^{(k)}, p_i^{(k)}\right) = H(e_i^{(k)}) + H\left(p_i^{(k)}\right).$$

If the probability of finding a particular string in the $k^{th}$ class is denoted by $P_k$, $H(P_k) = -\log_2 P_k$ bits are needed to identify class $k$ from Shannon's coding theorem.

For a typical state in the overwhelmingly most probable set of states, $P_k$ is close to 1, and $H(P_k)$ is small. However, this is only small relative to the number of bits neded to specify $s_{\text{typical}}$.

But in contrast, where the state corresponds to $k = 0$, $P_{k=0}$ is extremely low and $H(p_{k=0}) = -\log_2 P_{k=0}$ is large. In this case, most of the bits are captured in the probability term and not the specification of the highly improbable microstate. The extremely low contribution to the algorithmic entropy of $e_i$ and $p_i$ is compensated for by the massive number of bits needed to specify the probability term. The total contribution including the probability term ensures that the full algorithmic entropy of each state, irrespective of the class is the same, as demonstrated by the simple example in table 9.2. The following details the argument.

Let $n_e^{(k)}$ be the number of stored energy substrings, and $n_p^{(k)}$ be the number of momentum substrings in the class $k$. The total number of strings with the fixed energy in $k$ is $n_e^{(k)} n_p^{(k)}$. All combined strings in the subset are equally likely, and the probability of selecting a particular string, given the subset $k$, is $1/(n_e^{(k)} n_p^{(k)})$. The overall probability of this particular string in the full set is this probability given the set $k$, multiplied the probability of the $k^{\text{th}}$ subset in the full set. That is, if $\mathcal{P}_k(i)$ is taken to be the overall probability of selecting string $s_i$ within $k$, out of all possible microstates, including the most probable set, then $\mathcal{P}_k(i) = P_k/(n_e^{(k)} n_p^{(k)})$. It should be noted that $\mathcal{P}_k(i) = 1/N_t$ for all $k$ where $N_t$ is the total number of strings in the macrostate.

From Shannon's coding theorem, the algorithmic entropy, of a string $s_i^{(k)}$ from the set $k$, denoted by $H(s_i^{(k)})$, is within one bit of $-\log_2 \mathcal{P}_k(i)$ [2]. Hence, inequality (9.4) can be replaced by the more useful equation, which shows that the algorithmic entropy of the electronic and momentum states are separable for each probability class $k$:

$$H(s_i^{(k)}) = -\log_2 \mathcal{P}_k(i) = -\log_2 P_k + \log_2 n_e^{(k)} + \log_2 n_p^{(k)}$$

As $H(e_i^{(k)}) = \log_2 n_e^{(k)}$ and $H(p_i^{(k)}) = \log_2 n_p^{(k)}$ for all $i$ in $k$ and letting $H(P_k) = -\log_2 P_k$, it follows that;

$$H(s_i^{(k)}) = H(P_k) + H(e_i^{(k)}) + H\left(p_i^{(k)}\right) = H(P_k) + H\left(e_i^{(k)}, p_i^{(k)}\right). \tag{9.5}$$

This shows, as stated earlier, that the algorithmic entropies can be separated for each contribution in class $k$ and the contribution of the probability term pads out the total algorithmic entropy to ensure all microstates in the microstate have the same value. Improbable microstates just have a larger $-\log_2 P_k$ term.

As all microstates have the same algorithmic entropy, and a microstate in the most probable set of states is labelled 'typical', that is around the maximum value of $k$,

$$H(s)) = H(s_{\text{typical}}).$$

For a microstate in the most probable set of states, $H(P_{k=\text{typical}})$ is negligible compared with the bits needed to specify $e_{(\text{typical})}$, $p_{(\text{typical})})$ and ignoring the small $H(P_{\text{typical}})$ the algorithmic entropy of a typical string is,

$$H(s_{\text{typical}}) = H(e_{\text{typical}}) + H(p_{\text{typical}}). \tag{9.6}$$

In the set of all possible configurations, the typical configuration is algorithmically random relative to a low probability configuration.

*The probability bits can be identified as programme bits*
The previous analysis can be seen from another perspective. Given the characteristics of the isolated macrostate, and given the initial highly ordered microstate with $k = 0$, as illustrated in table 9.2, the programme $p_{k=0}$ enacting physical laws, drives the system's trajectory towards an increasing value of $k$. This leads to a corresponding increase in the combined algorithmic entropy of the stored energy and momentum states. Ultimately, the system settles in the most probable set of states for most of the time. Where the initial state is $\hat{s}_{k=0}$, the computation on a UTM $U$ corresponds to

$$U(p_{k=0}\hat{s}_{k=0}) = H(s_i^{(k)}) = \hat{s}_i^{(k)}, g_i^{(k)}.$$

Here string $i$ belongs to class $k$, while $g_i^{(k)}$ represents residual programme bits in the system that can either reverse the computation to regenerate the initial state, or take the system through to another state in the trajectory. Here, we make a clear distinction between programme states in $g$ and the observed microstate of the system $\hat{s}_i^{(k)}$. The overall trend is the most probable set of states. This implies, as outlined above, that

$$H(p_{k=0} \cdot \hat{s}_{k=0}) = H\left(\hat{s}_i^k, g_i^{(k)}\right)$$

and as

$$H(\hat{s}_i^k, g_i^{(k)}) = H(P_k) + H\left(e_i^{(k)}, p_i^{(k)}\right),$$

from equation (9.5). As we have shifted all non-programme bits to $s_i^{(k)}$ to represent the momentum and stored energy states, we can identify

$$H(\hat{s}_i(k)) + H\left(g_i^{(k)}\right) = H\left(e_i^{(k)}, p_i^{(k)}\right) + H(P_k)$$

Similarly,

$$H(p_{k=0}, \hat{s}_{k=0}) = H(P_{k=0}) + H(\hat{s}_{k=0}) = H(P_k) + H\left(e_i^{(k)}, p_i^{(k)}\right).$$

The number of bits in the reversible programme state is the same as the number in the log-probability term for a particular $k$ value. This ought to be so, as $-\log_2 P_k$ derived from Shannon's coding theorem must satisfy the converse of the Kraft inequality (the Kraft–McMillan inequality) which implies that a set of code-words (or instructions) can be found of the same length as the Shannon code length. As the system trends towards the most probable set of states, these residual programme bits, align with the probability bits and pad out the full algorithmic entropy for each microstate, ensuring all states have the same algorithmic entropy. Again it can be seen for a typical microstate in the most probable set of states the contribution of the residual programme bits will be extremely small.

*Degree of order*
For a string in class $k$, $H(P_k)$ bits need to be added to the specification of the string $e_i^{(k)}$, $p_i^{(k)}$, to create a typical configuration. $H(P_k)$ is a measure of the distance that the configuration of interest is from a typical state in the equilibrium set or random one. Hence, we can define the degree of order, i.e. $D_{\text{ord}}(s_i^{(k)})$ as the number of bits that need to be shifted from the stored energy states in a highly improbable configuration in class $k$, to the momentum states to generate a typical state.

$$D_{\text{ord}}(s_i^{(k)}) = H(P_k) = H(s_{\text{typical}}) - (H(e_i^{(k)}) + H(p_i^{(k)}) = \log_2\Omega - H(e_i^{(k)}, p_i^{(k)})$$

This follows, as $H(s_{\text{typical})}$ aligns with the logarithm of the number of states, irrespective of whether the number of states is taken to be all the states, or only the typical states.

This shows that when a microstate, corresponding to a fluctuation with probability $P_k$ subsequently returns to a microstate in the most probable set, $H(P_k)$ bits are transferred back to the momentum states increasing thermodynamic entropy by $k_B \ln 2H(P_k)$.

*The entropy of the Universe*
The above discussion helps to clarify any discussion on whether the entropy of the Universe is increasing from an algorithmic point of view. The inflation of the Universe implies the algorithmic entropy is increasing as space bits enter the system. However, if these space bits are generated by fundamental forces, or fields, already in the system, the total bits may be conserved. In which case, the Universe is isolated and is trending towards the most probable set of states, which is epitomised in the phrase 'the heat death of the Universe'. But if this is so, there is no increase in algorithmic entropy, rather programme bits specifying natural laws are being passed into the thermal states.

Nevertheless, it could be that the Universe is not isolated, and is coupled to an external system that is injecting (or removing) bits from the Universe. The Intelligent Design community would argue that this is so, or rather, they would claim 'information' is entering the Universe. Note however that the term 'information', as used by this community, refers to non-randomness or order and is actually the converse of the information defined in this book. It is order, or non-randomness that is assumed to enter into the Universe, as discussed in Devine [5]. The Devine paper argues that there is no evidence that this so-called information is necessary to explain the formation of complex living organisms. The Devine paper also points out that the claim by Dembski [6, 7] that a fourth law of thermodynamics, 'The law of conservation of information', is needed to argue that information cannot increase by natural process, is just the second law in disguise. The claim in effect is that algorithmic entropy cannot decrease. Despite this, at the grand scale, there may be coupling to systems outside the observable universe, increasing or decreasing the bits inside. Nevertheless, the bits in the greater total observable system would be expected to be conserved under the classical perspective.

*Are the programme bits real entities?*
At this point the reader (as did the author) might ask where are the programme bits in the programme $p_t$ that shift one state to another? While a simulation on a laboratory UTM needs to identify these bits, do they actually exist, or are they an artefact of the observer? The following has convinced the author that they do exist in a reversible system as physical entities with associated energy. This is because the bits and the structures that implement the programme can be re-constituted from the residual programme bits in a microstate in the most probable set of states. This can best be seen by considering a microstate $\hat{s}_{typical}$ of an isolated system that belongs to the most probable set of states. The bits specifying $\hat{s}_{typical}$ will primarily be momentum and position bits. The residual programme required for reversibility is then $g_{typical}$. However, $g_{typical}$, with the state settings in $\hat{s}_{typical}$ as an input, have all the characteristics of a primitive UTM that can simulate any other. In this case, the reverse programme re-constitutes both the original structures and the original state. That is, $g_{typical}$ and $\hat{s}_{typical}$ can undertake a real computation that outputs a high-level composite computational structure corresponding to the original initial state $(p, s_0)$ of the system. In which case, the bits and energy in the original state are conserved becoming bits and energy in the structures so formed. As a consequence, the high-level structures that implement $(p_t, s_0)$ in the real-world have the same number of bits and energy as the primitive instructions and gates existing in the a typical state in the most probable set of states. The bits do not disappear when energy and bits are packaged into a structural unit that implements a high-level computation. That is, the composite structure can always be specified in terms of the universal computing capability of the combined residual programme bits and microstate bits in a most probable configuration.

*The shortest computational path*
A critical question is whether the shortest algorithm to specify a particular real-world microstate is the one that reaches the microstate by a reversible trajectory, or is there a possible shorter algorithm.

Consider first the situation where a reversible UTM $U$ undertakes the computation $U(p_h, s_0) = \hat{s}_h, g$. The reversible trajectory to give $s_h$ or $(\hat{s}_h, g)$ is the shortest, as there can be no other path to this state. Hence $H(p_h s_0) = H(\hat{s}_h, g)$. But is there a shorter description of $\hat{s}_h$ which bypasses the need to generate the history or residual programme bits $g$? That is $H(\hat{s}_h) < H(p_h, s_0)$? The paragraph below shows that the reversible trajectory algorithm that generates each halt state provides the shortest algorithmic description provided all bits are tracked and discarded bits accounted for.

Consider the trajectory that emerges when hydrogen and oxygen are ignited. While the most probable set of states consists of water and heat, a rare unstable fluctuation could produce mainly ice, but as the temperature must rise, an ice state might only exist momentarily. The appearance of ice does not imply a shorter description of the more ordered state, as any shorter description of the ice requires a compensating longer description of the momentum degrees of freedom and residual programme bits as history. This indicates one cannot ignore the bits in the momentum degrees of freedom. However, if sufficient heat bits leave the system, what the observer might think of as a random fluctuation, now becomes part of a new set of the most probable states. If the residual bits in the ice system from this new most probable set are used to drive the system backwards in time, the initial state will be different from the original initial state of hydrogen and oxygen, and will be at a lower temperature. It will then have a shorter description as bits have been removed.

In essence, while there may be rare shorter algorithms that generate $\hat{s}_h$, these must be irreversible and for that reason do not adequately specify the state of a natural system.

A further point needs to be noted. Where a catalyst provides an alternative reversible trajectory, as more programme steps are required, the history of the process $g'$ will be greater. In this case, the appropriate $H(\hat{s}_h, g')$ will be greater than $H(\hat{s}_h, g)$. While the computation with the catalyst will still be reversible, the algorithm that generates both $\hat{s}_h$ and the new history string, $g'$, will be longer than the original algorithm that generates $\hat{s}_h$ without the catalyst as the system plus catalyst is larger. Even though the catalyst must be part of the initial state or initial programme, it is regenerated at the end of the process and can be ejected at the completion of the computation indicating there is no net entropy increase because of the actions of the catalyst. The algorithmic entropy must correspond to the measure extracted from the shortest path to generate $\hat{s}_h$ and then halt, not the most efficient path in a time sense. Once it is understood that the bits in a specific microstate are independent of the path taken to get to the microstate as was discussed earlier, it all makes sense.

### *Is the algorithm that tracks a replicating trajectory shorter than a copying algorithm?*

A tree can be defined at an instant of time from a replicating algorithm that generates each cell in the tree from the DNA instructions in the seed, while accessing external resources during each step of the growth process. At the specific instant, the algorithm halts. This happens either because the observer defines the halt requirement, or because a natural event terminates the growth algorithm. But can a tree be defined by a shorter algorithm that just copies each cell and its variations and places each in the correct position to build the tree? Again, it has been shown that the difference in bits between the final state and the initial state are independent of the path if all bits are accounted for. Provided bits are properly accounted for, the growth trajectory will be the shortest possible.

But replication processes are efficient in an algorithmic sense. A copying algorithm needs to specify in detail each cell, including its variations and its placement. This is unnecessary for replicating algorithm because the replicating algorithm in the genetic code, calls different switches depending on the environment of neighbouring cells and external inputs (such as the availability of water and light) to determine how the genes are expressed in the cells in different parts of the tree. Different cell variations, and even the position of each cell, are determined by the rules of growth arising from the computing software, and do not need to be separately specified. It is the different switches that distinguish a leaf cell from, say, one in the root system whereas a copying algorithm may not be as efficient in specifying variation of cell types. While the replicating algorithm discards bits in products such as carbon dioxide, water and heat, these are actually part of the computational history bits needed for reversibility. So while the copying algorithm can ignore these by-products, like carbon dioxide, there is significant mutual information between the DNA generating programme and these products.

In principle a growing tree is a reversible system, but waste bits exit the system throughout the growth process. As the waste bits drift away reversibility becomes highly unlikely in the life of the Universe. This leads to the conclusion that, building variation or diversity into structures in a system, increases the algorithmic entropy. But from the previous argument, it would appear to be algorithmically more efficient to generate any variation through the software (e.g. variation in DNA) rather than independently specifying a variation of the object itself at the structural level, as in the tree example. As Devine [3] has pointed out, it is plausible to conjecture that building the variation as switches to be interrogated by the software, decreases the entropy in a way that tends to compensate for the entropy cost of building diversity into near identical structures. With these understandings it becomes possible to track algorithmic entropy flows and therefore thermodynamic entropy flows in real systems, as will be discussed in section 10.9.

## References

[1] Esposito M and Van den Broeck C 2011 Second law and Landauer principle far from equilibrium *Europhys. Lett.* **95** 40004
[2] Zurek W H 1989 Algorithmic randomness and physical entropy *Phys. Rev.* A **40** 4731–51
[3] Devine S D 2009 The insights of algorithmic entropy *Entropy* **11** 85–110
[4] Devine S 2018 Algorithmic entropy and Landauer's principle link microscopic system behaviour to the thermodynamic entropy *Entropy* **20** 798
[5] Devine S D 2014 An algorithmic information theory challenge to intelligent design *Zygon* **49** 42–65
[6] Dembski W A 2002 *No Free Lunch: Why Specified Complexity Cannot Be Purchased Without Intelligence* (Lanham, MD: Rowman & Littlefield)
[7] Dembski W A 2002 *Intelligent design as a theory of information* (http://www.arn.org/docs/dembski/wd_idtheory.htm)

**IOP** Publishing

# Algorithmic Information Theory for Physicists and Natural Scientists

Sean D Devine

# Chapter 10

## How replication processes maintain a system far from the most probable set of states

It is shown how replication processes, as illustrated by a single bacterium in a supply of nutrients, reproduces itself by natural processes until the carrying capacity is reached and thereafter, maintains itself distant from the most probable set of states. Such a system is maintained in a homeostatic state against death and decay by continual replication. Once the resources are turned off, the system reverts back to the most probable set of states of decayed bacteria and degraded chemical species.

Replication systems, like the bacterial system are able to restore a system autonomously without external cognitive interventions. As death and decay drive the state of the system towards the most probable set, homeostasis is only maintained when energy, carrying computational bits in the form of species such as photons atoms and molecules etc, enter the system while degraded species and heat leaves. In which case, the system moves from one microstate in the viable or homeostatic region to another ejecting high entropy waste and replacing species and bits into the system. The net change in bits and energy in a replicating homeostatic system is zero.

An ecology, as a coupled and nested replicating system, is more ordered than a single species replicating system. Such interconnected systems are more resilient as fewer resource bits are needed to sustain the whole system and, the structures that are ejected from the system are more degraded. It is suggested that life is more efficient in maintaining the system further from the most probable set of states than no life, but at the cost of needing to pump out more waste. The concept of Chaitin's degree of organisation (section 10.9.1.2) is used to illustrate how variation increases the algorithmic entropy, but creates a greater capacity to survive

## 10.1 Maintaining a system distant from the equilibrium

This chapter uses algorithmic information theory to highlight the importance of replication processes in creating and maintaining a living system distant from equilibrium defined as the most probable set of states. The archetype of such a replication process, as is discussed in this section in detail, is the growth of a single bacterium in a supply of nutrients. When replicating systems are coupled, sharing resources or feeding off each other, the coupled system becomes further from equilibrium. This is because the resources, from an entropy perspective are used more effectively before degrading. The algorithmic approach looks at how replicating systems grow and how they are maintained, in terms of the computational bits that are carried into the system as stored energy, and the bits ejected as high entropy waste.

As some readers may wish to start with this chapter, relevant algorithmic information theory concepts are described briefly in the next section. If readers need more information they can refer to the earlier chapters,

### 10.1.1 Brief summary of the earlier exposition of AIT

Section 1.4 points out that $H$, the measure of the information content of a system is the algorithmic entropy measured in computational bits. The algorithmic entropy is defined as the length of the shortest, appropriately coded algorithm that generates a particular string on a universal Turing machine (UTM). This is possible as the physical laws driving a system from one state to another, are in effect computations on a real-world UTM. As algorithmic entropy differences are independent of the UTM used, the algorithmic entropy obtained from a computation on a laboratory UTM that exactly maps the real-world process, measures the same number of bits as the computation in the real-world. The flow of bits or information through the two computational systems are the same.

The provisional algorithmic entropy is the algorithmic measure that specifies a particular real-world configuration by specifying the structure of a system in terms of the requirements of the thermodynamic macrostate and then given the structure the particular microstate that is a variation of the structure. An illustration of the approach is to envisage a noisy image on a screen of black and white pixels. The structural information corresponding to a thermodynamic macrostate is the information that specifies the image, and given the image, the algorithm that then specifies the particular noisy variation of interest can be found.

However, there is a difference between the algorithmic approach and that of conventional thermodynamics. The provisional algorithmic entropy is the number of bits specifying the actual microstate, whereas the traditional entropies return a value for a thermodynamic macrostate, corresponding to myriads of microstates. But this is no different from assigning energy to a macrostate, while recognising that the energy is actually embodied in the particular microstate at an instant of time. In earlier chapters it has been shown that the number of bits defining the algorithmic entropy of a microstate in an isolated system is directly related to the thermodynamic entropy. The algorithmic entropy can provide insights into the natural world processes, as outlined in section 2.1 as, allowing for units, the provisional algorithmic entropy of a typical microstate in an equilibrium macrostate (outlined in chapter 4) corresponds to the thermodynamic entropy. Once this is recognised, one can easily move between the algorithmic measure and the conventional entropy description. This allows the provisional entropy to be used to track entropy changes and flows as the system evolves over time.

The use of the term 'equilibrium" needs to be clarified. In this book the terms 'the most probable set of states' or 'the equilibrium set of states' is preferred. When the system settles in the most probable set of states it is stable for a long period of time and corresponds to what is often called a local equilibrium. However, given sufficient time the system will degrade further to a new set of states known as the global equilibrium set of states. For example, if light from the Sun is blocked from reaching a forest, given sufficient time, the forest and its ecology will be reduced to the most probable set or the local equilibrium set of states consisting of mainly carbon dioxide, water, and minerals. Here, the discussion will focus on the most probable set of states, which corresponds to what is normally considered a local equilibrium.

The algorithmic approach provides a measure of the distance a natural system is from the most probable set of states where most of the bits are carried in the energy that specifies the momentum states and the temperature is a maximum. Where however, the bits are carried in the energy that specifies programme instructions implementing natural laws, and/or the stored energy states, the instantaneous microstate is distant from this equilibrium set. Such a microstate is said to be ordered, as it is highly improbable relative to the typical microstate in the most probable set of states. Once a system in an ordered microstate trends to the most probable set under the second law of thermodynamics, bits specifying the programme and stored energy components of the microstate are transferred to bits specifying the momentum states. The number of bits transferred to achieve this represents the degree of order of the initial state.

A highly ordered and therefore improbable microstate $\hat{s}$ of a system, can be defined with $H(\hat{s})$ bits, whereas a typical microstate in the most probable set requires $\log_2\Omega$ bits to be defined. Here, as discussed in section 8.6, $\Omega$ is the total number of available states. As outlined in section 9.3.2, the distance from equilibrium, or degree of order denoted by $D_{ord}$, is given by $D_{ord} = \log_2\Omega - H(\hat{s})$ bits. The degree of order is closely related to Kolmogorov's deficiency in randomness, except that the deficiency in randomness takes the size of the string representing $\hat{s}$ as given. The equivalent in algorithmic entropy terms would be to replace $H(\hat{s})$ by $H(\hat{s}||\hat{s}|)$.

A system can only be maintained distant from the equilibrium set of states if bits carrying stored energy flow into the system to reconstitute decaying structures, and heat and waste bits from the decayed structures are ejected to ensure bits do not accumulate in the system. When states are changed, the change in algorithmic entropy found by tracking the flow of computational bits into and out of the system, can be related to thermodynamic entropy flows by Landauer's principle [1] discussed in chapter 8. Landauer's principle states that, where one bit of information in a computational machine operating at a temperature $T$ is erased, at least $k_BT\ln 2$

Joules must be dissipated (see section 8.3). In a conventional computer this dissipation appears as heat passing to the non-computational parts of the system. As a consequence, where the length of the algorithmic description of the state of a real-world system changes because $\Delta H$ bits are reversibly removed, the corresponding thermodynamic entropy change is $k_B \ln 2\Delta H$.

The above points provide a basis for understanding how a natural system can maintain itself distant from the equilibrium set by natural processes. Not only can the provisional algorithmic entropy quantify the order embodied in a microstate of the system in terms of the number of bits needed to specify it, as the provisional entropy specifies the macrostate of a system, it also identifies the constraints on the system. The following sections explore the processes of degradation, and the requirements to re-generate the initial states for three natural systems. These are, the degradation by heat diffusion in a gas, the dissipation of energy in a photodiode, and the ignition of a hydrogen–oxygen system to form a chemical equilibrium with water (or steam). But first the degradation of a natural system is explored.

### 10.1.1.1 Degradation of natural systems

As a living system operates far from the local equilibrium set of states, it faces real-time degradation that drives the system to a microstate in the most probable set of states set under the relentless operation of the second law of thermodynamics (see chapter 9). In thermodynamic terms, the second law ensures that the entropy in such a system increases as the stored energy embodied in ordered structures becomes more dispersed and becomes unavailable to do work[1]. A living system must have in-built mechanisms to maintain itself in a so-called far-from-equilibrium configuration distant from the most probable set of states, by offsetting the degradation of the second law of thermodynamics. The mechanisms involve the ejection of disorder and the injection of high grade or stored energy into the system that carries the computational capability to create ordered structures. It is when these natural computation processes, operating under physical laws eject disorder that more ordered or low entropy structures are left behind. One can perhaps see this as a regulation process where the cost of maintenance is the cost of restoring the system to an initial macrostate.

The entropy changes of both living and non-living natural systems are constrained by the same laws. The later section 10.4 provides the general criteria for any system to be maintained distant from the equilibrium set. However, most systems, like the three inert systems described in this section, can only maintain themselves in the initial set of configurations under special circumstances. They cannot self-regulate, as to do so would require an autonomous process to replace the lost information. An inert earth (without life) will reach a steady state where the surface temperature is such that the radiation from the Sun exactly balances the heat radiation from the Earth. The inert earth, as a system, is broadly analogous to the

---

[1] Fortunately for life, the rate at which second law processes drive the system towards the most probable set of states, is constrained by rates involved in natural processes and barriers such as the chemical activation energy.

photodiode system. Both the Earth and the photodiode system are stable when the input and output energies balance. But this is not true regulation.

In contrast, the inert system with a living cell can autonomously maintain itself far from the most probable set of states. The cell does this by accessing stored energy species as nutrients and ejecting disorder as waste. As has been mentioned, Landauer's principle [1] showed that the thermodynamic cost of maintaining a non-equilibrium system in a homeostatic state requires the lost information in bits to be replaced, and excess bits that have entered the system to be ejected. Much of the self-organising capability of life on earth, or of a system of cells, would seem to be a consequence of the evolution of replicating structures. Replication processes provide a natural mechanism for true regulation, in contrast to the stable inert system. Section 10.3 deals with some conceptual issues around the reversibility of natural laws, while section 10.7.1 shows that, in contrast to inert systems, replication processes can naturally create and maintain a homeostatic configuration in structures far-from-equilibrium, i.e. far from the most probable set of states. This allows one to apply the entropy and energy requirements of the process of replication to very simple systems and carry the initial insights over to biologically more complex living systems.

## 10.2 Examples of the computational issues around the degradation of simple systems

There are some conceptual issues that need to be resolved to avoid confusion over the meaning of order and where order comes from. The following three simple representative thought experiments help to clarify the computational issues behind the processes that maintain a system distant from the most probable set of states under the influence of the second law of thermodynamics, as was discussed in chapter 9. The first and simplest example is where heat is removed from the system making the system more ordered. In a sense order is imported from the external environment. The second looks at maintaining a photodiode in an excited state, while the third looks at maintaining a hydrogen–oxygen mixture away from the most probable set. The last two examples describe systems which start in a configuration where the energy is stored in the form of high grade energy, but which later is redistributed throughout the system.

- Consider a gas in a container existing in an instantaneous configuration distant from the equilibrium set where a region of the gas is at a higher temperature than the bulk of the gas. The difference in temperature between the two regions creates an energy gradient and the second law will drive the system towards a uniform temperature. From an overall system perspective, while the specification of the initial configuration shows it is ordered relative to the final configuration, if the system is isolated, nothing has left the system and strictly the thermodynamic entropy is unchanged. Collisions between gas particles enact natural computations, diffusing the energy throughout the system and driving the system to the most probable set of states. If a region of the system is to be permanently hotter than the bulk, heat would need to be removed once the energy disperses, and compensating heat would need to be introduced, perhaps by radiation, to maintain the high temperature region of the gas.

- The second example of degradation is a photodiode where, initially, the electrons have been excited from the valence band to the conduction band. The macrostate of the system is defined by the set of microstates consisting of the excited electronic states, the vibrational states and other states of the system. The excitation produces a potential difference between the conduction and valence band that can, in principle, be used to heat the system either directly (through collision processes as the electrons return to the valence band), or indirectly by heating a resistor, which is part of the system and is connected to the photodiode. The photodiode system can also do work if the potential difference generated by the excitation is used to drive an electric motor which might also be within the system. Whether by doing mechanical work that dissipates heat, or producing heat directly without work, if left to itself the system will settle in the most probable set of states where most electrons return to the valence band increasing the temperature. Stored energy bits, specifying states in the conduction band, and programme bits specifying computational instructions, diffuse through the system to increase the bits in the momentum degrees of freedom and hence the temperature. In principle, the photodiode can be maintained away from the most probable equilibrium set by a flux of photons that continuously repopulate the conduction band, provided that the excess heat generated by the process is removed by passing heat to the environment.

- The third representative case is where a stoichiometric mixture of hydrogen and oxygen burns to form either liquid water or steam, depending on the initial temperature and pressure. After ignition, the system moves from the initial configuration and will settle in chemical equilibrium where

$$O_2 + 2H_2 \rightleftharpoons 2H_2O + \text{heat}.$$

A typical state in the chemical equilibrium belongs to the most probable set of states. In this situation, if the system is isolated, most of the hydrogen and oxygen will have been converted to $H_2O$, and the temperature will increase as stored energy is released to form water and heat. However, this process is reversible and, in itself, does not generate order. While still being part of the chemical equilibrium, given sufficient time, the microstate of the system will fluctuate away from the most probable set of states, or even recycle to the initial state. *Only when heat is lost* is it possible for the remaining system to become more ordered. The initial set of states can be maintained only if heat is expelled and external energy used to re-generate hydrogen and oxygen by, for example, electrolysing the water. This is unlikely to happen naturally.

If an isolated system is initially in a configuration distant from the most probable set of states, the second law of thermodynamics diffuses the energy through the system increasing the temperature driving the system to the most probable set of states. Ordering can only occur when the disorder is ejected as waste species, or as heat, leaving a more ordered structure behind. The critical factor is that diffusing energy through the system increases the temperature, creating a situation where excess entropy can pass to the environment. In the case of the photodiode and the hydrogen–oxygen system, high grade energy needs to be used to recreate the initial state. Maintaining a system off the equilibrium set, corresponds to maintaining an entropy gradient between the system and the equilibrium set of states. The physical laws that determine the trajectory of a real-world system through state space can be envisaged as the result of a computational process operating under algorithms embodied in these laws, as has been discussed in detail in section 9.3. As the thermodynamic cost of replacing the lost information becomes the cost of maintaining the system away from the equilibrium set, AIT provides a tool to enquire into the emergence and maintenance of order in these real-world systems.

## 10.3 Entropy balances in a reversible system

This section discusses the situation where a reversible isolated system moves from an apparently ordered state to a more disordered state, as outlined in chapter 9. However, there seems to be a paradox as the entropy cannot increase in an isolated system. Section 8.5.1 showed that the apparent increase in algorithmic entropy as the system moves from an improbable or ordered microstate, to a microstate in the most probable set, comes from the initial bit settings in the programme state with its halt setting. Strictly, the true initial state is $(p_h^*, s_0)$. This includes the observed initial state $s_0$ and the specification of the programme $p_h^*$ embodied in the real-world computational structures. Furthermore, if both sets of bits are tracked there is no entropy change for an isolated system. As was discussed in section 9.3, one can say that an ordered configuration is one that is distant from the equilibrium set, as most of the bits no longer specify momentum states.

Once the bit settings of the programme, $p_h$ that drive the system to the halt state are considered as part of the initial configuration, it is seen that $H(p_h, s_0) = H(s_h, \zeta)$, where $H(s_h, \zeta)$ is the entropy of the halt configuration including the history of the computation $\zeta$ that is needed to maintain reversibility. This understanding is implicit in the discussion by Zurek [2] and Bennett [3, 4]. Here, the notation $\zeta$ is used for the history information, rather than the measure $g$ in section 8.5.1, as here the history is not considered as garbage, but as being critical to the way the system evolves. If, however, all the information is accounted for in a reversible process, an equals sign is appropriate in equation (3.21) as there can be no entropy change. Reversibility is only lost when information corresponding to the history $\zeta$ is lost. This happens when excess heat is ejected from the system. In which case, the system's entropy decreases as the disorder in the momentum states is reduced.

The equivalent of equation (8.1) for the reversible situation where all entropy changes are tracked, then becomes

$$H(s_h, \zeta) = H(s_0) + H(s_h, \zeta|s_0^*). \tag{10.1}$$

This point is used to describe the entropy requirements of a homeostasis next in section 10.4.

For example, as is discussed in more detail earlier, there is no entropy change to the total system and, in principle, the system could revert back to the original state.

## 10.4 Homeostasis and second law evolution

As outlined previously in section 8.6, Zurek [5] has shown that where a system changes from the initial state $i$ to the output state $o$ by an external disturbance, corresponding to a change of $H(i) - H(o)$ bits, the loss or gain in bits needs to be reversed by a regulation or restoration process acting from *outside* the system.

In contrast, this section looks at the requirements for the restoration process to operate from within the system to maintain it distant from the equilibrium set of states. Such autonomous regulation is essential for a natural living system to be maintained in a viable region. The argument here is that autonomous regulation is not a fortuitous outcome of complex interactions of natural laws but, at least in simple cases, and perhaps in most cases, is accomplished by replication processes [6].

Before looking at replication processes as such, the thermodynamic information requirements for a system to maintain homeostasis are outlined.

### 10.4.1 Information requirements of homeostasis

As the provisional algorithmic entropy defines the common entropy of each microstate in a set of microstates with the same characteristics, the formalism can be used to determine the algorithmic processes that maintain a real-world system in a homeostatic state distant from the equilibrium set of states. Such a system is maintained in a stable region of the state space by the inflow of information and the outflow of waste while keeping the number of bits in the system constant. Two issues arise:

- how can such a homeostatic macrostate be sustained by a natural process when the second law of thermodynamics is driving the system to what is commonly termed equilibrium, i.e. the set of most probable microstates?
- what is the algorithmic entropy of a microstate in a homeostatic system distant from the equilibrium set of states?

The arguments in these sections follow Devine [6]. Homeostasis implies that the system's provisional entropy must not change, and therefore the system must be maintained by a regulation process in an attractor defining a viable macrostate. Section 4.2 showed the provisional entropy of a microstate consists of the algorithmic equivalent of the Shannon entropy of the set of all states, and a term that defines the structure common to all the microstates in the set. Furthermore, allowing for units, the thermodynamic entropy of the macrostate returns the same value as the provisional algorithmic entropy of any microstate $\epsilon_i$ in the macrostate. As a consequence, changes in the provisional entropy can be used to track the entropy flows in and out of the system.

In order to see how a stable, or homeostatic state, distant from the most probable set of states can be sustained, we first define the viable region of the system. This will be taken to be the macrostate $E$ consisting of a set microstates far from the equilibrium set, where the $i$th microstate is denoted by $\epsilon_i$. Each of these microstates specifies a configuration in the system's state space. In its viable region, the system moves through an 'attractor-like' region of the state space where each microstate $\epsilon_i$ has the same provisional entropy[2]. This attractor-like region maintains its shape as it drifts through a hypercube where the labels on the variables, but not the type of variables, are changing. That is, over time, one carbon atom will be replaced by another.

However, if a system is originally in a microstate $\epsilon_i$ distant from the most probable set of states, second law processes, acting within the system, shift the computational trajectory away from the viable macrostate $E$. The system can only be maintained in the viable region if the second law degradation processes can be countered by accessing the stored energy embodied in appropriate species (such as photons, atoms, molecules or chemicals) where the states are represented by the string $\sigma$ and, at the same time, ejecting disorder or waste represented by the string $\zeta$. Alternatively, work can create an entropy gradient, as happens for example when a heat pump produces a low entropy sink to absorb excess heat.

In a homeostatic set of states, the system moves from one state in the viable region to another as entropy is ejected, and replacement species enter the system. For the algorithmic entropy of a typical state in the homeostatic set of configurations to remain constant, the increase of bits at each step must continuously be ejected as waste; otherwise, bits would build up in the system. A snapshot of a particular state in the homeostatic stable regime will show a mix of structures; some highly ordered, some that are partially disordered, and some that can degrade no further.

### 10.4.1.1 The restoration process that counters the second law

The second law process that degrades the species and the restoration computation that re-creates order are best seen as two separate processes. Consider the first stage of the process as the second law disturbance that drives the system away from the viable region towards a non-viable configuration $\eta_j$. To maintain reversibility, $\eta_j$ must also include the states capturing the reversibility of the computation implied by the disturbance. This disturbance degrades the system's structures. From a computational point of view, this disturbance can be represented by the algorithm $p_{2ndlaw}$, the shortest algorithm that implements second law processes to shift the system to $\eta_j$. Because we are tracking bits reversibly, the shortest algorithm is the one that completely specifies the degraded state. In which case, the natural processes are equivalent to the following reversible computation on the reference UTM [6].

$$U(p_{2ndlaw}, \epsilon_i) = \eta_j. \tag{10.2}$$

---

[2] I don't think this is a true attractor as the labels on the variables change. That is, over time atom $i$ is replaced with another identical atom $j$.

As the maintenance process never halts, the algorithmic entropy is determined by bit flows. Any instruction to link subroutines that would be needed in the static case is not needed here, as was discussed in section 8.5. As nothing leaves the system at this stage, the algorithmic entropy $\eta_j$ of the system following the second law process is given by

$$H(\eta_j) = H_{\text{prov}}(\epsilon_i) + |p_{\text{2ndlaw}}|. \tag{10.3}$$

As in principle, the degradation is reversible, bits are conserved and provided all the history bits are taken into account in $\eta_j$, the equals sign is appropriate in equation (10.3). That is, the change of $H(\eta_j) - H_{\text{prov}}(\epsilon_i)$ bits comes from the bits in $p_{\text{2ndlaw}}$. What might be termed a regulation or restoration process counters the effect of the second law disturbance by the restoration algorithm $p_{rest}$ that acts on an input resource string $\sigma_j$ specifying the species at the start of the process, including the specification of the stored energy states, and the existing string $\eta_j$ specifying the non-viable configuration.

The net output for the restoration process is the final microstate $\epsilon_k$, with the same provisional entropy as $\epsilon_i$, and with an extra string $\zeta_l$ that is generated with $\epsilon_i$. In general, a computation like $p_{rest}$ generates $\epsilon_k$ and $\zeta_l$ together and therefore there is a high level of mutual information between the two components of the outcome. From equation (10.2), this restoration process is represented by the computation;

$$U(p_{rest}, \eta_j, \sigma_j) = \epsilon_k, \zeta_l. \tag{10.4}$$

From equation (10.4),

$$H_{\text{prov}}(\epsilon_k, \zeta_l) = H(\sigma_j) + H(\eta_j) + |p_{rest}|. \tag{10.5}$$

Equations (10.3) and (10.5) can be added, and after rearranging it is seen that the provisional entropy of the system has increased by $H(\text{waste})$;

$$H(\text{waste}) = H_{\text{prov}}(\epsilon_k, \zeta_l) - H_{\text{prov}}(\epsilon_i) = |p_{\text{2ndlaw}}| + |p_{rest}| + H(\sigma_j). \tag{10.6}$$

$H(\text{waste})$ is the number of bits that need to be ejected for the system to be restored to the original macrostate. This is the requirement for a system to self-regulate. As one would expect, the entropy of the waste string must include the bits embodied in the second law disturbance algorithm, the bits in the regulation algorithm, and the bits that have entered the system to define the microstate of the species carrying the source of stored energy. All this additional entropy as bits must be ejected if the system is to be returned to the initial macrostate.

In contrast to the Zurek approach discussed in section 8.6, for autonomous regulation the bits in the computations $p_{rest}$ and $\sigma_j$ involved in the regulation or restoration process are part of the system and need to be accounted for. Furthermore, equation (10.6) implies that, for autonomous regulation, the net decrease in bits due to the regulation process must equal the increase in bits that enter through the disturbance if bits are not to build up in the system. That is,

$$H(\text{waste}) - |p_{rest}| - H(\sigma_j) = |p_{\text{2ndlaw}}|.$$

However, the bits that are ejected from the system are more degraded in the sense that much of what were originally bits specifying stored energy or programme states become bits associated with the momentum states, increasing the temperature. The extraction of heat or waste from the system by the action of physical laws, is in effect a transfer of order into the system from the environment. The above argument also implies that the algorithmic entropy specifying a microstate in a homeostatic system is related to the bits in, less the bits out. Section 8.5 specifically addresses this issue using an argument closely related to that in this section.

Equation (10.6) shows that the ability of the system to maintain homeostasis does not directly depend on $H_{\text{prov}}(\epsilon_k)$, and therefore the system's distance from the equilibrium set of states. Rather, as is discussed by Devine [6] and implied by the requirements of equations (10.17), the rate at which the second order degradation processes can be countered by the restoration process depends on [6]:
1. the rate at which the concentrated source of energy can enter the system, and
2. the rate at which excess entropy can be ejected from the system.

These two requirements determine the entropy balance for the set of configurations far from the most probable set. The greater the rate that the system degrades, the further from equilibrium set the system must be, in order to eject sufficient waste such as heat. Also, the further the system is from the equilibrium set, the greater its capability to do work, as this depends on the entropy difference between the system and its surroundings.

As the second law programme embodied in the natural laws shifts the trajectory out of the homeostatic set of configurations increasing the entropy by $|p_{\text{2ndlaw}}|$, any regulatory or restoration programme, embodied in natural laws, such as a replication process, must turn the excess entropy into waste that can now be discarded in a manner similar to that described in section 8.6.

In order for a natural system to truly regulate, excluding human or animal cognitive responses, natural regulation processes must be wired into the system in some way. In the next section 10.7.1, it is argued that replication processes behave like a primitive form of regulation that requires no intelligent external interventions. This observation provides fundamental insights into living systems. True replication processes are able to naturally restore a system to a homeostatic state as, given adequate resources, the drive to create or maintain order is inevitable. Because replication drives a system towards a more ordered configuration, when degradation occurs, natural replication processes seek to access external resources to create or maintain the order.

As is discussed in more detail below, this is why the replication of bacterial cells in a broth of nutrients, creates a state far from the equilibrium set. Such replicating systems maximise the numbers of replicated units in a given environment. In so doing they counter the second law degradation provided resource inputs can be accessed and waste can be ejected, as shown in equation (10.6). These replicating systems settle in an attractor-like region of the state space with the same provisional entropy. As resources flow through the system replicas are created and destroyed. Outside the viable attractor region, the trajectory is highly sensitive to its initial state and the system behaviour is likely to be chaotic. The capability of replicating systems to regulate suggests that it should be no surprise that replication processes underpin the maintenance of living systems far from the equilibrium set of states.

## 10.5 Replication processes generate order to counter the second law of thermodynamics

The argument developed below is that replication processes, which generate algorithmically simple and therefore low entropy structures, are the major mechanism in generating and maintaining a living system distant from the most probable set of states. As understanding replication is important to understanding these systems, the following points are explored throughout this section.

- The critical point is that the algorithmic entropy of a system of replicated structure is low. Relatively few bits are required to specify such a system, as the algorithm only needs to specify the structure once and then replicate repeats of the structure by a short routine.
- Replication processes can create and maintain an ordered system away from the most probable set of states in an attractor-like region of the system's dynamical state space where all the states have the same provisional algorithmic entropy.
- Variation in a system of replicated structures leads to an increase in the algorithmic entropy. However, variation also provides a natural mechanism to stabilise the system against change, by allowing the system to evolve to a more restricted region of its state space. In other words, variation can maintain the system in a stable configuration through adaptive evolutionary-like processes. AIT provides a reasonably convincing argument that, in many situations, those variants that persist in a changing environment are those that use resources more efficiently, and have lower entropy throughputs.
- Coupled and nested replicator systems create greater stability against change by co-evolving as, from an entropy perspective, the interdependent replicated structures use resources more efficiently. This efficiency, called here 'entropic efficiency' would seem to be an important constraint on evolutionary selection processes. Nevertheless, while each replicated structure is efficient in this sense, the number of interdependent or nested replicated structures increases to ensure that overall, the high quality energy degrades more effectively than would otherwise be the case [7].

### 10.5.1 Replication as a process that creates ordered structures

As has already been argued, algorithmic information theory indicates that replication processes are key to generating much of the observed local order around us. In contrast to alternative structures, where each structure must be specified independently, a system of replicated structures is more ordered as the algorithm that generates the system is more compressed. As fewer bits of information are required to describe the structure and, as replication occurs through natural laws, provided resources are available and high entropy waste can be ejected, replication processes can both create and maintain order. In such a situation, replicated structures are more likely to emerge than similar structures produced by other natural process. Indeed, it seems that many natural systems rely on replication processes as a means of self-organisation and self-regulation. Given one replicator, others will form and a system of replicated structures can be maintained in a way that compensates for the second law of thermodynamics.

This can be seen by considering a system of $N$ repeated replicated structures that can be generated by a short algorithm of the form 'Replicate structure $N$ times" where the replicate instruction is embodied in the DNA in the cell. The algorithmic entropy of this algorithm corresponds to

$$H_{\text{algo}}(system) = |N| + |replicator\ description| \\ + |replicate\ routine|.$$

(10.7)

Relative to the large number of replicas that eventuate, and given common natural laws, the replicator description and replicator routines are short. The algorithmic entropy is dominated by the description of $N$ which only requires something like $\log_2 N$ bits. The system of replicated structures is ordered compared to a similar set of non-replicated structures. In the latter case, the algorithm needs to specify each of the $N$ structures separately, taking at least $N$ bits, rather than $\log_2 N^3$.

The process of replication is like a chain reaction that creates repeats of a particular structure using structural or stored energy. While replicated structures accumulate in the system, other physical processes, such as collisions or chemical reactions, driven by the second law of thermodynamics processes, will destroy these structures. However, replication processes, implementing equation (10.6), access high quality energy and eject disorder, and are able to restore such a system to the original ordered set of configurations. In general, replication involves physical or biological structures that reproduce by utilizing available energy and resources and, at the same time, ejecting excess entropy as heat and waste to the environment.

Physical examples of such replicating systems are a crystal that forms from a melt, a set of spins that align in a magnetic material, and coherent photons that emerge through stimulated emission. Biological replication includes an autocatalytic set, bacteria that grow in an environment of nutrients and the growth of a biological structure such as a plant.

The characteristic of a replicator is that, in a resource rich environment, the probability that a structure will replicate increases with the number $N$ of existing structures. Consider the situation where the probability of the appearance of a replicated structure is proportional to $N^x$ (where $x > 0$), then [8]

$$\mathrm{d}N/\mathrm{d}t \propto N^x.$$

---

[3] Note that here the word 'replica' will be used to denote those physical or biological structure that use external energy and resources to reproduce themselves. This means the biological cell is the replicating unit, not the DNA information string that is copied as part of the replicating process.

For this to happen it is assumed that entropy as waste products or as heat can be ejected so that entropy and waste does not build up within the system. For example, given a double helix of DNA in the right environment, the probability of a second double helix appearing is comparatively high. As the probability of replicated structures appearing increases with their occurrence, replication will drive the state point to a region of state space dominated by a large number of repeated replicated structures. Where resources are limited, the number of replicated structures grows over time until a state of homeostasis is reached; a state where the set of replicators and the environment reach a long-term stable relationship.

The focus here is on true replication processes where the presence of the replicated structure triggers more replicas[4].

A schematic representation of this process is the logistic growth equation

$$dN/dt = \hat{r}N(1 - N/K). \tag{10.8}$$

This equation, while trivially simple, captures the essence of replication. Here, $\hat{r}$ represents the usual exponential growth rate of replicated structures and $K$ represents the carrying capacity of the system. In the homeostatic state, replicas die and are born. As a consequence, $dN/dt = 0$ as the system is maintained in a homeostatic state by the flow through of nutrients and energy and the ejection of waste. The rate at which the system can access resources and eject waste determines where this homeostatic balance occurs. This is the situation where constant bits remain in the system. The replicating units create ordered structures and shift compensating disorder elsewhere to be ejected. For example, when spins become aligned in a magnetic material, disorder is shifted to the vibrational states (i.e. the temperature rises). The disordered vibrational states capture the memory of the computational process. Unless the corresponding latent heat can be removed, the system remains reversible and the spins will in time revert back to a more random configuration. In essence, replication processes use natural laws to self-regulate maintaining the system far from the most probable set of states, even though the replicated structures degrade under the second law of thermodynamics. Simple physical replication processes can be used to illustrate the key characteristics of natural ordering through replication.

As many living systems also need to do work generating heat, the thermodynamic cost of maintaining the system away from their equilibrium set of states increases. In order to fly, birds do work at a greater rate than mammals or reptiles. As a consequence, their body temperature is higher. While systems further from the equilibrium set have a greater capacity to do work, they need to be both more efficient in their use of the resources that are inputs to the computational process, and in ejecting disorder represented by the output string that exits the system. As is discussed later, evolutionary type processes acting on a system of replicated structures select variations that are more efficient in this sense.

---

[4] True replication requires that the presence of one unit creates a chain reaction to create more units. This contrasts with processes such as the combustion of oxygen and hydrogen, where the heat of combustion, not the presence of water, triggers the process.

## 10.6 Simple illustrative examples of replication

In contrast to the photodiode system or the hydrogen and oxygen system discussed above, replication process are naturally ordering processes. While many replicating processes occur in living systems, much can be learned about the process by considering two simple physical examples—the alignment of magnetic spins (i.e. magnetic moments) below the Curie temperature and the replication of photons by simulated emission. In the second example, stimulated emission provides ordered repeats of a structure by passing disorder to the electronic states of the atoms and then to thermal degrees of freedom. These examples are discussed in some detail below to clarify the entropy flows in an ordering process.

### 10.6.1 Replicating spins

For those unfamiliar with magnetic systems, in what follows the word 'spin' refers to the magnetic moment of a spinning electron. One can envisage these spins as micro magnets associated with a magnetic atom such as an iron atom. When these micro magnets are all oriented in the same direction, one says 'the spins are aligned', etc.

Above the Curie temperature, an aligned system of spins will become more disordered as thermal energy passes into the spin system. If the more disordered system is isolated, it will settle in an equilibrium set of states where the spins are only partially aligned. It is only when the temperature falls below the Curie temperature, with ejection of bits as latent heat, will order increase as spins align when ferromagnetic coupling between spins dominates the thermal energy.

The ideas can be illustrated by a simple model—the ordering of a 1D chain of spins. This model not only illustrates replication, but also is informative about what happens to the information or bits during the ordering process.

Let the configuration of the partially coupled 1D spin chain be specified by a string of $N$ disordered, or randomly aligned spins, denoted by $x$, where $x$ is either 1, representing a spin up, or 0 representing a spin down. Let the vibrational states be below the Curie temperature and be represented by a string of $N$ zeros signifying low temperature order. As the vibrational states are at a low temperature, there is an entropy gradient between the spin subsystem and the vibrational subsystem. The initial configuration $i$ consisting of a random set of spins and the ordered vibrational states is then represented by

$$i = 1xxx...xx000000....$$

The first character is a '1' and represents the particular spin that will be replicated in the sense that, under the right conditions, magnetic forces between spins will ensure the next spin is aligned with the first and so on.

From a computational perspective, the replication programme scans the string representing the spins finds a 1 and effectively replicates the orientation of this spin by ensuring the next spin is also a 1. Spin alignment is a spontaneous symmetry breaking process. For the ordering to continue, information (i.e. bits) carried by the spin states, must be transferred to the 00...00 vibrational states, disordering the vibrational degrees of freedom and raising the temperature. While the system is isolated, no entropy is lost and the vibrational states retain the memory of the physical process maintaining reversibility.

Let $U_1$ be the computation that maps the real-world computation aligning the next spin with the current spin. The overall ordering process can be envisaged as a repeat of this alignment process on the initial string $i$ down the spin chain. In which case, the output after N steps is

$$(U_1)^N i = o = 11111...11xxxxxx...xx, \tag{10.9}$$

where $x$ is a 0 or a 1. As was mentioned, the randomness has been transferred to what previously was the ordered section of the string representing the vibrational coordinates. If the system is below the Curie temperature after the energy transfer and remains isolated, the system settles in a stable set of aligned spins. Strictly, each aligned configuration is one of an equilibrium set of similar configurations, with the odd rare fluctuation that mis-aligns spins. If the system is no longer isolated and heat enters the system, the temperature rises. In order to re-order the system, disorder as heat must to be ejected and passed to a low temperature external sink, but at the cost of increasing the entropy of the rest of the Universe.

For large $N$, ignoring computing overheads, the algorithmic entropy $H(i)$ of the input string information content of the input string is given by

$$\begin{aligned} H(i) &\approx (N + H(N)) \quad (\textit{specifying the random } 1xxxx...x) \\ &+ \log_2 N + H(\log_2 N) + |0| \quad (\textit{Specify } 0, \ N \ \textit{times}). \end{aligned} \tag{10.10}$$

Here, self-delimiting coding requires the size of $|N|$ to be represented by $N + H(N)$ bits. Similarly, the coding for repeat structures is represented by $\log_2 N + H(\log_2 N)$ bits corresponding to $H(N) + H(|N|)$ bits.

The output string can be specified by a similar algorithm but where this time, the spins are ordered and the vibrational states disordered. That is, the algorithmic entropy becomes algorithm

$$\begin{aligned} H_{\text{algo}}(o) &\approx \log_2 N + H(\log_2 N) + |1| \quad (\textit{aligned spins}) \\ &+ N + H(N) + |0| \quad (\textit{disordered vibrational states}). \end{aligned} \tag{10.11}$$

At this stage, as nothing is lost from the system, reversibility is implicit in the history of the computation embodied in the final state. Hence $H_{\text{algo}}(o) = H_{\text{algo}}(i)$. Once the vibrational states lose heat to the external environment the algorithmic entropy can be lowered and the output becomes;

$$o' = 11111...1100...00.$$

The algorithm that shifts $i$ to $o$ is implicit in the physical laws acting within the system.

### 10.6.2 Coherent photons as replicators

Another simple example is the replication of coherent photons through stimulated emission. Consider a physical system of $N$ identical two-state atoms where a photon is emitted when the excited state returns to the ground state. The emitted photons can either be in a coherent state, or a set of incoherent states. The state space of the system initially consists of:

- the position and momentum states of the atoms;
- the momentum states of the photons;
- the excited and ground electronic states of each atom.

Assume the system of photons and particles are contained within end mirrors and walls and no energy loss occurs through collisions with the container. The initial ordered configuration will be taken to be the $N$ atoms existing in their excited states with the photon states empty.

If the lifetime of the excited state of the atom is short, only incoherent photons will be emitted with momentum vectors scattered over all directions. In addition, under second law processes, some excited atoms will return to the ground state via collisions or other processes before emitting a photon and in so doing increasing the thermal energy of the system. Ultimately the system will settle in the most probable set of states at a higher temperature with most atoms in the ground state.

On the other hand, if the lifetime of the excited states is long, stimulated photons becomes possible by photon replication. Once a stray photon aligned with the mirrors replicates, photons will continue to replicate until there is a balance between the number of excited atoms, the number of coherent photons and the very small number of incoherent photon states. A symmetry breaking process takes place as the stimulated photons have aligned momentum vectors, rather than being randomly oriented over all directions.

While the system is isolated, the algorithmic entropy is unchanged. A coherent photon may be absorbed, returning an atom to its excited state. Photon replicas die and are born as the system settles in an attractor-like region of its state space. The physical computation process for an isolated system is both thermodynamically and logically reversible.

The algorithmic description of an instantaneous configuration of this isolated system after a period of time will consist of the description of the atomic states; a description of the state of each incoherent photon; the description of the coherent photon state (consisting of replicas of the original stimulating photon); and the momentum states of the atom which are deemed to be random. Let the electronic states of the system be represented as a string where a '1' represents an excited atom, and a '0' represents the ground state. The input string, $i$, representing the initial highly ordered system of excited atoms with no photons takes the schematic form:

$$[\text{Atom electronic states}] \quad [\text{Photon states}]$$
$$i = [1111111111111111111] \quad [\text{empty}].$$

We will assume that the system is kept at a constant temperature, as it allows the momentum or vibrational states of the atoms, and the atomic positions to be ignored as only the change in algorithmic entropy is relevant. Once replication occurs, the system will consist of a mixture of atomic states and $n$ photons in a coherent state.

The algorithmic description of an instantaneous configuration of the relevant total system will consist of the description of the atomic states in terms of whether they are excited or in the ground state and the description of the $n$ coherent photon state. That is,

[Atom electronic states]  [Coherent photon state]

$o = [0011111011011010110]$  $[n]$.

The $n$ coherent photon state is more ordered than the incoherent states as the momentum vector is no longer randomly oriented. The memory of the photon creation process that is needed to maintain reversibility ultimately passes to the momentum states of the atoms and is lost as heat to the environment. Nevertheless, if photons can escape or collisions depopulate the excited states, the system will need to access an external energy source to re-excite some of the atomic states to compensate for the photon loss. The external source that excites the atoms could be an electrical discharge or a flash lamp. At the same time heat will need to be ejected. As the above examples illustrate, in general a replication process creates order by passing the disorder elsewhere; effectively partially randomizing other degrees of freedom.

## 10.7 The algorithmic entropy cost of replica variations

The previous sections considered the situation of identical replicated structures. However, many real-world systems consist of near identical structures. For example, the expression of a cell in the eye is not identical to one in the liver, yet both contain the same DNA coding. Depending on the source of the variation in the replicated structures, variation introduces an entropy cost that can be quantified by the algorithmic information theory approach. In the case of near identical replicated structures, the provisional algorithmic entropy identifies an entropy increase with the uncertainty arising from the variations. As a consequence, the algorithmic description is longer.

A simple example is the string formed by replicating the structure '10' to produce the string $101010...10$. Variation can be introduced by allowing both '10' and 'also 11' to be considered as valid variants of the core replicated structure. This string then becomes the noisy period-2 string discussed in section 4.3.4, where every second digit is random. Thus a valid system of replicated structures would now be any output string of length $N$ having the form $o = 1y1y1y1y...1y$, and where $y$ is 0 or 1. There are $\Omega_s = 2^{N/2}$, members of the set and as section 4.3.4 shows that the provisional entropy of the variants is

$$H_{\text{prov}}(o) \simeq N/2 + H(N/2) + |1| + |0|, \tag{10.12}$$

In general, the provisional algorithmic entropy, which is given in section 4.2, includes the length of the code that identifies the string within the set of $2^{N/2}$ variants, together with the specification of the pattern, or the model, that identifies the set itself.

By comparison, the provisional algorithmic entropy of the string $o = 101010...10$, a string which represents no variations in the replicated unit (i.e. 10 not $1y$), has the algorithmic entropy given by

$$H_{\text{prov}}(o) = H(N/2) + |10|. \tag{10.13}$$

The increase in the algorithmic entropy from $H(N/2)$ to $N/2 + H(N/2)$ is the increase in the uncertainty (i.e. the Shannon entropy) that arises by allowing variants of the original structure. While in this case $N/2$ is significant compared with $H(N/2)$, if the variation is included in software, as is the case for DNA where triggers determine which genes are to be expressed, variation can be introduced with little increase in entropy. In essence, the provisional entropy of living beings built from variations of a core replicated structure may not be significantly different from a structure with identical replicated units.

### 10.7.1 Natural ordering through replication processes

In contrast to an inert system that cannot maintain itself, equation (10.8) shows that replication processes can naturally generate and re-generate ordered structures with low algorithmic entropy, by ejecting disorder in the case of simple replication processes, such as the crystallisation of ice, or the alignment of spins. However, most replicating and ordering processes also require the input of high-quality or concentrated energy in addition to ejecting waste. The high-quality energy repackages the system, separating the heat and degraded species from the ordered regions, allowing natural processes to eject the waste. Equation (10.7) shows that replicating systems have a lower algorithmic entropy than a system of non-identical structures. The computational processes underpinning replication can be seen in the discrete form of the logistics growth equation (10.8). That is, the discrete equation below where $j$ represents the $j$th computational cycle.

$$N_{j+1} = N_j + \hat{r}N_j(1 - N_j/K), \tag{10.14}$$

This equation maps the process of generating replicated structures until $N$ reaches the carrying capacity $K$. In which case, the algorithmic entropy might be expected to be

$$H_{\text{algo}}(system) = |N| + H(|N|) + |generating\ algorithm|.$$

While this is only a simple example of a replicating system, any replicating algorithm operating under physical laws will have the same basic form. However, note here the need for the term $H(|N|)$ to allow for self-delimiting coding (see section 3.4.1.

As discussed above, the alignment of magnetic spins or the formation of a block of ice from water are simple examples of a replication process. Only when the ejection of heat drives the temperature of the system below the Curie temperature, or in the case of ice, below the freezing temperature, will a complete phase transition occur. However, because the vibrational states are the means by which heat is transferred to the environment, the specification of the instantaneous configuration of the vibrational and other states needs to be included in the description to properly track entropy flows. This can be seen with the particular example a crystal of ice. If each water molecule in the ice is denoted by $r$, the ice structure of $N$ molecules is represented by a string $r_1, r_2, \ldots, r_N$ where the label denotes the position of each molecule in the structure.

However, the vibrational states that are coupled with these also need to be specified. As a result, the full specification becomes $r_1, r_2, \ldots, r_N, w_0(T')$. Here, $w_0(T')$ represents an instantaneous specification of the vibrational, rotational, electronic states and degraded species in the waste string that ultimately must be ejected from the system to inhibit reversibility. At each step of the replicating process, energy is passed from the structure to the vibrational states and then to the external environment. The ejection of waste allows the ordered structure to emerge as the temperature of the system returns to the original temperature $T$.

In the general case, the replication process, imitating the discrete form of the growth equation (10.14), can be seen as a computation that acts on an input string $\sigma$ ($=\sigma_1, \sigma_2 \ldots \sigma_N$), representing the resource string embodying stored energy and minerals, but also the structure $r_1$ which is to be replicated. The full input can be represented by $i = r_1 \sigma$, while the output is the system of replicated structures together with a waste string. If the replication cycle loops $N$ times, $N$ replicated structures will emerge.

$$U(\mathrm{p}_N, r_1, \sigma) = r_1 r_2 r_3 \ldots r_N, w_0(T'). \tag{10.15}$$

In this process, the number of replicated structures $r_1$, $r_2$ etc, increases where the subscripts identify successive structures.

Other states that contribute to the algorithmic entropy of the replicated system, originally at temperature $T$, are essentially unchanged at the end of the replication process.

Originally, vibrational, rotational, electronic states, which can be represented by $\phi_i(T)$, become $\phi_j(T')$ when the degraded waste is formed and the temperature rises. After replication, the new waste string, $w_0(T')$, representing degraded species is ejected. When this happens, $\phi_j(T')$ separates into $\phi_k(T) + w_0(T')$. The string $\phi_k(T)$ left after the ejection of $w_0(T')$, is equivalent to $\phi_i(T)$ and the number of bits is unchanged as $|\phi_k(T)| = |\phi_i(T)|$. The algorithmic entropy contribution of these states can be ignored. Overall, with the ejection of waste, the provisional entropy is lower and the structure is more ordered.

A replicating living system follows the same laws as an inert replicating system. This can be seen with the simple illustration of the growth of bacteria in a flow of nutrients which eventually settles in a stable situation, provided that waste products can be eliminated. Equation (10.8) is a schematic representation of the process which drives the system towards a stable set of configurations as the bacteria replicate until their numbers reach the carrying capacity of the system. The carrying capacity depends on the rate the nutrients are replenished and the rate at which bacteria die, producing the waste products that need to be ejected. In order to understand the computational processes that reflect this replication process, the following algorithm equation describes a replicating trajectory that embeds many micro steps into a larger replicating subroutine.

Here the parameter $N$ will define the number of times the replication routine is called to append a further replica to the string '$STATE$' and at the same time, resources are depleted before finally halting. While the replication process is a parallel computing process, it can be written in a schematic linear form. The number of replicated structures, $N$, doubles and, for each doubling of $N$, grows until the resources fall below the minimum value to continue replication. That is, when '$RESOURCES < MINIMUM$' the algorithm halts.

$$
\begin{aligned}
&STATE = r \\
&N = 1 \\
&FOR\ I = 1\ to\ N \\
&\quad ACCESS\ NEW\ RESOURCES \\
&\qquad IF\ RESOURCES \\
&\qquad < MINIMUM\ GO\ TO\ HALT \\
&\qquad REPLICATE\ r \\
&\qquad DEPLETE\ RESOURCES \\
&\quad STATE = STATE,\ r \\
&\qquad EJECT\ WASTE \\
&NEXT\ I. \\
&N = N + N \\
&GO\ TO\ FOR \\
&HALT
\end{aligned}
\tag{10.16}
$$

The '$FOR$' loop generates $N$ repeats of the fundamental replicating unit $r$. Once this has happened $N$ doubles and the process repeats and continues repeating until resource are no longer available. If $N_{max}$ is the final values of $N$, the final output is $STATE = r, r, r, r, \dots , r$ with $N_{max}$ repeats of the basic unit $r$. The replication process is reversible if nothing escapes the system.

As has been mentioned, another example that models typical behaviour is a system of identical two-state atoms in a gas where stimulated emission, in effect, orders the photons emitted from the excited atoms (see section 10.6.2) to form coherent photons. In contrast to the crystallisation case, stimulated emission requires the input of high quality energy embodied in the excited atomic states to feed the replication process, as well as the elimination of heat. A symmetry breaking process takes place as the stimulated photons have aligned momentum vectors, rather than being randomly oriented.

As has been discussed in section 9.3.2, when all is taken into account, a replicating algorithm is more efficient in specifying a structure than one that just copies, particularly as variation can be included in a replicating algorithm much more simply than copying different variants. The replicating algorithm that generates the tree from the genetic code in the seed does not require the particular variation to be determined for each cell type and position in the tree. The algorithm is efficient as it uses the same genetic code in the DNA, but calls different routines depending on the environment of neighbouring cells, and external inputs such as water, light and gravity, to determine which actual variation is expressed as part of the development process.

## 10.8 A replicating living system

The following argument tracks the degradation process and the restoration process of a living system from both a computational and a phenomenological point of view. We assume that the system is initially in a stable viable configuration denoted by $\epsilon_i$ that specifies the $N$ repeated structures and also the other degrees of freedom associated with the system. The set of stable configurations all have the same provisional entropy. This implies that the number of replicated structures is fixed, nevertheless, there are many different ways the thermal energy can be distributed amongst the other degrees of freedom such as the vibrational states of the system. The overwhelming majority of possible configurations will have the same number of replicated structures.

The second law degradation process removes the replicated structure as indicated by equation (10.2), i.e.

$$U(\mathrm{p}_{2\mathrm{ndlaw}}, \epsilon_i) = \eta_j.$$

This computation shifts the system to the non-viable configuration $\eta_j$ that has fewer replicated units. From the phenomenological perspective, the replicated structures are destroyed at a rate given by $\alpha N$ that depends on the number present. The regulation computation given by equation (10.4) accesses the resource string $\sigma$ to re-generate the structure. The rate at which this can happen is usually limited by the rate at which the resource structures enter the system. This is taken to be $\sigma_0$ structures per unit time. From the computational point of view the non-viable configuration $\eta_j = r_1, r_2, \ldots, r_{N-M}, w(T')$, where $M$ replicated structures have been degraded, creating the waste string $w(T'')$ that captures the history of the process to date. The corresponding restoration programme $\mathrm{p}_{reg,M}$ that loops $M$ times to re-generate the $M$ structures and ejects the waste $w(T')$ and waste produced by the replicating process gives

$$U(\mathrm{p}_{rest,M}, \eta_j, \sigma_1, \sigma_2, \ldots, \sigma_M) = r_1', r_2', \ldots r_N'.$$

The overall waste ejected includes the bits causing the replicas to decay; the bits in the regulation algorithm $\mathrm{p}_{rest,M}$ that restores the number of replicated structures from $N - M$ to $N$; together with the bits specifying the extra resources that have been added. That is, all extra inputs need to be ejected to stop the build up of the waste in the system.

While the growth characteristics align with equation (10.14), the logistics growth equations do not adequately track the resource flows for the replication process. A more realistic approach that identifies the replication dependence on the resource availability is the Holling type-II functional response. This is similar to the Monod function or the Michaelis–Menten equation or the interaction of a predator and its prey (which in this case is replicator–resource interaction). Two coupled equations, detailed in equation (10.17), capture the essence of a replication.

As mentioned, the equations below include a term $\alpha N$ to capture the decay or destruction of replicated structures due to second law effects in the growth equation. The assumption is that the removal of structures (i.e. their death) at any time is proportional to their number with the proportionality constant $\alpha$. Also, the constant flow through of the resources $\sigma_0$ needed to feed the replication process is included. These equations imply the computational waste material can be ejected. As is mentioned later, the inability to eject waste efficiently can limit the replication process. With these understandings, let $N$ represent the number of replicated structures and let $\sigma$ represent the number of resource units that are required to feed the replication process. In which case,

$$dN/dt = \frac{\hat{r}\sigma N}{(b + \sigma)} - \alpha N$$

$$d\sigma/dt = -\frac{\hat{r}\sigma N}{\gamma(b + \sigma)} + \sigma_0. \tag{10.17}$$

The parameter $\gamma$ represents the number of replicated structures produced from the consumption of one resource unit, i.e. $-\gamma\Delta\sigma \approx \Delta N$. The maximum growth rate is the initial growth rate $\hat{r}$ when $\gamma\sigma \gg N$, whereas $b$ is the resource level at which $\sigma = b$ and the growth rate is halved. The conditions for a stable long-term homeostatic state occur when the two derivatives approach zero. In which case, the number of replicated structures increases, tending to a long-term value $N_\infty = \gamma\sigma_0/\alpha = K$ where $K$ can be identified as the carrying capacity of the system, which in this case is not imposed externally, but determined by the system itself.

Equations (10.2) and (10.15) are the computational equivalent of the replication process captured by equation (10.17). In each unit of time, $\sigma_0$ resources flow into the system, maintaining the length of the resource string, $\sigma$. In the stable configuration, the resources are just sufficient to replace the $\alpha N$ replicated structures that decay over that period. From a computational point of view, the long-term description of the replicated structures becomes $r_1 r_2 r_3 ... r_K$ with $K = N$. The length of the algorithmic description of the string of replicated structures produced by a copying routine would be close to $|r_1 r_2 r_3 ... r_K, | = |r_1^*| + \log_2 K + H(\log_2 K)$. That is, one replicated structure needs to be specified by $r_1^*$ and the specification repeated $K$ times. Here, the asterisk indicates that this is the shortest description of the replica. On the other hand, if the length is derived from the replicating algorithm rather than the copying algorithm, the dominant contribution would come from $|r_1^*| + \log_2 N + H(\log_2 N)$. The optimum number of replicated structures will emerge when $N = K$ as $\log_2 N = \log_2 K$.

Replicating systems act as pumps that eject entropy to form the ordered state. When, for example, water crystallises through a replication process, rather than cooling slowly, a spike of latent heat is generated which passes to the environment more rapidly because of the increased temperature difference between the system and the environment. Similarly, when high quality energy is converted to waste species in the replication process, the ejected waste is more efficiently transferred to the environment compared with other processes.

While the real-world replication is a complex parallel computing process, the approach described above captures its essentials. Provided the creation rate of replicas exceeds their decay rate, the number of replicas will grow until the system settles in a stable set of configurations. In this homeostatic situation, the carrying capacity of the replicated structures is constrained either by the rate at which the waste can exit the system, or by the rate the resource inputs are available to replace decayed replicas.

Many living systems also need to do work. While systems further from the most probable set of states have a greater capacity to do work, they need to be more efficient in resource use and in ejecting waste. As is discussed below, evolutionary type processes acting on a system of replicated structures select variations that are more efficient in this sense.

## 10.9 Selection processes to sustain a natural system

Genetic diversity, coupled with biological selection processes, is key to the emergence of structures better adapted to the environment. This section looks at selection processes from a computational point of view, showing that diversity in the replicated structures, while better maintaining the system distant from the equilibrium set in an adverse environment, also drives the emergence of different structural types. It is argued that not only can a system of replicated structures counter second law degradation processes by replacing decaying species, if there is sufficient variety among near identical replicas, adaptation processes can counter more virulent disturbances impacting on the system. For this to happen, variations in the replicated structure must emerge at a time that is fast relative to the external environmental changes. This adaptation can be viewed as a form of regulation as in general, organised systems consisting of variations of a simple replica are more stable against change as the set of viable configurations is larger. However, it is a viable set that is expanding its horizons as diversity increases over time, primarily through changes to the genetic code by copying errors, crossovers, gene transfer, and more general mutations. Changes in the genetic information are equivalent to small modifications of the algorithm that generates the replicated structure, thus increasing diversity. New resources flowing into an open system of replicas are in effect additions to the input string expanding its state space. Similarly, resources flowing out of the system lead to a loss of information and a contraction of the state space. Consider the replicator–resource dynamics where a disturbance threatens the viability of the system of replicated structures. The disturbance, which could involve an inflow or outflow of species or energy, will vary the computational paths undertaken by the system. Some variations of the replica may become less likely, while others become more likely in the changing environment. Those best adapted will dominate the replica mix as they are more efficient in processing resources. Examples might be where the variant of one tree species is better able to cope with drought, or the emergence of drug resistant bacteria. This resource efficiency will be termed 'entropic efficiency'.

In essence, a system of replicated structures that has sufficient diversity increases the ability of the system to survive in an adverse environment.

Nevertheless, it needs to be recognised that selection processes reduce diversity in the short term as a system with fewer variations has a lower algorithmic entropy. But as in a living system, diversity inevitably reappears over time due to genetic mutations and genetic recombination, one can argue that these adaptive processes determine a long-term trajectory leading to the biological evolution of the system. One can consider that these adaptive processes are a form of quasi-regulation as they tend to maintain the system within the viable set of configurations.

The insights of Eigen and his co-workers [9, 10] on the emergence and growth of self-replicating polynucleotides can be applied to more general replicating systems. In the polynucleotide case, copying errors provide variations in the genetic code, some of which, through selection processes, dominate the molecular soup. Interestingly, Eigen shows that a distribution of closely interrelated polynucleotides, which he terms a 'quasi-species', dominate the mix rather than one particular variant. New structures can emerge if there is sufficient diversity among near identical replicas, as adaptation processes can counter more virulent disturbances impacting on the system.

A simple model, based on predator–prey dynamics (or in this case the equivalent replicator–resource dynamics), provides useful insights on how variation and selection processes enable a system to adapt when two variations of a replicating structure compete for limited resources. When this happens, it will be no surprise that where there are limited resources, the variant with the highest carrying capacity will dominate the mix. As is shown below, the carrying capacity depends on the efficiency of the replication process in the sense of efficient use of resources, and also the variant's capability to withstand the onslaught of second law processes. The argument could be articulated in terms of the interactions between two subspecies in a competitive environment using coupled versions of equation (10.8). This approach, which gives rise to the Lotka–Volterra equations, shows that Gause's law of competitive exclusion applies and the variation with the greatest carrying capacity is the one that survives [11]. However, in the case discussed here, the carrying capacity is not an external parameter but depends on how efficiently replication processes use resources and also the variant's capability to withstand the onslaught of second law processes. Consequently, coupled versions of the Lotka–Volterra equations are inappropriate.

Eigen's approach [9] is more realistic. From a computational point of view, where living systems compete for resources, the biological selection processes that optimise the system's use of resources operate at the genetic level. This reduces the information input needed to define the structure. This also establishes the requirements for a stable equilibrium, where there is a constant flux of monomers corresponding to the resources that feed the process. Eigen's results are essentially the same as the following simple discussion, which is based on the simple predator–prey model addressed in section 10.7.1. In the approach here there are two variants of the basic replica with numbers $N_1$ and $N_2$ competing for the resources $\sigma$ that feed the replication process. The first two of the following equations capture the growth rate of the two variants, given their respective decay rates $\alpha$ and the additional parameters $c_1$ and $c_2$ that represent the impact of one variant on the other. Here, a negative $c_1$ indicates that $N_2$ enhances the growth of $N_1$. The last equation captures the rate the resources change, given the resource consumption by the variants and the constant inflow $\sigma_0$ of new resources.

$$dN_1/dt = \frac{\hat{r}_1 \sigma N_1}{(b_1 + \sigma)} - \alpha_1 N_1 - c_1 N_1 N_2$$

$$dN_2/dt = \frac{\hat{r}_2 \sigma N_2}{(b_2 + \sigma)} - \alpha_2 N_2 - c_2 N_1 N_2 \qquad (10.18)$$

$$d\sigma/dt = -\frac{\hat{r}_1 \sigma N_1}{\gamma_1 (b_1 + \sigma)} - \frac{r_2 \sigma N_2}{\gamma_2 (b_2 + \sigma)} + \sigma_0.$$

While these equations are similar to the equations for predator–prey relationships (see [12]), the last equation has a term $\sigma_0$ to indicate resources are supplied to the system at a constant rate (see [9]). Another assumption is that the waste generated by this process is able to be ejected by the system.

The equations show that the system settles in a region determined by the rate the resources are consumed by the replication processes, rather than an externally given carrying capacity. The requirement for a non-periodic stable solution is that all the derivatives become zero. However, as outlined in more detail in the supplementary material in reference [6], if say $dN_1/dt > dN_2/dt$, for realistic starting values of $N_1$ and $N_2$, because $\gamma_1 > \gamma_2$ and/or $\alpha_2 > \alpha_1$, both subspecies grow initially. But eventually $N_2$ ceases to grow and ultimately decreases as the term $c_2 N_1$ drives $dN_2/dt$ through zero. Once this happens, the population of subsystem $N_2$ goes to zero while $N_1$ trends towards its maximum value. Assuming variant 2 becomes zero, the limit of $N_1$, i.e. $N_{1\infty}$ is $N_{1\infty} = \gamma_1 \sigma_0 / \alpha_1$ indicating that the carrying capacity of the variant dominating the system is $K = N_{1\infty}$. This is the variant with the highest replication efficiency and the lowest decay rate due to second law effects (i.e. the highest $\gamma/\alpha$). As this is the variant needing the lowest entropy throughput, resource fitness corresponds to what has been termed 'entropic efficiency'. The result can be generalised to more than two variants as shown by equation (II-47) of Eigen [9]. The above equation gives essentially the same result as Eigen for the stable long-term configuration. However, Eigen's approach shows that a closely interrelated quasi-species dominates the mix rather than just a pure variant. In the Eigen approach, $\phi_M$ is set to equal the average growth rate and death rate over all the variants. Here, $\phi_M$ corresponds to $\gamma \sigma_0$.

Variety in the replicating units allows the system to be viable in a changing environment. While increasing the variety in the replicated structures increases the entropy of the system, variety stabilises the system against environmental change. But, if the variation is coded at the genetic level, rather than at the structural level, for most living systems, the selection processes will operate at the genetic level. Just as genetic algorithms mimic real-world selection processes, the algorithmic approach sees these real-world computations as genetic algorithms.

While chance rather than physical laws, may be the determining factor in many evolutionary selection processes, entropic efficiency may still be important in semi-stable environments. The question is whether such entropic efficient selection processes, considered here, are widespread. Nevertheless, one can envisage the situation where a process that selects for entropic efficiency might be perceived as a process that selects for behaviour. For example, separated structures that have some movement might be selected to increase movement enabling the structures to move together or apart to control the overall temperature. From the computational perspective, variants having this movement would be more entropically efficient in a changing environment. Hence what might be seen as adaptation at the biological level can be interpreted as a drive for entropic efficiency at the algorithmic level. Another example might be those bees that have developed the ability to warm their hive by beating their wings when the temperature drops. Presumably, this behaviour driver arises as regulation has been built into the genetic code's software through selection processes that operate on individual bees. The effect is that entropic efficiency of the whole system of bees has increased. What might be seen as adaptation, or 'survival of the fittest' at the biological level can be interpreted as a drive for entropic efficiency at the algorithmic level. This is a drive that uses replication processes, based on natural laws, to regulate the system. In general terms, variation in the core replicated structure can be selected by the environment to provide an autonomous response to external factors and so can be seen as quasi-regulation process.

However, while the system selects the variant that optimises the entropic efficiency of each replica, the overall entropy exchange with the environment does not decrease as the number of structures in the system increases to counter any gain at the level of an individual structure. This is consistent with Schneider and Kay [7] who argue that the emergence of biologically complex structures is a move from the most probable set of states. Living systems are more effective than inert structures in dissipating energy, by degrading high quality energy and in countering entropy gradients. Schneider and Kay show that evaporation and transpiration of the constituents of an ecology are the major forms of energy and entropy dissipation. From the perspective here, when species die and the stored energy is reprocessed, and further degraded by species lower in the food chain, further evaporation and transpiration takes place. This perspective would see that replication is the driver of more efficient dissipation at the system level.

Selection processes that favour one particular variant of the replica reduce the provisional entropy of the system over the short term. Over the long term further variations may well increase the provisional entropy for future selection processes to act on the system.

What does this mean in terms of the regulation equation (10.6)? The input string $\sigma$ includes the nutrients to maintain the replicas and the waste needs to be ejected to the lower temperature sink in the environment. The principles are captured in a set of bacteria in a nutrient mix that exists in a set of viable configurations by accessing the nutrient and ejecting waste heat and materials to the external, cooler environment. Clearly if the nutrients become unavailable, or the temperature of the environment rises or an antibiotic enters the bacteria food chain, most bacteria will die and those better adapted will survive and dominate the population. From a computational point of view certain computations terminate, whereas others do not.

### 10.9.1 Adaptation and interdependence of replicas in an open system

Open systems of replicated structures can become interconnected and interdependent leading to more efficient resource use. Such interconnections can emerge when the waste string $\zeta$ of one system becomes the resource input $\sigma$ in another. Fewer resources are needed to maintain the combined systems. The predator–prey is one such relationship as the stored energy in one system (the prey) is used as the resource input to the other. The predator is just a highly efficient method of degrading the high quality energy embodied in the prey. Alternatively, mutualism can occur when two different species enhance each other's survival.

In general, a structural map of such interconnected and nested structures identifies the information or computational, flow diagram. Where repeats of algorithms are identified, these can be mapped as subroutines to show how the overall algorithm can be efficiently organised. The flow diagram maps an interconnected structure with interconnected subroutines, thus shortening the algorithmic description. Even though real-world computations are parallel processes, they can be configured to produce a serial computation process where routines pass information to each other.

Figure 10.1 shows two systems $A$ and $B$. Where there is no information or bit flows between the systems, corresponding to no resource flows, the overall algorithmic entropy is $H(A) + H(B)$ as in the left-hand side of the figure. However, if the computation of $B$ is shorter when surplus information from $A$ is passed to $B$, the overall algorithmic entropy is

$$H(A, B) = H(A) + H(B|A^*) < H(A) + H(B). \tag{10.19}$$

Bit flows between two subsystems reduce the overall throughput of bits needed to sustain the full systems.

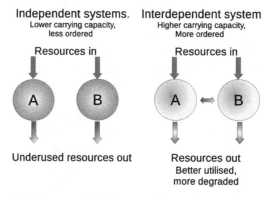

**Figure 10.1.** Resource sharing increases the carrying capacity and order.

It follows that because $H(A, B) < H(A) + H(B)$, the order is greater, as for a given set of inputs, the discarded entropy in the waste string is greater. In the more sophisticated case, where routines share resources between subsystems that are either part of a nested hierarchy, or are linked horizontally, the system can be sustained with fewer bits as waste bits are more degraded. The sharing process extracts more high grade energy from the resources in what otherwise would be under-utilised waste. As fewer external resources are needed to maintain interdependent systems, they are more viable further from equilibrium. In a resource-constrained environment, interdependence will emerge in preference to alternatives. Coupled systems are more stable against input variations and the overall entropy cost of maintaining the system distant from the most probable set of states is less.

A simple example might be when clustered systems reduce heat loss. Another simple example of interdependence is where photons that exit in one laser system are used to create a population inversion in another laser system. In which case, less information is lost to the environment with the combined system, than when the two lasers operate independently. Where overall resources are constrained, and there is sufficient variety in the second system (e.g. sufficient line width overlap between the lasers) this system can adapt by settling in more restricted areas of its state space. A collection of mutually dependent structures amalgamate to form a larger system that is further from the most probable set of states.

Adami's concept of physical complexity, as a measure of viability of low entropy structures [13] supports this observation. He states 'In this case, however, there are good reasons to assume that, for the most part, co-evolution will aid, rather than hinder, the evolution of (physical) complexity, because co-evolution is a slow, rather than drastic, environmental change, creating new niches that provide new opportunities for adaptation'. Where such structures are possible, selection processes would ensure they become likely. The situation where one set of constituents enhances the survival of another can be captured by equation (10.18) by making $c_1$ negative and $c_2$ zero. With appropriate values of the parameters the coupled systems can settle in a stable population regime.

Observationally, it appears that, in comparison to independent structures, a system of nested subsystems (such as a forest ecology nesting species, with an individual of a species nesting organs, and organs nesting cells) is more viable further from the equilibrium set, as the waste of one part of the system is the resource input for another. Nesting also allows specialisation of function, with little increase in algorithmic entropy, particularly if the output of a nested algorithm depends only on the information inputs. As has been mentioned in section 9.3.2, the algorithm that describes the trajectory that generates the structure, such as the algorithm embodied in the seed of a tree, is likely to be shorter than one that describes the structure in its final tree. As the above argues, overall there is less need for waste to be ejected per nested unit because of the mutual dependences and the efficiency in ejecting disorder (such as heat) is higher.

### 10.9.1.1 Mutualism and life

As selection processes favour entropically efficient replicating structures, the reduced dependence on external resources means the carrying capacity of interdependent nested systems is higher than systems where interdependence does not exist. As the coupled systems co-evolve by using resources more efficiently, in a resource-constrained environment the coupled systems are more stable against input variations. These factors suggest that such a system searches for entropically efficient configurations to maintain survival of replicated structures. Under resource constraints, interdependence is more likely to eventuate. Their mutual attractor region will not drift through state space at the same rate as similar, but uncoupled, systems. Where such structures are possible, they would seem to be likely. Interdependence as mutualism, or interdependence between systems of replicas increases the order driving the organised system further from the equilibrium set.

This argument has been applied to coupled biological systems ([6]) which suggests that life on earth is more efficient in maintaining a system further from the most probable set of states than no life, as life creates its own autonomous capability to survive and adapt. The caveat is that a concentrated source of energy such as photons from the Sun must be accessible, and waste must be able to be ejected. However, there is a cost, as life drives the whole system further from the most probable set of states at the expense of being a more efficient dissipator of energy. Observationally it appears that, in comparison to simpler structures, a system of interconnected and nested systems (such as a forest ecology nesting species, with species nesting organs, and organs nesting cells) is more viable far from the equilibrium set, as the waste of one part of the system is the resource input for another.

Overall, less waste per unit structure is ejected, as Schneider and Kay [7] argue that a system of hierarchical structures, such as a complex ecology, is more effective in degrading high-quality energy than simpler or inert structures and pumps out more useless energy at a greater rate. Hierarchical and interconnected systems make better use of the resources, but at the expense of driving their universe more quickly to an equilibrium set of states, as high-quality energy is processed more efficiently. At each step in an interconnected hierarchy, waste ejected by one system can be degraded by a lower system in the hierarchy. This happens when insects, fungi or bacteria degrade plant material far more rapidly than would happen if the degradation was to be driven by non-living processes. However, while resource use is more efficient in nested systems, as the population of the coupled structures increases, the overall degradation of the input resources is both more rapid, and more complete, than would otherwise be the case. More resources are consumed as the population of different replicated structures grows to more efficiently process high-quality energy. In a nutshell, individual replicated structures seek entropic efficiency, but at the system level, the population rises to increase overall dissipation. The more coupled the system, the greater the organisation, but on the above arguments, the overall degradation of the input resources is both more rapid and more complete than would otherwise be the case.

### 10.9.1.2 Degree of organisation

When structures are nested, resources are shared, as subroutines in the natural world pass information as bits between the nested structures. As equation (10.19) indicates, the nested algorithms not only form a short description but, because they pass information to each, less waste information is ejected per structural unit. However, if an observer is focussing on the detail, the observer may not recognise the structure in the nested system at higher levels of scale. Little high-level structure is apparent when observing a tree at the molecular level, and the algorithm specifying the instantaneous position, momentum and stored energy states of every molecule would be horrendously long. It is only at a much larger scale that the organisation of the tree can be recognised as a collection of cells and, at an even greater scale still, higher level structures identified. Figure 10.2 illustrates a nested system of inter-dependent replicated structures (see Devine [14]). At the smallest scale denoted by $d_0$, no pattern is discernible as organisation cannot be recognised. The system can only be described by an algorithm that specifies what appears to be a random arrangement of fundamental structures that may be indistinguishable from a local state in the most probable set of states.

Chaitin's [15] introduces the concept of 'd-diameter complexity' to quantify order at different levels of scale. This is helpful in understanding nested structure and the entropy cost of introducing variety. While the smallest scale is characterised by $d_0$ where no pattern is discernible, as the system is observed at increasing levels of scale, $d_0 \rightarrow d_1 \ldots d_{n-2}, d_{n-1}, d_n$, more structure is identified and the algorithm describing the system becomes shorter.

Using this approach, Chaitin [15] quantifies the degree of organization ($D_{org}$) as the loss in bits when a structure is specified at a higher level scale compared with a lower scale. Hence $D_{org}$ at scale $d$, which is higher than the smallest scale $d_0$, the scale at which the algorithmic entropy $H_{max}$,

$$D_{org}(d) = H_{max}(X) - H_d(X).$$

As scale $d_0$, in practice will correspond to the local equilibrium, $H_{max}$ is indistinguishable from $H(s_{equil})$. In which case, $D_{org}$ is effectively the distance from

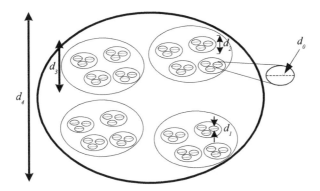

**Figure 10.2.** Nested structures at scales $d_0$, $d_1$, $d_2$ and $d_3$.

equilibrium, denoted by $D_{\text{ord}}$, as was discussed earlier in section 10.1.1. When no organization at all exists, the scale is irrelevant, and the algorithmic entropy is the same at all levels of scale, as shown by the dotted horizontal line given by $H_{\text{max}}$ in figure 10.3. If, at each level of scale, the nested structures are identical, the stepped black line in figure 10.3 illustrates how the number of bits needed to specify the system drops at each step as at each step, more order is identified. However, where variations in the replicated structures occur, as happens with different cell types at the same scale, the steps are smoothed in the dashed line. Diversity increases the provisional entropy at each level of scale.

But diversity can be built into a structure when an algorithm, such as that embedded in DNA, calls different routines depending on the settings of switches in the genetic code. Doing so requires a very little increase in the algorithmic entropy of the DNA. As software variation occurs at lower levels of scale, it would appear to be algorithmically more efficient to generate the variation through the software (e.g. variation by switches in the DNA,) rather than independently specifying variants of similar structures. It is plausible to conjecture that the nesting of structures, decreases the algorithmic entropy in a way that more than compensates for the entropy cost of building in diversity into the system [14]. Indeed, this may be an inevitable consequence of selection processes acting on structures. Identical replicated structures with high $D_{org}$, have less ability to adapt to environmental change, than systems with variation or greater diversity. The cost of allowing variation is a lower $D_{org}$.

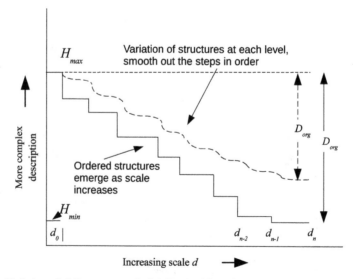

**Figure 10.3.** Variation of $d$-diameter complexity ($D_{org}$) with scale; — nested replicators with no variation; – – – – nested replicators with variation; - - - - no organization at any scale [14].

## 10.10 Summary of system regulation and AIT

AIT identifies the algorithmic entropy or the information content of a system by the minimum number of bits required to describe the system on a UTM, while Landauer's principle [1] holds that the reversible erasure of one bit of information corresponds to an entropy transfer of $k_B \ln 2$ to the environment. Together these understandings provide a consistent way of looking at the thermodynamic cost of maintaining a system in a stable set of configurations distant from the equilibrium set [5]. As only entropy differences have physical significance, the number of bits needed to reversibly shift a system from one configuration to another, multiplied by $k_B \ln 2$, corresponds to the equivalent thermodynamic entropy change of the system. In thermodynamic terms, where a disturbance or a second law degradation process, threatens the viability of a system by increasing the algorithmic entropy by $H$ bits or equivalently the thermodynamic entropy by $k_B H \ln 2$ Joules per degree Kelvin, the thermodynamic cost of restoring the system is to remove $k_B H \ln 2$ Joules per degree Kelvin.

Furthermore, it is argued that, as a system of replicated structures can be described by few bits, natural replication processes use all the available resources to generate simple ordered structures with low algorithmic entropy. This perspective allows one to recognise that a natural replication process can be envisaged as computation on a real-world UTM that is able to generate order far from the most probable set of states. Not only can replicating processes generate order, these processes can self-regulate or self-organise as they can naturally compensate for second law degradation by accessing external resources as inputs to re-generate degraded replicated units while ejecting entropy as waste, fulfilling the requirements of Landauer's principle.

When there is a changing environment, and there is diversity among replicating units, selection processes act as an autonomous quasi-regulation process. The replica variant that persists is likely to be the one that is more entropically efficient in terms of its use of resources and its capability to eject waste. In these cases, environmental fitness carries with it a requirement to optimise the entropic efficiency of the structures in the system. Entropic efficiency means the entropy cost of maintaining the system is minimised, as the system settles in a configuration far from the equilibrium set that is as close to reversible as possible. However, while selection processes do allow a system to return to something close to the original config-uration, over time the system drifts or evolves to new configurations as new variations appear.

Similarly, where interdependence between different replicated structures is possible, simple calculations suggest that selection processes will favour the variants that exhibit interdependence. Hierarchies of replicated structures would seem likely to emerge as selection processes favour those that waste fewer resources. But, as the numbers of such structures increase the overall energy, dissipation is higher and, while the hierarchical system persists, it hastens the degradation of the high quality concentrated energy that feeds the living process. As Schneider and Kay show [7], an ecology consists of myriads of self-replicating efficient units. But, because species lower in the food chain consume the waste of higher species, the overall degradation of the system is greater than would be the case for a non-living system, or even a simpler living system. Living systems hasten the death of the Universe.

Where a system needs to do work, it must be maintained further from the equilibrium set of states and again replicating process can maintain the system in a suitable stable configuration.

The results are general and can in principle apply to any system. However, in many real-world situations, there will be insufficient understanding of the details of the system to quantify the cost of maintaining the system far from the most probable set of states. Nevertheless, the approach may well be useful in understanding incremental changes to real systems and provide broad descriptions of some system behaviour. While there is more to a living system than replication or entropy flows, just as energy constraints determine system behaviour, so entropy requirements constrain structural possibilities.

# References

[1] Landauer R 1961 Irreversibility and heat generation in the computing process *IBM J. Res. Dev.* **5** 183–91

[2] Zurek W H 1989 Algorithmic randomness and physical entropy *Phys. Rev.* A **40** 4731–51

[3] Bennett C H 1973 Logical reversibility of computation *IBM J. Res. Dev* **17** 525–32

[4] Bennett C H 1988 Logical depth and physical complexity *The Universal Turing Machine–A Half-Century Survey* ed R Herken (Oxford: Oxford University Press) pp 227–57

[5] Zurek W H 1989 Thermodynamics of of computation, algorithmic complexity and the information metric *Nature* **341** 119–24

[6] Devine S D 2016 Understanding how replication processes can maintain systems away from equilibrium using algorithmic information theory *Biosystems* **140** 8–22

[7] Schneider E D and Kay J J 1994 Life as a manifestation of the second law of thermodynamcis *Mathl. Comput. Modelling* **16** 25–48

[8] Szathmary E and Maynard Smith J 1997 From replicators to reproducers: The first major transitions leading to life *J. Theor. Biol.* **187** 555–71

[9] Eigen M 1971 Selforganization of matter and the evolution of biological macromolecules *Naturwissenshaften* **58** 465–523

[10] Eigen M, McCaskill J and Schuster P 1988 Molecular quasi-species *J. Phys. Chem.* **92** 6881–91

[11] Gause G F 1934 *The Struggle for existence: Systems thinking and thinking systems* (Baltimore, MD: Williams and Wilkins)

[12] Alebraheem J and Abu-Hasan Y 2012 Persistence of predators in a two predators–One prey model with non-periodic solution *Appl. Math. Sci.* **6** 943–56

[13] Adami C 2002 What is complexity *BioEssays* **24** 1085–94

[14] Devine S D 2009 The insights of algorithmic entropy *Entropy* **11** 85–110

[15] Chaitin G 1979 Toward a mathematical definition of 'life' *The Maximum Entropy formalism* ed R D Levine and M Tribus (Cambridge, MA: MIT Press) pp 477–98

**IOP** Publishing

# Algorithmic Information Theory for Physicists and Natural Scientists

Sean D Devine

# Chapter 11

# Sustainability requirements of a viable economy distant from equilibrium

Algorithmic information theory (AIT) is used to explore an economy from a whole system perspective with a new paradigm where resources and environmental costs are endogenous to the system. An economy is seen as a living system, distant from the most probable set of states, which is the ultimate decayed state that eventuates when energy sources dry up.

The simplest economy is taken to be a replicating family of autonomous hunter–gatherers who reproduce until they reach the carrying capacity of the system. The specification of the system at the carrying capacity is orders of magnitude shorter than one that specifies the disordered state that eventuates when all units die and decay. Like the bacterial system discussed earlier, or the human body, which is a system of replicated cells, the resources that sustain the replicating hunter–gatherer community, are the computational instructions as bits, embodied in the stored energy in food and minerals consumed by the replicating units. Sophisticated economies use their resources more efficiently than simple economies and, as a consequence, are further from their thermodynamic equilibrium, in contrast to the neoclassical view that sees an economy settling in an equilibrium where economic forces balance.

Because it is impossible to articulate the growth in the complexity of an economy in detail, a narrative is used to explore the economic system in terms of the large-scale drivers showing how order increases from an algorithmic perspective, in terms of bit flows, or information and resource flows.

The autonomous hunter–gatherer replicating unit, after many generations, of trial and error, learning and cognitive processes, forms higher order replicating units, shifting the system further from the thermodynamic equilibrium. This happens when simpler units, such as the hunter–gatherer community, learn to cooperate through trade and, with further development, amalgamate to form ordered structures, such as tribes, firms, cities and nations. At each stage of development resources are used more efficiently. Innovation, such as dwellings and clothes, increase resource efficiency. Innovation, leading to tools that amplify human labour, creates more order than would otherwise be possible. It is seen that replication processes initially increase the carrying capacity corresponding to Lotka's maximum power principle, but later, replication processes drive increased energy efficiency, leading to the maximum entry production principle (section 11.5.7). The distance the economy is from its degraded or decayed state is a measure of its order; however, the greater the distance, the more resources are needed to sustain it.

This approach contrasts with the neoclassical view of an economic system. What might be seen as an economic equilibrium from a neoclassical viewpoint, here is seen as a living system sustained in a homeostatic state distant from the decayed thermodynamic equilibrium set of states. The behaviour of a living economy is different from that implied by the neoclassical view of equilibrium. When an economic system settled in a homeostatic stable configuration is disturbed, it does not necessarily return to the initial state once the disturbance is removed.

Three distinct forms of computation exist in an economy. The first is the routines embodied in the human anatomy to digest food and fight disease. The second is the cognitive routines of human agents, either as individuals or as amalgamated units. These are the codified routines analogous to the routines of evolutionary economics. But the number of bits capturing the cognitive routines are extremely small relative to the third form of computation, which are the routines embodied in the laws driving natural processes. However, when a cognitive algorithm calls a natural subroutine, such as smelting iron, the number of bits in the process of smelting iron is massively larger than the number of bits in the cognitive routine. Hidalgo *et al* (section 11.5.7) call the cognitive routines 'know-how', as know-how manages economic activity like a central processor of a computer that calls large-scale routines embodied in the natural world. Hidalgo *et al* argue that Singapore as an economy is much more effective than Pakistan, as Singapore, like a central processor, controls a large computational trade network. A high GDP can be seen to be a consequence of an ordered economy, not the driver of one.

As resources are endogenous to the algorithmic approach, the understanding of Ayres, can be extended to provide insights into the debate between the bioeconomists and the neoclassical economists about economic growth. Other scientific approaches to an economy, such as control information developed by Corning and Klein and low entropy human systems as discussed by Chaisson (section 11.9) can be interpreted from an AIT perspective. In the long run, unless renewable energy sources (including nuclear) are used, resource and environmental constraints are likely to constrain the economy. The rise of atmospheric carbon dioxide disturbs the balance of the economy and from the algorithmic perspective is seen as a failure to effectively eliminate waste from the system to maintain it distant from thermodynamic equilibrium.

The algorithmic approach has a role to play in terms of our environmental choices that need to be made. For example, it is impossible to lift the poorer nations of the world out of abject poverty without increasing energy use, with the consequential threats to the homeostatic state of the global economy.

## 11.1 Introduction

How can a country the size of the USA support 329 million people when simple hunter–gatherer communities ranging over the same territory, would number perhaps a few hundred thousand?

Following Devine [1], this chapter argues that an economy, like an ecology, is a computational system that exists in a highly improbable state distant from the most probable set. In that sense it is said to be far from thermodynamic equilibrium. Natural laws, triggered by the cognitive actions of human agents can be envisaged as computational processes that can sustain the economic system distant from thermodynamic equilibrium by the input of stored energy carrying computational bits, and the ejection of bits carried by degraded species and heat. The principles outlined in sections 10.1 and 10.4.1, show how AIT can interpret a sophisticated economy, such as that in the USA, as a complex living system, distant from its thermodynamic equilibrium. However, here thermodynamic equilibrium is taken to mean the most probable set of states that eventuates when all energy flows through the system cease in contrast to the neoclassical idea of economic equilibrium. From the algorithmic perspective, the carrying capacity of the US economy is greater precisely because it can be sustained further from equilibrium by energy inputs. Such an economy exists in a homeostatic non-equilibrium state, sustained by real-world computational processes that carry bits into the system as stored energy, separating order from disorder, and ejecting disordered high entropy structures as heat and waste.

Section 10.4.1, applied AIT to a living biological system to provide a measure of the distance of a homeostatic living system from its most probable set of states that is commonly known as the thermodynamic equilibrium. In so doing, the approach is able to identify the thermodynamic requirements to sustain such a system. An economy can similarly be seen as a living system, and it is shown that the more sophisticated the economy, the more ordered it is, as it is further from this equilibrium. The more effectively such an economy uses resources, the better are its performance in term of GDP, its carrying capacity and the well-being of its participants.

The algorithmic approach offers a new economic paradigm that treats an economy from a whole system perspective [1]. Resource and environmental issues become part of the conceptual framework, i.e. endogenous to the system. This leads to the understanding that, compared with simpler economies, the US economy must be more effective in accessing resources to maintain viability. The algorithmic approach not only provides a set of tools to determine the thermodynamic requirements for a system to be maintained distant from equilibrium, but also provides insights into the trade-off between energy use and environmental costs as the economy grows. In so doing the approach contributes to the debate between environmental economists [2–4] and neoclassical economists [5, 6].

The AIT approach avoids the constraints of neoclassical economics, which relies on the received understanding that resource scarcity and externalities such as pollution can be adequately captured by the price mechanism to ensure optimum economic performance.

## 11.2 A reminder of the principles of AIT

As some reading this chapter may not have covered all of the previous chapters, the key principles of AIT are summarised below.

### 11.2.1 Natural laws as computations

The key understanding of AIT is that the natural laws that drive real-world behaviour can be understood as computations on a real-world universal Turing machine (UTM). As one UTM can simulate another, these natural processes can in principle be exactly simulated on a standard laboratory UTM to within a constant.

In which case, when appropriately coded, the number of bits in the algorithm that shifts the state of a system to another state, measures the algorithmic entropy change that has taken place. Just as computational gates in a laboratory computer enact physical laws to determine outputs, given particular inputs, so too the molecular species in a living system implement natural laws. The programme instructions in the real-world computer are embodied in the stored energy states of species, of which DNA is one of the most obvious examples. Provided all bits are tracked to ensure reversibility, Landauer's principle [7] shows that each bit of information in the algorithm defining the algorithmic entropy is carried by $k_B \ln 2 T$ Joules, whether implemented in a real-world, or a laboratory computer. Here, $k_B$ is Boltzmann's constant and $T$ the temperature of the computational system. This is discussed in detail in chapter 8 and in Devine [8]. As entropy is a function of state, only entropy differences matter, and the number of bits in the algorithm that specifies a system and then halts, is independent of the UTM that implements the algorithm as the machine dependence cancels. The number of bits is identical to the number obtained by tracking the flow of bits in and out of the system at the halt instant, as shown in section 8.5.3. This is similar to the way one might track the final state of a tree from the DNA instructions in the seed cell, and the information flows embodied in the resource inputs and waste outputs as the tree grows.

The second law of thermodynamics captures the reality that the computational processes, acting within an isolated system, embodying structural order far-from-equilibrium, drive the system to a disordered set of states known as the most probable set, or equilibrium set of states. However, over the time frames of interest, the equilibrium set of interest is a local equilibrium, rather than a global equilibrium. The computational instructions that implement the second law are associated with structures that store energy. Once the energy is released, as bits are conserved (section 8.5.1), the temperature increases when bits shift from the stored energy states to the momentum or thermal states. As section 10.4.1 outlined, the requirements to sustain a system in a non-equilibrium state is that the bits embodied in stored energy states entering the system, must balance the bits in heat and waste that exit the system. The relationship between computations and natural processes can be seen in table 11.1.

The algorithmic entropy, or the information in bits, denoted here by $H$, is closely related to the Shannon and thermodynamic entropies as shown in section 7.2.2 and discussed in chapters 8 and 9. Further discussion can be found in [9–11]. As only the entropy difference between two states has physical significance, in principle a laboratory UTM can be used as a ruler to measure information distances in bits between two real-world configurations.

### 11.2.2 An illustration based on an image on a screen

The manner in which bits specify a structure can be seen with the illustration of an image consisting of black and white pixels on a 10 megapixel screen. If there is no structure or pattern the image will be just a random array of black and white pixels, represented by a 1 for a black pixel and a 0 for a white. In which case, a string of 1's and 0's of length 10 megabits is needed to exactly specify each pixel in a particular random image. Contrast this with an ordered image representing a photograph. Such ordered images might well be generated by about 1 megabit. As this is significantly fewer than the bits needed to specify the random array, it shows that order is simpler to describe, requiring fewer bits than disorder [8].

Imagine, that the second law of thermodynamics, randomly degrades bits in the ordered image, replacing a black pixel by a white one and vice versa, and in so doing generates heat. Ultimately, the image would become a random array of black and white pixels, showing how order trends to disorder. Such a decaying image can only be sustained in the ordered state if bits can enter the system to keep regenerating the image. Not only does this require an input of energy to reset each bit, it also requires the ejection of the heat released as random bits are replaced.

The difference between the number of bits needed to specify a random array of 10 megapixels and an ordered photograph of 1 megapixel, corresponds to the degree of order, i.e. 10 megabits less 1 megabit. This specification of a two-dimensional

**Table 11.1.** Algorithmic order and structural order ([1]).

| Algorithmic order<br>Information and bits | Matching characteristics of structural order<br>Organisation and resources |
|---|---|
| Short algorithmic description<br>= Low algorithmic entropy<br>= Ordered system | Organised structure |
| Nested and interconnected subroutines<br>  (see figure 11.2) | Nested and interconnected structures mapped by a<br>  simple flow diagram |
| Fewer information bits describe system | Fewer resources are needed |
| Information bits pass between routines | Resources flow between system components |
| Disorder as bits ejected | Waste and low-grade energy is ejected as heat |

structure demonstrates the same principles as those that drive a living system, as is described next.

*Degree of order in a living system*

The image of pixels specified by an algorithm captures the essentials of a sophisticated living system. If $H_{ord}$ is the number of bits needed to specify exactly an ordered living system, and $H_{rand}$ the number of bits that specifies a configuration in the equilibrium or most probable set of states, the difference in bits between the ordered outcome, and the random one is called the degree of order, denoted by $D_{ord}$ as is discussed in section 9.3.2. If there are $\Omega$ possible states in the system, the value of $H_{rand} = \log_2 \Omega$ is the computational equivalent of the Shannon entropy. For the 10 megapixel array, there are $2^{10\,000\,000}$ possible states and hence $H_{rand} = 10$ megabits. The degree or order, which is in effect the distance bits from equilibrium, is given by

$$D_{ord} = \log_2 \Omega - H_{ord}.$$

Table 11.2 shows the connection between algorithms in bits and the energy flows that create and maintain a system such as an economy analogous to maintaining an image on a screen.

*Notation*

Those who have skipped earlier chapters need to be aware that scientists use the words 'information' and 'complexity' in a way that is completely opposite to the way mathematicians use these words. Scientists, from an intuitive perspective, see a more complex system as one that is not simple, but is highly structured and ordered. Such systems are often said to contain more information. On the other hand, the convention here follows that of mathematicians, who see disordered systems as more complex than the highly structured or ordered ones. Similarly, as information refers to the number of bits needed to describe a system or structure, the more disordered the structure, the harder it is to describe and the greater is its information content in bits. The intuitive concept of information often used by scientists, is closer to the idea of the degree of order or distance from equilibrium outlined in the previous section.

**Table 11.2.** Algorithms that map ordering through natural processes.

| Algorithms that implement natural processes | Natural processes |
|---|---|
| Human routines call algorithms that drive natural processes. | Humans utilise concentrated energy as food or fuel. |
| Algorithms separate order from disorder. | stored energy separates order from heat and waste |
| Waste containing heat bits ejected leaving ordered bits behind | Waste and heat ejected, leaving order behind. |

Here to ensure there is no misunderstanding, the term 'sophisticated economy' will be used to replace what others might call a 'complex economy'.

### 11.2.3 Replication processes create natural order

The human body is a highly ordered system produced by replicating individual cells, as discussed in chapter 10 and section 10.5.1. Replication is a computational process where the instructions in bits are carried into the system as stored energy, while high entropy heat and waste bits are ejected.

The simplest replicating system that illustrates the thermodynamic principles underpinning the creation and the long-term viability of a far-from-equilibrium living system is a simple bacterial system existing in a flow through of nutrients (see section 10.7.1).

Initially, consider a single bacterium in a nutrient flow. The energy in the nutrient carries the computational bits to enable the bacterium, and its offspring, to replicate by implementing the instruction in its DNA. As the number of bacteria grows, death and decay will remove bacteria from the system, creating waste and generating heat. This is analogous to the way the image in the above illustration decays. At the carrying capacity, determined by the death rate and the flow of nutrients, the system is maximally ordered, settling in a homeostatic state where the replication rate equals the death rate.

While a more detailed algorithm that is tied into the availability of resources is outlined in section 10.7.1 and equation (10.16), the following provides a simple argument. At the carrying capacity, where the number of bacteria equals $N$, the bacterial system can be specified by a short algorithm (embodied in the bacterial DNA) consisting of a routine of the form,

*From Nutrients REPLICATE bacterium N times.*

Given the specification of the nutrients, the length of this algorithm consists of the length of the replicating algorithm (in the DNA) plus about $\log_2 N$ bits [11]. However, if the nutrient flow is stopped, the system will revert to a disordered local equilibrium of randomly distributed chemicals that can only be specified by an horrifically long algorithm as there is no structure or order. As a consequence, the bacterial system can only be maintained against decay, if the decayed products are ejected as waste and heat, and new resources enter the system to provide the computational information needed to generate new bacteria.

As was discussed in section 10.7.1, where replicating systems are coupled so that resources are shared, the carrying capacity is higher and the system, like an ecosystem, is further from equilibrium as resources are used more effectively.

## 11.3 An economy seen as a replicating system

As section 10.7.1 discusses, the bacterial system, which is an archetypical replicating system, shows how replication processes generate and maintain a living system distant from equilibrium. The creation of order by replication can be seen as a computational process that accesses programme information in the nutrients, together with the replicating programme in the replicating unit, in order to reproduce, while ejecting waste and heat. As mentioned, humans are a collection of replicated cells generated by their DNA given appropriate resource inputs. Similarly, a human family is a higher order replicating collective, which is even further from equilibrium.

This insight allows the simplest economy to be seen as a replicating system of independent hunter–gather families. These families, which here will be termed economic agents, form the basic replicating unit that, like the bacterial system, replicates or reproduces, increasing their number until the carrying capacity is reached. This is determined by the availability of resources as food. At the carrying capacity, like the bacterial system, the hunter–gatherer economy is maximally ordered, as it is furthest away from the state of decay that would eventuate if all participants died, and their bodies decomposed. Equation (10.7) shows that the number of bits needed to specify an ordered system such as the hunter–gatherer community, is extremely short relative to the number of bits needed to specify the disordered state, corresponding to the death and decay of the hunter–gatherer community. This disordered state usually referred to as the equilibrium state, consists of a random arrangement of minerals and chemicals specifying the most probable set of states of the system. At its core, an economy is a collection of units that create order by replication. The degree of order depends on the available resources and the decay rate of the replicating hunter–gatherer families.

The thermodynamic requirements to maintain an economy in a viable state are identical to those of an ecological system, as was discussed in section 10.5.1. Like the bacterial system, or even a human body, the computational resources that sustain the replicating hunter–gather system are in the bits embodied in the stored energy as the food and minerals consumed by the replicating units. Equally important is the need for degraded waste in the form of heat, sweat, carbon dioxide, water, excrement and corpses to be ejected. From an environmental or ecological perspective, the availability of resources with stored energy enhances the simple economic system, enabling it to maintain or increase order. But if resources become scarce, or pollution cannot be adequately ejected, the economy is under threat.

Just as simple replicating biological systems can increase the carrying capacity by sharing resources, forming higher order replicating units, so too a more sophisticated economic structure can emerge as happens when replicating hunter–gatherer units trade, when they innovate to create dwellings and tools, and when they become interdependent by amalgamating to form tribes, firms and cities. Initially, order is crystallised in the form of the carrying capacity of the families, but once cognitive processes make decisions, different ordered structures appear. In which case, at each step the economic system becomes more ordered, and further from the decayed equilibrium state as more resources become available, or resources are used more effectively. Over many generations, due to selection processes and the cognitive behaviour of the economic agents, highly ordered structures, as seen in a first-world economy, emerge. The order can be recognised at this level, by the complex flow diagram that maps the algorithms capturing human behaviours, as they initiate real-world computations.

The drive for increasing order manifests itself in two different ways, as is discussed later. The first is the drive to increase the carrying capacity corresponding to Lotka's maximum power principle (MPP) [12, 13]. The second, while increasing the carrying capacity, encourages energy efficiency leading to the maximum entropy production principle (MEPP).

A more sophisticated economy, with its dependence on fossil fuels and minerals, has more serious issues to face. When the waste, such as carbon dioxide, cannot be adequately ejected, disorder accumulates driving the system from its highly ordered state.

The distance an economy is from its local equilibrium, or decayed state, is a measure of its order. The greater this distance, the greater the degree or order, but the greater the resources needed to sustain it. This is no different than the observation that a human existing in a viable state is more ordered and more distant from equilibrium than an ant, but the human must access more resources to survive.

### 11.3.1 The contrast with a neoclassical economy

The underlying viewpoint here is that an economic system exists in a state which does not correspond to the traditional neoclassical concept of an economic equilibrium [14]. In neoclassical economics, the economy is assumed to reach its optimum capability at an economic equilibrium where economic forces balance. However, once energy considerations are taken into account, what might be considered a neoclassical equilibrium is instead seen to represent a living system, like the human body or an ecology, that exists in an ordered viable, homeostatic state far from equilibrium. As has been mentioned, once all energy resources are turned off, death and decay processes implementing the second law of thermodynamics will drive the far-from-equilibrium system to its local thermodynamic equilibrium corresponding to the most probable set of states devoid of economic life. While the neoclassical equilibrium approach is a convenient construct, it assumes feedback mechanisms exist to counter even significant disturbances. If an economy were truly an equilibrium there could be no economic growth. In contrast to the neoclassical equilibrium, significant deviations from a homeostatic, stable configuration are path dependent and are usually irreversible. The significance of path dependence from an institutional perspective has been noted by Arthur [15, 16].

Because the homeostatic state is an attractor, maintained by the in-flow of resources and the out-flow of waste, in the short term, the homeostatic state appears to be similar to a stable equilibrium. That is, for mild disturbances, the economy might well adapt in the short term, and revert to something like the original state once the disturbance is reversed. For example, if some economic agents die through drought in a hunter–gatherer economy, when the rains return the number of agents might return to the pre-drought situation. However, if, for example, oil scarcity causes oil prices to rise in a more sophisticated economy, the far-from-equilibrium economy does not necessarily return to the previous stable state once oil prices fall.

Rather, the economy moves to a new situation after having adapted to alternative fuels or having become more fuel efficient. Nevertheless, economic agents produce, consume and trade, make investments and strategic choices, exactly as expected, from a neoclassical or evolutionary economic perspective. But for such an economy to grow, order must be created through computational processes driven by useful or stored energy.

This perspective argues that a developed economy, as in the United States, is a highly ordered interconnected set of structures, (in the form of firms, institutions and infrastructure) having low algorithmic entropy, and which is able to be sustained distant from its local thermodynamic equilibrium, by using stored energy and ejecting high entropy waste.

## 11.4 Order creation through the know-how of economic agents

The above principles provide an understanding of how information embodied in an economic system, drives growth and creates order, as seen in the complexity of its structures and interconnections. From the AIT perspective, an ordered economy with the same basic constituents as a less ordered economy needs fewer bits to be described on a reference UTM, as can be seen by the order in a structural map representing the economy. The more sophisticated the economy, the more information is stored in its structures, and the greater the resources needed to sustain it. When a human eats, breathes or consumes water and minerals, it is the programme bits that determine whether the human system can be sustained. Food, water, minerals, etc, are analogous to plugging different memory sticks into a laboratory computer. The computer accesses the memory sticks to get the needed instructions. Similarly, the waste ejected as carbon dioxide or heat corresponds to another memory stick that is removed once it accumulates all the used programme resources. By so doing, it frees the computer from clutter, allowing the computation to continue. Similarly, an ordered economy can only be maintained distant from its local equilibrium in a homeostatic state by what can be seen as computational processes where bits, carried by the stored energy, regenerate the economy while disordered waste is ejected. As illustrated in table 11.2 [1], there is a one-to-one correspondence between the information measured in bits embodied in the economy, and the energy flows in and out, as each computational bit must be carried by a unit of energy.

*Resources → stored energy → information as instructions → order.*

The critical units of an economy are the agents or the actors that initiate economic actions. At the simplest level the agent is a hunter–gatherer family, at a higher level a tribe, a firm or a city and at the national level an economy. At the fundamental level, the agent is a replicating unit, which through selection processes and cognitive actions, generates more sophisticated agent structures, as is outlined later.

The key point is to see an economy as a computational system that is shaped by the cognitive processes of agents and real-world natural processes. In practice, it would be impossible to track the binary algorithms that might generate or specify an economic system. However, this is unnecessary, as the algorithmic understanding can be used to identify the thermodynamic forces at work without going into detail. This can be seen by recognising that there are three types of computational processes that shape an economy, shifting it from one state to another, as outlined in the following three points.

1. The routines in real-world natural processes.

   These are the routines in the natural world that capture the computational processes implementing natural laws such as the burning of wood and the growing of a plant from seed. When different species and structures enter the economic system, computational instructions in the form of bits in the stored energy states and in the position and momentum states are carried into the system to initiate programmes in the economy. Because bits are conserved if tracked [8] (see section 8.5.1), it is the computational processes undertaken by the bits that are significant. It is what these species do, not what they are, that is important. The economy is driven by the human agent managing these natural processes.

2. Background routines.

   From a computational perspective, the human agent is maintained through instinctive routines such as 'eat, 'reproduce', etc. When a human agent takes the decision to eat an apple, a cognitive programme which can be denoted by 'EAT APPLE' is initiated. The 'EAT APPLE' routine calls deeply embedded routines within the human body that turn the resources in the apple to energy and, in so doing, sustain the human agent. These deeply embedded human routines, which are necessary for human survival, include routines such as extending muscles or fighting disease that are common to all agents. The number of bits in the decision processes that trigger some of these routines are negligible relative to the deeply embedded bits in the computational action that digests the food, etc. The background routines are those that have no economic significance and can be taken as given and do not directly impact on the economy.

3. Cognitive routines of agents.

   In addition to these instinctive routines, cognitive routines that Hidalgo [17] sees as 'know-how', call the appropriate computational routines in the natural world. These critical routines, existing in the mind of economic agents, shift the economy from one state to another by organising the information embodied in the external resources, to create or maintain ordered structures. These 'know-how' routines trigger natural computational processes. Examples are the cognitive process (analogous to the routines called by the Central Processing Unit in a computer) that might call real-world routines such as 'BURN WOOD' or 'PLANT SEED' or 'SMELT IRON'. When initiated, these routines burn wood, grow food and create iron. Hidalgo [17] refers to the quantity of know-how embodied in human cognitive processes as 'personbytes'. However, relative to these real-world routines, the number of bits captured in the know-how routines are negligible. Furthermore, such routines can be learned at very little cost, passing from agent to agent, and the most effective routines will become common because of environmental selection processes.

While these know-how routines involve very few bits, they can be expressed as routines analogous to the routines of evolutionary economics [18], or as noted by Arthur *et al* [19], the heterogeneous expectations of the agents in the simulation of the stock market. Other routines might be related to learning such as 'imitate other agent's behaviour'. In principle, the know-how routines can be represented by equivalent binary programmes that capture human action.

The information approach, that encapsulates agent behaviour in computational routines, provides particular insights into such questions as resource dependence, sustainability, and the drivers of an effective economy.

The primary behavioural driver in a simple economy of agents, such as hunter–gatherer communities, is to reproduce (replicate) until the system reaches a homeostatic or stable state determined by the system's carrying capacity. The system becomes further from equilibrium as the carrying capacity increases, for example when clothing or fire extend the viable range, or tools increase hunting effectiveness. This may happen by chance, or through cognitive processes that encapsulate know-how in better routines. However, it is not the aim here to investigate the processes whereby humans arrive at these routines, or to specify them in detail, but to recognise that they are part of the economy's computational processes, and the discovery of these routines is part of the adaptation processes of human agents.

*A Galois connection*

A Galois connection is the term used to relate partially ordered objects in one set, to those in another. Once a Galois connection is established between partially ordered sets, ordering is preserved. In the set of allowable flow diagrams of an economy, a city nests smaller units such as firms. Each firm can be represented as a more detailed flow diagram of subunits, until at the fundamental level a human agent who, through actions, initiates real-world computations. As a Galois connection can be established between the structures in the flow diagram, and the (enormous) number of bits specifying particular economies, a flow diagram that shows more order, corresponds to an economy that can be described with fewer bits at the fundamental level.

Similarly, a computational routine in a high-level language in the form of 'EAT APPLE' aligns with the binary implementation of the instructions, conserving order between computational languages even if the details cannot be specified. Similarly, if economic systems are ordered by the difference between the input energy and the waste energy discarded, the ordering is preserved with economic systems that are ordered through bit flows. This allows us to use a narrative to discuss an economic system in terms of an overarching flow diagram or network, that calls routines at one level, nests subroutines at another level, that itself nest sub-subroutines and so on.

## 11.5 A narrative to capture economic development

### 11.5.1 The hypothetical steps to greater economic sophistication

As has been mentioned, the more abstruse mathematics and physics underpinning the algorithmic approach (see [1, 8, 11]) can be put to one side, allowing the focus to be on the information issues relevant to the survival of an economy with resource and environmental constraints. As is discussed further in more detail, one can explore the emergence of a typical advanced economy by a narrative that tracks the information flows in and out of the system through hypothetical stages of development. This happens when a simple economy of autonomous, hunter–gatherer families evolves over many generations to form a large-scale, more ordered and more connected economy, but in so doing the economy becomes more resource dependent. By whatever means, trial and error, cognitive processes or downright competition, a simple hunter–gatherer economy over millennia, becomes a sophisticated nation. Key is increasing or maintaining order by using information resources in stored energy in the species that enter the system. In principle, a modern economy can be seen as the endpoint of computational processes that generates an advanced economy from a primitive one.

Ordered structures emerge when information efficiency increases. This can happen through developing trade networks, and through forming collectives such as tribes, firms, cities and nation states. This order is analogous to the order in a rich ecology, which because of interdependency and shared resources, is further from equilibrium. This is schematically shown in the hierarchical map of figure 11.2. As more resources become available, or because resources are used more effectively, the structures that emerge are more ordered. The more effective economies eventually dominate the economic landscape. The fundamental difference between a complex and a simple economy is not just that the GDP is higher, but that the complex economy is more ordered and more distant from equilibrium. The human agent, and the interdependent agent structures that form, are the actors that shape economic life.

During much of this development trajectory, the major driver is increasing the carrying capacity of the basic units such as the human family. Replication at the family level leads to replication at the higher level of the firm, with resource competition driving more highly ordered and connected structures. However, more recently in human history, with reproductive choice and discretionary wealth surpluses, the economic focus shifts from increasing the carrying capacity, to improving agent well-being by creating ordered artefacts, either as possessions, or as tools to create further order.

The more ordered the economy, the better organised it is in terms of resource flows and the subroutines that characterise the behaviour of the economic structures at each level of scale.

With this understanding, an economic narrative emerges that uses terms like order, disorder, distance from equilibrium, information requirements of sustainability, information flows and resource flows. These provide a conceptual framework to explore a sustainable economy.

### 11.5.2 Independent agents

The simplest level of an economy can be envisaged as a collection of independent agents consisting of self-sufficient hunter–gatherer families who will reproduce (replicate) until the sustainable carrying capacity is reached in a manner similar to the bacterial system previously outlined in section 10.7.1. This simple economy is ordered, as it is maintained in a homeostatic state by accessing food resources and ejecting waste. In a simple hunter–gatherer economy, when new resources are needed, or when waste becomes a problem, the actors move on. Agents use simple routines (such as hunting routines) categorised as know-how to sustain themselves. There is no controlling agency and GDP is meaningless for self-sufficient agents. Constituents of the agent-family have finite lifetimes, determined by natural causes and the carrying capacity of the system. At the carrying capacity, the birth rate equals the death rate. If there are environmental changes affecting energy access, the birth and death rate will adjust to maintain the system. Without the information resources embodied in the food energy, the agents die, the economy dies, and the whole system reverts to its local equilibrium.

### 11.5.3 Agent adaptation

At the next level of sophistication, the agents can compete with each other for scarce resources. Variety, as the viable system's model would argue [20, 21], increases the resilience of the system of agents. Variety allows agents operating under more effective routines to dominate the economy as they make better use of the information bits in the resources. If one agent innovates, the routine 'IMITATE INNOVATIVE AGENT' can be passed from agent to agent. In which case, learning can increase the carrying capacity of the system. At the carrying capacity, the system maximises its use of the exergy flowing into the system, corresponding to Lotka's maximum power principle [12, 13], which is in effect a 'maximising power intake principle' (see discussion [22]). The principle is a direct consequence of replication processes and selection.

If two similar replicating systems, such as two hunter–gatherer communities compete for the same resources, the one with the highest replicating efficiency and the lowest death rate will completely dominate the system as it maximises the utilisation of exergy increasing the order, analogous to the growth of self-replicating polynucleotides discussed in section 10.9 and references [11, 23, 24]. This could be the agent type that has learned how to produce food more efficiently from the same inputs, or even types who require less food because of structural differences. Agents who do not adapt are removed, and the system uses resources better [11]. Following environmental change, selection processes will ensure those with the best capability mix, dominate the system. By increasing the carrying capacity, order increases. The approach shows how the system settles in a region where the number of agents is determined by the rate the resources are consumed, rather than an externally given carrying capacity [11]. In contrast to biological evolution, variation need not be blind, as it can arise through strategic insights and intelligent responses of economic agents.

### 11.5.4 Trade increases order

From an algorithmic perspective, order increases when programme bits that enter one part of the economy, pass to subroutines of another part of the economy rather than being ejected as waste bits. The simplest example is trade. In an ecology, the equivalent of trade is a symbiotic relationships between species. Trade increases the order of an economy, as trade makes better use of the information in the stored energy resources. From an algorithmic point of view, trade is equivalent to sharing information between the routines associated with different agents. Fewer information bits embodied in the stored energy need to enter the system to define the more ordered system [11]. As information resources that would otherwise be discarded are utilised, trade increases the efficiency of resource use. Order increases if potatoes can be traded for carrots rather than be left to rot as the carrying capacity is higher. More energy can be utilised for the same inputs. Figure 11.1, which is the economic equivalent of figure 10.1, identifies how information is better used when agents can trade, as bits in stored energy are shared. This information drives the system further from equilibrium as what would have been waste is better utilised. What finally leaves the system is more degraded and more disordered, containing less useable energy. One can conclude that, in a resource-constrained environment, interdependence through trade is the major alternative to conflict between agents.

Trade can extend to providing information and services where the value of the trade is primarily in software as know-how or information, embodied in labour and organisational capability. As Paul Romer has stated, 'the value is in the recipe" [25]. The know-how as software, calls routines in the natural world to generate order.

However, stories, poems, art and other creative activities, embody order that can be transferred directly to the human imagination, rather than increasing societal order as a whole. In so doing they increase personal utility. The energy cost of production of, what might be called, 'creative goods', is low when participation is shared. Because of the lower energy burden on the economy, humankind might be better to find fulfilment in order embodied in information, rather than material artefacts.

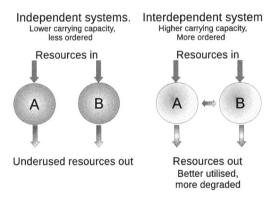

**Figure 11.1.** Agent sharing through trade increases the carrying capacity and order.

### 11.5.5 Trade in artefacts

The next stage is where stored energy and human know-how are used to created ordered objects which here will be called artefacts. Artefacts have a different function than tools, which are discussed below. In the simplest economy, manual labour can create an artefact, such as a carved wooden object, while disorder is expelled as heat, chips, and the waste, in the form of carbon dioxide, sweat and excrement. Artefacts as economic goods or possessions, increase personal well-being, rather than increasing the carrying capacity. Simple examples are a piece of jewellery, or a carving. More sophisticated examples are possessions where the value lies primarily in beauty, the comfort offered, the status that possession brings. Artefacts are valuable as they embody order and because they require know-how, and often significant energy to be produced. In which case, the creation of artefacts drives the economy further from equilibrium. The price of an artefact may only be roughly correlated with the order embodied in it, but also may be determined by aesthetics, and the status of possession. In modern societies, the focus has shifted from increasing order through increasing the carrying capacity, to increasing order through the creation of artefacts that increase perceived well-being. But as discussed immediately below, an artefact has greater value when it is used as a tool or a machine.

### 11.5.6 Order created by innovation, tools and machines

A distinction needs to be made between ordered artefacts, as discussed in the previous section, and tools that are the source of further order creation. Ordering through technological innovation can include better farming practices, such as extracting resources from waste, or using fertiliser, irrigation, and creation of tools such as a plough or spear. When an animal, rather than a human pulls the plough, valuable food resources are protected, as the animal feeds on grass. The carrying capacity increases as an alternative energy source is available.

Tools and machines, which access new computational pathways, amplify the capabilities of an agent, by accessing fuel to create new computational pathways. This significantly increases the order and carrying capacity of the system, by driving it further from equilibrium. Wood can be burned to warm a community, while clothes and dwellings allow the community to survive over a wider area, increasing the order. However, this is usually at the cost of greater resource and greater waste expenditure. Energy is needed to drive such innovations but, to be sustainable, carbon dioxide, minerals and waste must pass to the environment. In contrast to artefacts as possessions, the value of tools and machines, lies in their use to create further order, driving the system further from equilibrium. Smarter technologies (such as computational technologies) can maintain or increase order using less energy and therefore generate less waste, while some technologies can use resources more efficiently to minimise waste.

Hidalgo [17] sees the equivalent of this ordering process as crystallised imagination. He illustrates this with the idea of a medicinal pill. The pill embodies know-how and imagination that is a consequence of human ingenuity. From the computational viewpoint the swallowed pill activates real-world computations managed by human capability to bring about desired changes in our body, sustaining order by restoring the survival capacity of a human being. Similarly, tools arise through technological innovation. From a computational point of view, know-how, as a suite of routines in the human brain, triggers the algorithms representing the natural laws, to rearrange the system and pump out disorder.

An artefact such as a car or a cell phone becomes primarily a tool when it increases labour productivity or when, like a home, it increases survival by providing protection and conserving energy. As society develops, resources are invested in tools, by diverting resources from consumption. This approach sharpens the distinction between investments that increase order and those that do not. Order-creating investments include investments in technologies that produce artefacts and tools that enhance human capability through learning and discovery. Innovation that creates new technologies is an evolutionary process [18]. However, as learning allows other agents to use technological know-how, computational capability diffuses through the economy at very little cost, enabling the whole system to function at a higher level. The high quality of life evident in developed economies relies on tools and external energy to enhance the value of labour, while learning allows technological know-how to diffuse through the economy at very little cost, but always with the proviso that degraded waste must also be ejected.

When the economy becomes more complex, observationally it seems that the order per agent increases, as the agent chooses to focus on increasing ordered possessions and productive tools. That is, by increasing personal utility, rather than instinctively increasing the carrying capacity by increasing offspring. This change in driver is critical to the modern economy.

### 11.5.7 Amalgamation and nesting of agents to form new agent types

As economic sophistication increases, agents develop mutually beneficial interconnections to form more ordered collective structures that can be envisaged as higher-level computational units.

Hidalgo [17] (p 157) developed the concept of economic complexity which is linked to computational know-how, arguing that more complex and more ordered products depend on larger and more intricate networks, enabling successful economies to trade in more diverse goods. Hidalgo and Hausman [26] illustrate this with a measure that distinguishes the more diverse economy of Singapore from Chile and Pakistan in terms of the ubiquity of the Singaporean products, and the diversity of its export countries.

This is consistent with the viewpoint here that these intricate networks are highly ordered structures critical to a modern economy, driving the economy further from equilibrium than less connected structures. It is the know-how that manages these highly ordered network structures to create ordered products.

Large networks store a large amount of know-how and knowledge. As economic complexity increases, agents develop mutually beneficial interconnections to form more ordered collective computational networks. The complex economy is richer

Information bits as
concentrated energy in

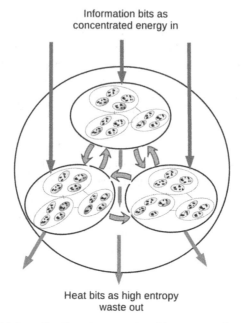

Heat bits as high entropy
waste out

**Figure 11.2.** Resource and information flows in a nested and interconnected economy. Adapted from [1].
© 2018 by the author. CC BY 4.0.

because it has richer interconnections and is therefore more ordered than a simple hunter–gatherer economy. Figure 11.2, extracted from Devine [1], illustrates how primitive agent structures can become interconnected to form highly ordered productive structures. Firms, cities and nation states share informational resources horizontally and vertically between subsystems through trade and other relationships. The structural map of an ordered economy shows how routines, as know-how, can harness routines in the natural world to generate ordered productive structures. Cities pass information to other cities, or farmers provide food to cities, while within the cities, firms pass informational resources and goods embodying order to customers. A better structurally designed network is more computationally efficient, using the available information resources more effectively, extracting maximum benefit from resources, while ejecting more disorder as bits in the degraded waste. This structural order is critical to a modern economy driving it further from equilibrium.

The emergence of large structures interconnected over significant distances requires infrastructure in the form of transport systems, power, communication systems, as well as waste removal systems. Effective infrastructure makes better use of the information resources embodied in the useful or stored energy by facilitating the production and the distribution of goods and services. When transport shifts objects from one place to another to allow resources to be used elsewhere, it corresponds to the computational equivalent of a robotic device, transferring instructions in hardware from one computational system to another.

Both central planning and market signals can drive infrastructural ordering. The US adapted economically to its large geographical area, increasing scale and scope by harnessing coal as a cheap fuel, leading to the emergence of connected infrastructures, and giant companies [27]. Such structures are highly ordered using the available information resources more effectively, extracting the maximum benefit from these resources. However, from an information throughput perspective the process was very inefficient.

Financial institutions are critical components of an interconnected economy. Financial institutions are computational high-level agents that exchange information with other institutions and structures. Money behaves as a numerical code to signal the resource value and to allocate resources to computational agents to implement routines. These are the routines that determine how, and to whom, and under what conditions resources such as fuel, artefacts and machines are allocated.

Effective allocations should target underlying growth aligned with increasing the order of the economy, rather than increasing investment allocations to fixed assets such as existing housing. If this does not happen, the economy ultimately will need to correct. The approach here sharpens the distinction between investment that increases order, and investment that does not. Order-creating investments include investment in the production of ordered artefacts, and investment that enhances human capability through learning and innovation.

The argument here is not that such structures are inevitable (although in an open society with sound institutions they are more likely to occur), but that when they do occur, the sophistication of the economy increases as it becomes more ordered, and more distant from equilibrium. Selection processes are likely to favour agents who become more strategically connected, by amalgamating lower level structures as information resources are better used. An economy never quite gets to its maximum entropy production state, as residual energy in waste still exists that can be processed by the birds, rats and microbes that degrade the rubbish in tips. However, the total eco-biosystem seeks to maximise entropy production, driving everything to equilibrium more rapidly than a much simpler system.

*MEPP further increase in order*
While replication and selection processes drive the economic system to maximise power throughput, according to Lotka's maximum power principle [12, 13], another set of processes that interconnect different parts of the economy maximise the entropy production of the whole system.

The critical point is that, where information trickles through more structures before being ejected as waste, the resources are being used more effectively, and therefore the economy is more ordered. Similarly, in a highly connected economy from a computational perspective, the waste from one component of the system still retains residual programme information that can become the resource input for another, extracting more value from the useful energy before being discarded [28]. The more highly connected and ordered the economy, and the more hierarchical its structure, the greater the entropy in the final waste output, whether it is measured in bits or in thermodynamic terms The ecological argument of [29] shows that a more complex ecology, formed by natural selection process, degrades the useful energy more effectively, and pumps out more useless energy as heat at a greater rate than a simple ecology. However, while an ecology has some of the characteristics of an economy, the ecology tends to have fixed inputs.

This allows the evolutionary stages of an economy to be understood in terms of the Maximum Entropy Production Principle. Hermann-Pillath in figure 2.15 [22], shows the relationship between the Jayne's MaxEnt principle [30, 31], Lotka's maximum power principle (MPP) and the maximum entropy production principle, while the associated discussion identifies these principles as a manifestation of the second law of thermodynamics in non-equilibrium systems from a whole system perspective. Here, these principles arise as a consequence of selection processes in coupled replicating systems.

## 11.6 Are there resource limits to economic growth?

A critical strategic issue is whether economic growth can continue indefinitely or whether there are natural limits. As AIT treats energy and resources as the part of the system that carries the information in bits, it provides a tool to help resolve a historic confrontation between the neoclassical economists represented by Solow [5] and Stiglitz [6], and the bioeconomist [4, 32]. The bioeconomics school believes that economies are constrained by the so-called 'entropy law' [3]. This leads Georgescu-Roegen [4] to claim that the economy is constrained by the need to access 'low entropy' and eject high entropy waste to maintain stability. However, Georgescu-Roegen has poorly articulated a crucial issue, borrowing his argument from an earlier edition of Schrödinger's book *What is life?* [33]. Shrödinger later apologised for oversimplifying by using the term 'low entropy', pointing out that it was free energy, not low entropy, that drives life. The ox, as a far-from-equilibrium system, does not directly import low entropy, but is sustained by accessing free energy from grass as fuel, and excreting waste containing heat. Goergescu-Roegen [34] further lost credibility by introducing a problematic fourth law of thermodynamics to argue material resources also degrade irreversibility [35].

On the other hand, Solow [5, 36] and Stiglitz [6, 37], argue that, as resources are depleted, the substitution of capital for labour can lead to technological improvements which compensate for the resources used. They use the economic tool called the 'production function' to model how labour and capital can increase productivity. But Daly [32] is unconvinced, and reiterates Georgescu-Roegen's [38] view that Solow and Stiglitz' production function argument is a conjuring trick and an inevitable consequence of its homogenous form, thus avoiding the problem, or shifting it too far into the future. While the production function approach is too simplistic, the problem is not so much the production function, but rather that neoclassical economics is predicated on an equilibrium view of an economic system. Until energy and resources are included as part of the economic framework, problems such as those identified, are inevitable. In summary, the stand-off was not effectively resolved as the conceptual framework was not adequate to cross differing paradigms. Some progress has been made in the debate by including energy in the production function, a recent example being that of Kummel [14].

Since the controversial work of the bioeconomics school, Ayres [2, p 39], from the point of view of Shannon Information Theory, has provided a more robust approach to these concerns. Trained as a mathematical physicist, Ayres' contribution to understanding of the thermodynamics of economic growth is highly significant. He [2] identifies confusions over terms such as entropy, low entropy, negative entropy, order, disorder, complexity and information; confusions that inhibit the conversation (see also [39, 40]). Ayres [35], in trying to further the conversation, drew attention to the role of information and its relationship to energy and entropy. His insights can be interpreted within the AIT outlined above, to identify the resources used to sustain a living system in terms of the useful information carried in the form of stored energy[1].

The approach of this chapter in a sense starts where Ayres left off. By applying AIT to an economy, the limits of the neoclassical approach are identified, and Ayres' ideas are placed within a more versatile conceptual framework. Importantly, Ayres [41] draws attention to the thermodynamic entropy equivalent of one bit of information. If one bit of uncertainty is added or removed, the thermodynamic entropy change is $k_B \ln 2$.

Ayres [2] argues that the Shannon measure of uncertainty is not the critical information measure. Instead, he introduces the concept of 'D-information'. This is the reduction in uncertainty in bits when an observer gains more evidence about the state of the system, indicating that it belongs to a subset of the original possibilities. If the subset is more ordered, this measure aligns with the degree of order used here (see section 11.2.2). The gain in bits in moving from a configuration in this ordered subset of possible configurations, to one in the equilibrium set or most probable set of states, corresponds to D-information. This increase in bits corresponds to the difference between the Shannon entropy of the ordered subset, and the Shannon entropy of the equilibrium set of states.

Ayres [2] also defines the term 'physical information' for information that is stored in the energy states of real-world structures. From the algorithmic perspective, this is the programme information that carries the computational instructions driving the system's trajectory, separating order from the waste to ultimately eject high entropy waste as heat and degraded chemical species. Physical information provides the available energy, or exergy, corresponding to a generalised Gibb's free energy, able to do useful work [4, 42].

Ayres uses another term, 'Survival Relevant Information', denoted by SR, to refer to physical information that is relevant to evolutionary selection processes. Ayres sees all SR information, good or bad, as embodied in the programmes that impact on, for example, an economic system. While Ayres seems to restrict this concept to just the structural information representing capability in genes or, in the economic case, know-how, the algorithmic approach would also identify the grass that maintains the ox as also relevant to survival. The perspective here would not

---

[1] In the literature, the relevant energy can be called exergy, useful energy, free energy, etc. Here, 'stored energy' is used simply to refer to energy stored in molecular structures that is available to undertake computations to shift one state to another.

only include the know-how as Ayres does, but also the real-world programmes that the know-how organises to bring about change.

Ayres [35] has a more moderate position than the bioeconomists. He suggests solar energy is sufficient in principle to meet energy needs into the foreseeable future. With this view it then becomes possible to increase energy to compensate (at least to some extent) for decreasing mineral resources. Because in the long-term resources may be scarce, ultimately, as he notes [35], the future may need to recycle and mine the partially degraded waste from its past.

Critically, Ayres [2] has identified that, from an entropy perspective, manufacturing processes have become more efficient over the centuries. He observed that in the 19th-century economic value was added by harnessing information in chemical transformations by inefficient processes. A century later value added was mainly through harnessing information through more efficient morphological transformation. More recently, value tends to be added through symbolic information, effectively in the form of software. Ayres and Warr [43] then suggest that since 1970, as economic growth has been higher than the inputs of capital, labour and work, entropy as symbolic information is becoming more important. Seeing information in terms of programme bits gives a better understanding of Ayres' insights. The order or information in a manual typewriter is morphological, whereas a PC embodies order mainly in the software and, as a tool, can achieve far more than the typewriter.

This suggests that, rather than embodying variation in production system in hardware, variation based on software can be used in flexible production systems driving versatile robotic systems.

While technological advances can increase the efficiency of resource use, and recycle waste with residual stored energy, new technologies increase demand for useful or stored energy in the first instance. But this requires learning to be used effectively. AIT complements Ayres' approach and can provide insights into the trade-off between energy use and environmental costs to sustain a far-from-equilibrium economy. Also, it provides a useful tool with which to engage with more traditional views. The rise of atmospheric carbon dioxide that disturbs the balance of the economy is seen as a failure to effectively eliminate waste.

## 11.7 Order and GDP

The fundamental difference between a sophisticated economy and a simpler one is not just that the GDP is higher, but that the sophisticated economy is more ordered and more distant from equilibrium. It can only survive when bits in stored energy states enter the system to restructure it and by ejecting stored energy and waste. The algorithmic approach distinguishes the increase in GDP, which primarily is a measure of the value of trade, and the increase in order associated with increased effectiveness when resources are used more efficiently. Nevertheless, one would expect there to be a rough correlation between increased GDP due to more efficient use of resources (or due to accessing new resources) and the consequential increase of order. A more sophisticated economy will have a higher GDP because increased trade, with the creation of interconnected networks, utilises stored energy better. But it does not follow that an increase in GDP corresponds to an increase in order and therefore economic effectiveness. When long-term GDP increases are not correlated with an increase in order, a correction may be needed. The algorithmic approach suggests the following different categories of economic activity.

1. A static economy where there is neither an increase in GDP or order. In a simple economy high-value energy as food or fuel sustains the population and maintains the productive capability, replacing artefacts and agents that decay and degrade. However, as only maintenance is required there is no increase in order or GDP.

2. However, even when there is minimal growth, the economy can still become more ordered, improving well-being when artefacts and tools are passed from one generation to the next. The order increases because, as the ordered artefacts last longer, they accumulate in the economy.

3. Where the market price of fixed assets, such as housing increases, leading to increased returns on the asset, GDP is rising, but there is no gain in order. Instead, a disproportionate share of the benefits of the economic output flow to the owners of the fixed assets.

4. In the long term, further order is created when innovation leads to investment in new technologies, with accompanying up-skilling of the work force. The creation of new technological platforms, as epitomised by the ICT technologies, generate increasing economic order that is aligned with an increase in GDP, as rates of return increase [44].

5. Technologies may appear to substitute for resources, but as tools and machine require more energy, there is a cost. Greater awareness of the operational constraints of an economy will help societies to maintain their way of life with responsible management of both the concentrated energy input, and waste minerals.

## 11.8 Complementary approaches to human systems

As outlined below, the approaches of control information [45] and energy flows in low entropy systems [40, 46] provide further insights into the thermodynamics of living systems.

### 11.8.1 Control information

Corning and Kline express concerns over the loose terminology in discussions centred around the bioeconomics school [39, 45, 47]. They argue that the Shannon idea of information as uncertainty is blind to any functional basis the information might have. Instead they introduce the idea of 'Control Information', which from a cybernetic perspective is 'The capacity (know-how) to control the acquisition, disposition and utilization of matter/energy in purposive (teleonomic) processes' [45, 47]. In practice, they take control information, $I_{CI}$, as

$$I_{CI} \propto (\ln A_{usef} - \ln A_{cost}),$$

where $\ln A_{usef}$ refers to the natural logarithm of the available useful stored energy, while $\ln A_{cost}$ is the natural logarithm of the energy expended to harness this energy. From this perspective, driving a car has high energy returns, but there is little energy cost involved for humans to control the process. Riding a bicycle also has a low cost, but has much lower energy returns. As a consequence, the control information $I_{CI}$ is lower.

The AIT measure of information avoids the problems of information as uncertainty identified by [39, 45, 47], as the programme bits execute a function in the real-world. $H_{CI}$, the AIT equivalent of $I_{CI}$, is the difference in bits between the algorithm that controls the process ($H_{cost}$), and the algorithm that implements change ($H_{usef}$). This is the combination of the human know-how and the real-world subroutines that achieve a specific purpose (such as smelting iron), less the cost in doing so. As for a process where all bits are tracked reversibly, and as there are $k_B \ln 2T$ Joules per bit, $I_{CI} = k_B \ln 2T H_{CI}$, where $H_{CI}$ is the control information in bits. That is, the algorithmic equivalent is

$$H_{CI} = H_{usef} - H_{cost}.$$

However, the concerns in the current paper are not about energy efficiency or profitability, but the long-term sustainability of the economic processes. An economy is less under threat from resource constraints when bicycles are used for transport compared with motor vehicles, even though the control information or information profitability of motor transport is higher.

### 11.8.2 Energy flows in low entropy systems

Chaisson [40, 46] has developed a big picture view of the common features of a complex systems ranging from the grand scale of the cosmos, to societal complexity. As mentioned earlier, the preferred approach here to avoid ambiguity, would be to used the word ordered system, distant from equilibrium rather than the term 'complex system'.

Chaisson notes that, as complex systems (using his term) are islands of low entropy, the entropy in the environment must be increasing. Chaisson suggests that the idea of information is of little use in quantifying complexity in the general case. Instead, he sees entropy decreases in complex systems as dependent on energy flows. Human society with its machines is among the most energy laden systems known. His complexity measure of 'energy rate density' is the amount of (free) energy available for work that passes through a system in unit time and unit mass [40, 46].

From the perspective of AIT, this energy carries the programme bits that transform the system. In which case, the energy rate density can be converted to the 'bit rate density' in terms of the programmes that drive the system further from equilibrium. In other words, Chaisson's narrative closely aligns with the arguments here, once it is seen that the energy rate density is related to the ' bit rate density' by $k_B \ln 2T$ joules per bit. Chaisson notes, for example, that the energy rate density ranges from 4 Joules s$^{-1}$ $kg^{-1}$ for a hunter–gatherer society to 200 Joules s$^{-1}$ $kg^{-1}$ for a modern society. The cultural evolution of sophisticated gadgets can be traced by the rise in energy rate density. He observes that the energy rate density rises sharply over time for a complex system and then tapers off. The approach here would see this rise as a consequence of bit flows increasing until the carrying capacity of a particular system is reached. Once this happens there is little further rise until biological or cultural evolution creates a new structure in the system shifting it further from equilibrium.

## 11.9 Implications of the algorithmic approach

This leads to the core assumption of this paper. A more effective economy is more ordered than a simpler economy. But because more informational resources are needed to sustain it, the effective economy needs a higher input of stored energy to maintain its ordered state. This highlights the constraints that inhibit potential growth and provides an alternative perspective to explore different options. It highlights the fact that the current carrying capacity on earth may not be able to increase much without destroying the order underpinning our quality of life. The following are some implications.

- Know-how routines are a key factor in understanding how to optimise decisions dealing with environmental and resource issues. New technologies and technological change are essential if we are not to disrupt the Earth's economy with a consequential crash in well-being. But always the question is 'Can we increase order at minimal disruption to the overall system?' It is unlikely that mining from Mars or the Moon will ever increase our overall order. Choices related to energy and information must clarify our economic decisions. For example, irrespective of whether cryptocurrencies have any value in facilitating trade, the energy cost of mining each new bitcoin increases rapidly and is now at 17 megajoules per dollar [48]. The question is whether new technologies, like cryptocurrencies, extract more resources from the planet than they contribute in terms of increased well-being.

- As the processes that sustain an economy in an ordered state, distant from equilibrium, are critical for the viability of an economy, is there a simple measure (not GDP) that indicates viability and economic sophistication? Perhaps a proxy for the order of an economy could be derived from the trade networks. Hidalgo *et al* [17, 26] have related a country's fitness to the complexity of its products in trade networks, not just their diversity, but the expertise and technological infrastructure required to produce them. Similarly, Krantz *et al* [49] have used the maximum entropy principle to extract country fitness from trade networks. These measures are more likely to be correlated with the order than is GDP.

- In the early stages of economic growth from a low base, environmental degradation increases, but when per capita income rises, environmental degradation falls. But some of this is a consequence of production shifting to poorer economies that carry the environmental costs. Developing economies may also learn how to avoid the pitfalls of historic pollution experienced by the developed economies. Furthermore, more detailed economic modelling reinforces the concern that structural changes that favour growth, may also increase pollution [50] contrary to what the Environmental Kuznets curve implies [51]. For a discussion of these issues, see Stern [52].

If only renewable energy sources are used, the degradation may stabilise. However, where energy from fossil fuels is used to create and maintain order, the increase of atmospheric carbon dioxide is inevitable [52, 53]. Irrespective of how much per capita income grows, carbon dioxide levels are unlikely to fall in our lifetimes.

## 11.10 Conclusions for economic systems

In contrast to the neoclassical understanding of economic equilibrium where economic forces balance, once energy is considered, it is seen that an economy is far from its local thermodynamic equilibrium and can only be sustained in a homeostatic or stable state, with the input of stored energy and the expulsion of degraded waste. Without energy, the economy dies, ultimately decaying to its local thermodynamic equilibrium, devoid of economic life.

The algorithmic approach sees an economy as a computational system [1], where the computational instructions can be tracked, as bits embodied in human know-how, and as bits in the energy states of the resources accessed by the economy. The thermodynamic process by which stored energy enters the system and waste is ejected driving the system further from thermodynamic equilibrium, corresponds to $k_B \ln 2T$ Joules per bit. More ordered economies are better economies, as they use fewer computational bits embodied in the economy to extract the maximum benefit from resources, before degraded waste carrying bits as heat is ejected.

Critical to the operation of an economy are the bits in human know-how. Know-how, rather like the operation of the Central Processing Unit of a computer, can initiate ordering processes through manipulating the information bits embodied in the natural world states. Know-how can initiate further ordering processes through trade, through innovation by creating new technologies, and forming highly organised economic structures to add value. As more ordered economies better use their resources, they are more effective. The approach clarifies some of the issues raised by the bioeconomics school [4, 32, 38, 42], providing an overarching economic perspective that can integrate other economic perspectives. By drawing attention to the role of useful or stored energy and evolutionary technological change and the need to eject waste, it clarifies the strategic choices to determine how best to improve societal well-being using limited natural resources.

While in practice it is impossible to specify an economy in detail, a structural map or flow diagram can encapsulate the order, as the diagram indicates when fewer bits are needed to specify the economy. Furthermore, once the energy throughput of an economy is established, the energy flow can be converted to bit flows. The degree of order is the increase in bits from the relatively few bits needed to specify an ordered economy and the massive number of bits needed to specify the decayed equilibrium state. The algorithmic approach has a role to play in discussion of our long-term environmental problems, not so much by identifying what must be done, but by identifying what cannot be done.

# References

[1] Devine S 2018 An economy viewed as a far-from-equilibrium system from the perspective of algorithmic information theory *Entropy* **20** 228

[2] Ayres R U 1994 *Information, Entropy and Progress: A New Evolutionary Paradigm* (Woodbury, NY: American Institute of Physics)

[3] Daly H E 1993 Sustainable growth: An impossibility theorem *Valuing the Earth: Economics, Ecology, Ethics* (Boston, MA: MIT Press) pp 267–73

[4] Georgescu-Roegen N 1971 *The Entropy Law and the Economic Process* (Cambridge, MA: Harvard University Press)

[5] Solow R M 1997 REPLY:Georgescu-Roegen versus Solow/Stiglitz *Ecol. Econom.* **22** 267–8

[6] Stiglitz J E 1997 REPLY:Georgescu-Roegen versus Solow/Stiglitz *Ecol. Econom.* **22** 269–70

[7] Landauer R 1961 Irreversibility and heat generation in the computing process *IBM J. Res. Dev.* **5** 183–91

[8] Devine S 2018 Algorithmic entropy and Landauer's principle link microscopic system behaviour to the thermodynamic entropy *Entropy* **20** 798

[9] Zurek W H 1989 Algorithmic randomness and physical entropy *Phys. Rev.* A **40** 4731–51

[10] Bennett C H 1982 Thermodynamics of computation—A review *Int. J. Theor. Phys.* **21** 905–40

[11] Devine S D 2016 Understanding how replication processes can maintain systems away from equilibrium using algorithmic information theory *Biosystems* **140** 8–22

[12] Lotka A 1922 Contribution to the Energetics of Evolution *Proc. Natl. Acad. Sci. USA* **8** 147–51

[13] Lotka A 1922 Natural selection as a physical principle *Proc. Natl. Acad. Sci. USA* **8** 151–4

[14] Kümmel R and Lindenberger D 2014 How energy conversion drives economic growth far from the equilibrium of neoclassical economics *New J. Phys.* **16** 125008

[15] Arthur B 1989 Competing technologies, increasing returns, and lock-in by historical events *Econ. J.* **99** 116–31

[16] Douglass C N 1993 *Lecture to the memory of Alfred Nobel* https://www.nobelprize.org/prizes/economic-sciences/1993/north/lecture/

[17] Hidalgo C 2015 *Why Information Grows: The Evolution of Order, from Atoms to Economies* (New York: Basic Books)

[18] Nelson R R and Winter S G 1982 *An Evolutionary Theory of Economic Change* (Cambridge, MA: Belknap)

[19] Arthur W B, Holland J H, LeBaron B, Palmer R G and Tayler P 1997 Asset pricing under endogenous expectations in an artificial stock market *The Economy as an Evolving System II. SFI Studies in the Sciences of Complexity* vol XXVII (Reading, MA: Addison-Wesley)

[20] Beer S 1979 *The Heart of Enterprise* (Chichester: Wiley)

[21] Beer S 1981 *Brain of the Firm* 2nd edn (Chichester: Wiley)

[22] Herrmann-Pillath C 2013 *Foundations of Economic Evolution. A Treatise on the Natural Philosophy of Economics* (Cheltenham: Edward Elgar)

[23] Eigen M 1971 Selforganization of matter and the evolution of biological macromolecules *Naturwissenshaften* **58** 465–523

[24] Eigen M, McCaskill J and Schuster P 1988 Molecular quasi-species *J. Phys. Chem.* **92** 6881–91

[25] Romer P M 2002 Economic growth *The Concise Encyclopedia of Economics* https://www.econlib.org/library/Enc/EconomicGrowth.html

[26] Hildago C A and Hausmann R 2009 The building blocks of economic complexity *Proc. Natl. Acad. Sci. USA* **206** 10570–5

[27] Chandler A 1977 *The Visible Hand* (Cambridge, MA: Harvard University Press)

[28] Devine S 2017 The information requirements of complex biological and economic systems with algorithmic information theory *Int. J. Design Nature Ecodyn.* **12** 367–76

[29] Schneider E D and Kay J J 1994 Life as a manifestation of the second law of thermodynamics *Mathl. Comput. Modelling* **16** 25–48

[30] Jaynes E T 1957 Information theory and statistical mechanics *Phys. Rev.* **106** 620–30

[31] Jaynes E T 1979 Where do we stand on maximum entropy *The Maximum Entropy formalism* ed R D Levine and M Tribus (Cambridge, MA: MIT Press) pp 15–118

[32] Daly H E 1997 FORUM: Georgescu–Roegen versus Solow/Stiglitz *Ecol. Econom.* **22** 261–76

[33] Schrödinger E 1944 *What is Life? The physical aspect of the living cell* (Cambridge: Cambridge University Press)

[34] Georgescu-Roegen N 1986 The entropy law and the economic process in retrospect *Eastern Econ. J.* **12** 3–25

[35] Ayres R U 1999 The second law, the fourth law, recycling and limits to growth *Ecol. Econ.* **29** 473–83

[36] Solow R M 1974 The economics of resources or the resources of economics *Am. Econ. Rev.* **64** 1–14

[37] Stiglitz J E 1974 Growth with exhaustible natural resources: Efficient and optimal growth paths *Rev. Econ. Stud.* **41** 123–37

[38] Georgescu-Roegen N 1979 Comments on the papers by Daly and Stiglitz *Scarcity and Growth Reconsidered* ed V K Smith (Baltimore, MD: Johns Hopkins University Press) pp 95–105

[39] Corning P A and Kline S J 1998 Thermodynamics, information and life revisited, part I: To be or entropy *Syst. Res. Behav. Sci.* **15** 273–95

[40] Chaisson E 2001 *Cosmic Evolution: The Rise of Complexity in Nature* (Cambridge, MA: Harvard University Press)

[41] Ayres R U 1998 Self-organization in biology and economics *Technical Report* RR-88-1 International Institute for Applied Systems Analysis

[42] Georgescu-Roegen N 1977 Inequality, limits and growth from a bioeconomic viewpoint *Rev. Social Econ.* **XXXV** 361–75

[43] Ayres R U and Warr B 2005 Accounting for growth: The role of physical work *Struct. Change Econ. Dyn.* **16** 181–209

[44] Romer P M 1994 The origins of endogenous growth *J. Econ. Perspect.* **8** 3–22

[45] Corning P A 2002 Thermoeconomics: Beyond the second law *J. Bioecon.* **4** 57–88

[46] Chaisson E J 2015 Energy flows in low entropy complex systems *Entropy* **17** 8007–18

[47] Corning P A and Kline S J 1998 Thermodynamics, information and life revisited, part II: 'Thermoeconomics' and 'control information' *Syst. Res. Behav. Sci.* **15** 453–82

[48] Krause M J and Tolaymat T 2018 Quantification of energy and carbon costs for mining cryptocurrencies *Nat. Sustain.* **1** 711–8

[49] Krantz R, Gemmetto V and Garlaschelli D 2018 Maximum-entropy tools for economic fitness and complexity *Entropy* **10** 743

[50] Neve M and Fagnart J F 2017 Pollution, defensive expenditure and the desirability of economic growth *Proc. EAERE2017—23rd Annual Conf. of the European Association of Environmental and Resource Economists*

[51] Kuznets S 1955 Economic growth and income inequality *Am. Econ. Rev.* **49** 1–28

[52] Stern D I 2004 The rise and fall of the environmental Kuznets curve *World Dev.* **32** 1419–39

[53] Kaika D and Zervas E 2013 The Environmental Kuznets Curve (EKC) *Energy Policy* **62** 1392–402

# Chapter 12

## AIT and philosophical issues

Algorithmic information theory (AIT) provides insights into learning and artificial intelligence as learning and artificial intelligence are impossible where there is no consistency or pattern in what is observed. The minimum description length approach, discussed earlier in chapter 5, shows the best fit to the data is found by the physical model which provides the most compressed version of the data, satisfying both Occam's razor and the Epicurus principle. But while the approach may fit the data it does not necessarily provide the true model. Hutter, in section 12.1, extending these ideas, has combined the idea of universal sequence prediction with a decision theoretic agent by a generalised universal semi-measure.

Chaitin has argued from his proof of Gödel's theorem, that where empirically observation suggests an undecidable statement reflects the world as it is, new axioms could be added to the formal mathematical system provided these are not contradicted by the evidence. It might not be mathematics as we know it, but the process might work.

The Universe seems to behave as if is a digital computer. As discussed in section 12.3, LLoyd explores this idea, looking at a matter dominated universe and the radiation dominated Universe. In both cases, the number of bits needed to describe the operation of the Universe is about the same. Even if the Universe is a quantum computer, the strong Turing thesis implies that under the circumstance where there are no infinities, every finitely realisable system can be simulated by a Turing machine (TM). While there is some disagreement, it would seem reasonable to assume that, above the Planck scale, digital computations can effectively describe physical processes given that the states of the computer, can be considered discrete to within quantum limits.

In section 12.3, Wolfram argues that the order we see in the Universe arises through simple computational processes, analogous to those undertaken by a cellular automaton. This would suggest a trial and error search could find simple generators of the Universe. If this can be done, the Universe would only be pseudo-random. Another approach is that of Chaitin (see section 12.3) who discusses the intelligibility of the Universe in terms of AIT. But if the theory of everything (TOE) was uncovered there would be no certainty that a deeper explanation might exist.

Section 12.3 draws attention to the suggestion of Calude and Meyerstein that the string specifying the Universe may not be lawful but rather random, as if produced by a toss of a coin. If such a random outcome is infinite, every possible sequence will occur. Perhaps we humans just happen to be living in an ordered part of this random sequence. Others discuss whether the human mind can ever fully understand the physical world. Perhaps the mathematical Universe might be too algorithmically complex for the human mind, but the physical Universe might not be. We can make sense of the Universe, but our ability may be limited by the storage capability of the human mind, or perhaps because of insufficient time to undertake the computational steps needed, or because Gödel's theorem might constrain human understanding.

Yet it is a surprise that scientific reduction seems to work remarkably well. Perhaps many subroutines of the Universe are so algorithmically simple, that the human mind, a miniscule subset of the Universe, can make sense of such routines. While we may use phenomenological laws to select plausible explanations of parts of the Universe, we may never be able to discern or explain organised systems at a macro level.

The book closes by identifying some issues that need to be addressed further. The approach is classical and the reversibility of natural systems is assumed. While a workable approach to the resolution of the phase space needed to define a bit, is found, there are some underlying issues that need further exploration.

## 12.1 Algorithmic descriptions, learning and artificial intelligence

AIT provides some practical insights into learning and artificial intelligence. One can take an intuitive view of learning as a process by which an agent, when given data associated with some phenomenon, can make sufficient sense of the data to partially predict future outcomes. Learning is impossible where the observations show no pattern or structure. As these observations cannot be compressed, each future outcome is a surprise. Leibnitz [1] has argued that the best theory compresses data more effectively than alternatives. As a consequence, the better the theory, the better the learning that takes place and the better it can predict future outcomes. As the fields of learning and artificial intelligence are specialist disciplines, only the flavour of the algorithmic insights can be outlined here. Hopefully, those who are interested can delve deeper into the topic.

Two lectures by Solomonoff [2, 3] review the connection between compression, learning and intelligence. Learning can be interpreted within an AIT framework. In particular, the outcome of a learning process is as effective as the minimum description length procedure. As has been outlined in section 5.3, the minimum description length (MDL) approach argues that the best fit to observed data is found by the physical model that provides the most compressed version of the data. It was pointed out the approach satisfies both the simplicity embodied in Occam's razor, and the breadth of Epicurus' principle, as the approach seeks the simplest explanation without rejecting possible causes. However, there are some deeper questions surrounding MDL. Vitányi and Li [4] have pointed out that data compression using MDL is almost always the best strategy for both model selection and prediction, provided that the deviation from the model is random with respect to the envisaged probability hypothesis. What this means is that to be effective, there can be no identifiable order or pattern in the deviations. As was mentioned in section 5.3, the ideal approach to MDL can be derived from a Bayesian approach using the algorithmic universal distribution of section 3.9 as the prior probability of different hypotheses. That is, the prior is $2^{-H_i}$, where $H_i$ is the length of the algorithm that specifies the hypothesis $i$. The hypothesis that maximises the Bayesian probability is the one that minimises the sum of two terms. The first of these terms is the algorithmic specification of the hypothesis as a model, while the second, given the model, codes the deviations from the model by a code that satisfies Shannon's noiseless coding theorem (section 3.4). This minimisation outlined in section 5.3 corresponds to finding the algorithmic minimal sufficient statistic (section 4.3.1) or the provisional entropy of the data (section 4.2).

Barron and Cover [5] apply the approach to selecting the most appropriate probability distribution to explain a set of random variables drawn from an unknown probability distribution. They show that the two-part MDL approach will eventually find an optimum data distribution from the class of candidate distributions. However, the approach is one based on having an effective strategy to find potential models, rather than having any belief about the simplicity of the true state of the world. In contrast to the original Bayesian approach, MDL makes no assumptions about the underlying distribution, or any subjective assessments of the probabilities. As Grünwald points out [6], MDL is asymptotically consistent without any metaphysical assumptions about the true state of things. Furthermore, the practical MDL approach is an effective method of inductive inference with few exceptions.

Vereshchagin and Vitányi [7] show that the structure function determines all stochastic properties of the data: for every constrained model class it determines the individual best fitting model in the class, irrespective of whether the 'true' model is in the model class. In this setting, this happens with certainty, rather than with high probability as in classical statistics. It becomes possible to precisely quantify the goodness-of-fit of an individual model with respect to individual sets of data.

Hutter [8–10] combines the idea of universal sequence prediction with the decision theoretic agent by a generalised universal semi-measure. Induction is optimised when the agent does not influence the outcome, whereas combining this with decision theory allows the agent to interact with the world. The model he proposes is not computable, but computable modifications of it are more intelligent than any time or space-bound algorithm.

## 12.2 The mathematical implications of algorithmic information theory

Chaitin [11] argues that, as there are mathematical statements that are true but not provable, mathematics should be taken to be quasi empirical, rather than the usual *a priori* approach. This would allow new axioms to be added to the formal mathematical structure where there is some reasonable evidence to support either the truth or falsifiability of the unknowable statements. Chaitin [12] argues that Einstein saw mathematics as empirical, even suggesting that the integers are a product of the human mind. Chaitin also argues that, while Gödel, with his Platonic world view, saw mathematics as an *a priori* activity, Gödel does state that: 'If mathematics describes an objective world, there is no reason why inductive methods should not be applied the same as in physics'. This leads Gödel to argue that a probable decision about the truth of a new axiom is possible inductively. Where such a possible axiom has an abundance of verifiable consequences and powerful impacts, it could be considered as an axiom in the same sense that a hypothesis is accepted as a physical theory. The implications are that mathematics, by judiciously selecting axioms that appear to be true for good empirical reasons, but which are not yet provable, can decide 'truth' empirically.

## 12.3 How can we understand the Universe?

Those researchers, who see the evolving path of the Universe as a computational process, raise the possibility that the Universe is itself a digital computer. The first to do so was Leibnitz according to Chaitin [1], as Leibnitz believed in digital physics. More recently, such notables as John Wheeler (quoted in [13]) coined the phrase 'It from bit', while Ed Fredkin [14, 15] sees the fundamental particles of the Universe as processors of bits of information. At the Planck scale of $1.6 \times 10^{-35}$ m, quantum effects dominate, and the Universe would seem to behave like a quantum computer almost by definition.

Seth Lloyd [16] (see also [17]) explores the idea of the Universe as a computer as it processes information in a systematic fashion. He suggests the Universe may perform quantum computations where every degree of freedom registers information while the dynamical interactions between degrees of freedom process information. Lloyd puts bounds on the processing capability of the Universe. If gravitation is taken into account, the total number of bits is $\approx 10^{120}$. Similarly, the number of operations $\approx 10^{120}$. These are simple polynomial functions of the constants of nature, $h$, $c$, $G$ and the age of the Universe. The number of operations within time horizon $t$ is the Planck time, where gravitational effects are of the same order as quantum effects. Lloyd looks at a matter dominated Universe and a radiation dominated Universe, and has found that the formulae for describing the operations and the number of bits are about the same in both cases. It is not the purpose of this work to delve deeply into the points Lloyd makes, but to point readers to the possible ramifications of seeing the Universe in such a way.

Even if the Universe is a quantum computer, the strong Church–Turing thesis implies that, under the circumstances where there are no infinities in the Universe, every finitely realisable system can be simulated by a finite TM [18]. However, there are arguments against a digital physics based on continuous symmetries and the implication of hidden variables [19].

Even so, it would seem reasonable to assume that, above the Planck scale, digital computations may effectively describe physical processes. The internal states of the computer can be considered discrete within quantum limits. Similarly, there is little difficulty in envisaging the Universe as a computer that steps through a trajectory in its reasonably well-defined state space. For example, the behaviour of say a gas in a container can be seen as a computing process when collisions move the system from one microstate to another.

Paul Davies in *The Fifth Miracle* ([20] (p 95)) states that the Universe has the same logical structure as a computer. He argues from algorithmic information theory that physical laws show pattern, and therefore are information poor, noting that the term 'information' is used in the sense that the laws are algorithmically simple. The data embodied in laws is assumed to be compressible. On the other hand, Davies suggests the genome is information rich and is close to random. (It should be noted that algorithms exist to compress DNA for information storage purposes. So the genome is certainly rich, but not necessarily close to random.) Davis then argues that the genome is highly specific because it arose from evolutionary processes through random mutations and natural selection. This leads to a compressed, but specific, information structure. Personally, I think that replication processes, as I argue in chapter 10, are a natural way to generate ordered structures.

Wolfram [21] puts forward a stronger view and argues that the order we see in the Universe arises through simple computational processes, analogous to those undertaken by cellular automata. If so, the Universe is not random but pseudo-random, as the complex structures that emerge do so through relatively simple computational processes. Wolfram then surveys simple computational worlds, hoping to find insights into the computational processes of the Universe itself and claims a theory of everything (TOE) is in principle possible by trialling different simple computational machines. He believes that interpreting the Universe in digital form is likely to provide better insights than the more conventional mathematics based on continuum dynamics. Interestingly, in chapter 12 of his book, Wolfram [21] provides a detailed account of AIT.

Another approach is that of Chaitin [13], who discusses the intelligibility of the Universe in terms of AIT. He quotes Weyl who drew attention to Leibnitz' claim that physical laws must be simple. Chaitin supports Weyl's belief that simplicity is central to the epistemology of science and gives examples from a number of eminent scientists about simplicity and complexity. These scientists support the view that a belief that the Universe is rational and lawful is of no value if the laws are beyond our comprehension. Is then a TOE possible? Such a TOE would maximally compress the observable universe. Chaitin quotes Barrow [13] in arguing that, even if a TOE was uncovered, there would be no certainty that a deeper explanation might exist. This possibility appears to contradict Wolfram's views outlined above that a simple generator of physical reality might be possible. However, there is no contradiction as Chaitin points out. The TOE that he and Barrow are describing is an algorithmic description, effectively limited by Gödels's improvability, whereas Wolfram suggests systematically searching for simple generators of the Universe starting with the most simple.

Calude and Meyerstein [22] raise the question as to whether the Universe is lawful or not. Their conclusion is that the Universe is lawless in the sense that there is no overall structure implied by the word 'law'. Their argument in effect is saying that the human mind is not capable of grasping the behaviour of the Universe. While these authors refer first to the historical perspectives from Plato to Galileo, their own argument focuses on the strong articulation of Gödel's theorem that shows the set of unprovable but true statements is large, improvability is everywhere. The arguments are interesting and capture Chaitin's statement that: 'God not only plays with dice in quantum mechanics, but even with the whole numbers'. Calude and Meyerstein [22] suggest that the Universe may best be described by what they call a lexicon produced by say the toss of a coin. Within this infinite lexicon, every possible sequence will occur. Sections of this string representing our Universe may be partially ordered, and we can hope that this ordered part of the lexicon may be partially explained by science. But elsewhere the string may be random. However, where we do make sense it will only be for that part of the lexicon that is ordered. Calude and Meyerstein argue that as the human mind can never fully understand mathematics, the human mind can never fully understand the physical world. We are part of the system and we do not have the energy resources needed to probe the relativistic Universe. On the other hand, Casti and Karlqvist [23] have the hope that, while the mathematical Universe might be too algorithmically complex for the human mind, in principle the physical Universe might not be.

**Why can we make any sense of the Universe?**

We do seem to be able to make sense of the Universe, but our capability to do so would seem to be limited for three reasons.

- The storage capability of the human mind is limited. Even if this is extended through external storage and processing of information (such as was done in the proof of the four colour theorem), there will still be finite limits to the amount of information humans can process. If computers do the processing for us, will we have the same confidence in the result if our minds are unable to process the information directly?
- Even if humans can access adequate storage, they might have insufficient time to undertake sufficient computing steps to come up with an adequate understanding of say a law of the Universe. This is analogous to the fact that it may take longer to calculate the weather than the Universe takes to generate the observed weather.
- Finally, the Gödel limit may well constrain human sense-making. Even if the other problems did not limit human rationality, the above arguments, implicit in Gödel's theorems, indicate that most of the statements that characterise the behaviour of the Universe might well be unprovable to us, either as

individuals or as a collection of humans. In effect, if scientific understandings are based on formal logical processes, most theorems will be beyond us.

The question then arises as to why we are able to make any sense of anything. As Einstein, quoted by Chaitin [13] said: 'The most incomprehensible thing about the Universe is that it is comprehensible'. It could be that sense-making through physical laws is not really rigorous in the formal system sense and therefore is not limited by Gödel's theorem. We may have explanations that work, but which might at some level not require consistency, but rather a lesser form of certainty, perhaps embodied in a probability. It could be that our brains are quantum computers and are not constrained by Gödel's theorem. However, the following argument suggests that reductionism, which is core to much of our sensemaking, works because the observable universe is relatively simple.

While the scientific reductionist approach seems to be extraordinarily successful in making sense of the Universe, despite the attacks of some philosophers and postmodernists, this is a surprise.

Yet we do seem to be able to make sense of the world by reducing the whole, which appears impenetrable, to smaller manageable components. Surely this is because the world is structured that way. In other words, the surprise is not that the Universe is complex, but that it is algorithmically simple. This is a simplicity that allows the observed Universe to a large extent to be reduced to simple laws. These laws are so simple that they can be processed by a finite brain that is insignificant relative to the rest of the Universe. Such simplicity seems to arise because small parts of the Universe can be described simply. I can describe algorithmically the behaviour of a falling stone; a stone which is part of a much greater whole. My algorithmic description of a falling stone can be seen as a subroutine in a much more complex algorithm. But to a large extent, the inputs of the rest of the Universe make little difference to the result. The rest of the Universe impacts on the falling stone mostly as small perturbations. While we may not have the computational capacity to understand the system in its entirety, we appear to have the capacity to understand the much less algorithmically complex subroutines that are structures nested within structures or order nested within order, and can model the manner in which these subroutines are integrated into the whole. This suggests that we can make sense at a particular level of nesting, because the algorithmic complexity of the system at the level of nesting is less than the algorithmic complexity of our cognitive processes. At our level of inquiry, many of the subroutines describe highly ordered systems with low algorithmic complexity. Such an approach may not always work, but in practice it seems to work surprisingly often. However, in reconstituting the subroutines, we often need to allow for apparently random contributions, i.e. contributions that are outside our capability to comprehend. External impacts may often appear as randomness. Whether hidden laws, noise, or quantum uncertainty, what seems to us like chance events in the macro world often only have a minor impact on the part of the Universe we can make sense of.

Perhaps we can rely on phenomenological ways of sense making that avoids the Gödel dilemma. The implicit or explicit axioms of phenomenological laws may have empirically selected one of two possible unprovable truth statements or even selected a path through a binary tree of unprovable truth statements. This may allow us to describe highly algorithmically organised systems at the macro level to a moderate degree of satisfaction. Nevertheless, it may be impossible to relate these higher level understandings to more fundamental understandings because of our cognitive limitations. When the whole cannot be explained by combining the parts, it might be because our brains cannot reduce the phenomenological understandings to a strict formal logical process.

It could even be that the uncertainty principle arises through such a process. While, the great physicists and mathematicians, including Gödel, have been sceptical about any relationship between his theorem and the uncertainty principle, and while the formal framework of quantum physics does not allow for hidden variables, who knows?

## 12.4 Closing thoughts

This book shows how the algorithmic approach to thermodynamics can be expressed in a coherent form. However, like statistical mechanics, there are difficulties and some underlying issues. The approach here requires the systems to be both classical and reversible. The conservation of bits in a closed system, or in an open system when bits are tracked depends on reversibility. While the ejection of bits from a system removes reversibility, from a wider system perspective, reversibility is in principle possible, but not in the timeframes of interest. However, this argument, while plausible, may not be satisfactory.

Coupled with this is the deterministic nature of the trajectory of the system. But determinism is only recognisable from the perspective of an external observer who has sufficient computational capacity to exactly simulate the trajectory. Determinism, like reversibility, does not seem to be meaningful from within the system. If a system that includes me as an observer jumps back in time to yesterday, I cannot know, as my brain states will have reversed to yesterday's brain setting. This may imply that time is related to the trend to the most probable set of states.

But, could the Universe I exist in as an observer, see water in a stream run uphill. This would imply that time is going in one direction for me the observer, and in the opposite direction for the water subsystem that I am observing. Perhaps many have pondered this and come up with a satisfactory solution. From the perspective here, such an outcome might be valid, but highly improbable. If we define forward in time as a move of the system towards a greater number of states, we as an external observer are more likely to see a forward movement in time rather than a reverse one, as from a probability perspective, fewer time-reversed states exist. The number of states increases as stored energy and programme bits are released to increase the number of momentum states.

Another issue is the basis for the resolution of the phase and state space, that defines the minimal size of a computational bit. The Gács entropy approach [24, 25], which in practical terms aligns with the algorithmic entropy used here, may resolve this. However, here the uncertainty principle is taken to be the ultimate limit of the resolution of the phase space and therefore defines the minimum size of a bit.

However, Shannon's ultimate limit also specifies the minimum size of a computational bit in terms of the noise spectral power density, $k_B T$, as outlined in section 8.3. Are these two approaches consistent? Related to this is the argument that bits are conserved. Just as the conservation of energy only applies to systems above the quantum limit, the same may be true of bits. As the energy of a system is proportional to the computational bits that exist through $k_B T$ where $k_B$ is Boltzmann's constant, $k_B T$ rather than the temperature, may be more fundamental.

Despite these assumptions, and uncertainties, algorithmic information theory can be applied to non-equilibrium thermodynamics consistently and coherently.

# References

[1] Chaitin G J 2005 *Meta Math! The Quest for Omega* (New York: Pantheon)

[2] Solomonoff R J 2005 *Lecture 1: Algorithmic Probability* (http://world.std.com/rjs/iaplect1.pdf)

[3] Solomonoff R J 2005 *Lecture 2. Applications of Algorithmic Probability* (http://world.std.com/rjs/iaplect1.pdf)

[4] Vitányi P M B and Li M 2000 Minimum description length induction, Bayesianism, and Kolmogorov complexity *IEEE Trans. Inform. Theory* **46** 446–64

[5] Barron A and Cover T 1991 Minimum complexity density estimation *IEEE Trans. Inf. Theory* **37** 1034–54

[6] Grünwald P D 2005 A tutorial to the minimum description length principle *Advances in Minimum Description Length: Theory and Applications* ed P D Grünwald, I J Myung and M A Pitt (Cambridge, MA: MIT Press)

[7] Vereshchagin N K and Vitányi P M B 2004 Kolmogorov's structure functions and model selection *IEEE Trans. Inf. Theory* **50** 3265–90

[8] Hutter M 2000 A theory of universal artificial intelligence based on algorithmic complexity (http://arxiv.org/abs/cs.AI/0004001).

[9] Hutter M 2005 *Universal Artificial Intelligence* (London: Springer)

[10] Hutter M 2007 Universal algorithmic intelligence: A mathematical top-down approach *Artificial General Intelligence* ed B Goertzel and C A Pennachin (Berlin: Springer) pp 227–90

[11] Chaitin G J 2006 The limits of reason *Sci. Am.* **294** 74–81

[12] Chaitin G J 2003 *The Limits of Mathematics* (London: Springer)

[13] Chaitin G 2004 On the intelligibility of the Universe and the notions of simplicity, complexity and irreducibility *Grenzen und Grenzüberschreitungen, XIX. Deutscher Kongress für Philosophie, Bonn, September 2002* ed W Hogrebe and J Bromand (Berlin: Akademie) pp 517–34

[14] Fredkin E 1990 Digital mechanics *Physica* D 254–70

[15] Fredkin E and Toffoli T 1982 Conservative logic *Int. J. Theor. Phys.* **21** 219–53

[16] Lloyd S 2002 Computational capacity of the Universe *Phys. Rev. Lett.* **88** 237901

[17] Lloyd S 2006 *Programming the Universe: A Quantum Computer Scientist Takes On the Cosmos* (New York: Knopf)

[18] Deutsch D 1985 Quantum theory, the Church-Turing principle and the universal quantum computer *Proc. R. Soc. Lond., Ser.* A **400** 97–117

[19] Digital physics (http://en.wikipedia.org/wiki/Digital_physics).

[20] Davies P C W 2003 *The Fifth Miracle: The Search for the Origin of Life* (London: Penguin)

[21] Wolfram S 2002 *A new kind of science* (Champaign, IL: Wolfram Media)

[22] Calude C S and Meyerstein F W 1999 Is the Universe lawful? *Chaos Solitons Fractals* **106** 1075–84

[23] Casti J L and Karlqvist A (ed) 1996 *Boundaries and barriers* (New York: Addison-Wiley)

[24] Gács P 2004 The Boltzmann entropy and random tests, Boston University Computer Science Department http://www.cs.bu.edu/faculty/gacs/papers/ent-paper.pdf

[25] Li M and Vitányi P M B 2008 *An Introduction to Kolmogorov Complexity and Its Applications* 3rd edn (New York: Springer)

CPSIA information can be obtained
at www.ICGtesting.com
Printed in the USA
BVHW012239161120
593331BV00003B/11